Advance Praise for

BOB SEGER'S HOUSE AND OTHER STORIES

"In *Bob Seger's House and Other Stories,* the editors honor the great tradition of Michigan storytelling and mythmaking—the tales we tell each other to help us understand our world, to keep us alive. These stories cover a diverse range of characters, times, places, and styles, displaying the abundant wealth of writing talent with Michigan connections. No matter where these stories take place, they're grounded in spirit and heart."

—Jim Daniels, author of *Eight Mile High, Birth Marks,* and other books

"This is a vital and engrossing collection of stories from some of the most important voices in contemporary American fiction. That these authors and characters all have strong ties to Michigan provides an intriguing connection between the stories, and collectively the stories paint a wonderfully varied and compelling portrait of the state and its diverse cultures. Yet these are not just great *Michigan* writers; they are great writers, period. This anthology could hold its own with any recent collection of contemporary American fiction, and the authors in these pages have rightfully earned many of the nation's most revered literary achievements."

—Valerie Laken, author of *Dream House* and *Separate Kingdoms*

"This collection of new stories from my home state is alive with a sense of what it means to be a writer in a place as diverse as Michigan. From the U.P. where people live against the hard edge of weather, to the sometimes equally harsh streets of Detroit, or the suburban landscapes of Ann Arbor and Grand Rapids, these are stories of a quiet yet fierce grace to remind us what it means to be alive."

—Dan Gerber

T0306901

Advance Praise for

BOB SEGER'S HOUSE AND OTHER STORIES

"Who knew Michigan was so wide, deep, weird, and full of second chances? Well, I did— and you did too, but we haven't seen such literary stories all in one epic collection. Picking up this book is like taking the Rand McNally of the state and crinkling it up and mashing it together to make new roads, lakes, and cities. The Michigan that is here in these pages is entirely new yet familiar. Funny how that works when it comes to art. You can go from the Upper Peninsula and all the way downstate and never leave the page, all the way to Seger's."

—Doug Stanton, *New York Times* best-selling author

BOB SEGER'S HOUSE AND OTHER STORIES

MADE IN MICHIGAN WRITERS SERIES

GENERAL EDITORS

Michael Delp, *Interlochen Center for the Arts*

M. L. Liebler, *Wayne State University*

ADVISORY EDITORS

Melba Joyce Boyd, *Wayne State University*

Stuart Dybek, *Western Michigan University*

Kathleen Glynn

Jerry Herron, *Wayne State University*

Laura Kasischke, *University of Michigan*

Thomas Lynch

Frank Rashid, *Marygrove College*

Doug Stanton

Keith Taylor, *University of Michigan*

A complete listing of the books in this series can be found online at wsupress.wayne.edu

BOB SEGER'S HOUSE

ITED BY Michael Delp AND M. L. Liebler

WITH A FOREWORD BY Charles Baxter

Wayne State University Press
Detroit

AND OTHER STORIES

© 2016 by Wayne State University Press,
Detroit, Michigan 48201.

All rights reserved. No part of
this book may be reproduced
without formal permission.

Manufactured in the
United States of America.

20 19 18 17 16 5 4 3 2 1

ISBN 978-0-8143-4194-0 (paperback)
ISBN 978-0-8143- 4195-7 (ebook)

Library of Congress Cataloging Number:
2016931830

∞

Publication of this book was made possible
by a generous gift from The Meijer Foundation.
Additional support provided by Michigan
Council for Arts and Cultural Affairs and
National Endowment for the Arts.

Designed and typeset by Bryce Schimanski
Composed in Arno Pro

CONTENTS

FOREWORD

Charles Baxter

HERE IS A TRUE STORY. RECENTLY I FOUND MYSELF AT a party in Manhattan. Somehow I managed to strike up a conversation with another guest about the particular locales where we had lived. After all, the where-are-you-from conversation is standard-issue party behavior and usually harmless. As it turned out, this woman had spent much of her life in Delaware. *Delaware!* What did I know about Delaware? The conversation threatened to collapse as I stood there and tried to think of one single relevant fact. "A beautiful coastline!" I lied, having never seen the Delaware coastline but believing in my heart that it *must* be beautiful thanks to the Atlantic Ocean. From somewhere deep down I then dredged up a factoid. "R. Crumb was born there, right?" I said delightedly, pleased to remember the great cartoonist. "Mr. Natural himself."

"He lives in France now," she said. "And you? Where have you lived?"

"Michigan," I said. "For thirty years." From the blank look on her face, I knew we were now having a Woody Allen conversation. "You know: Detroit? Ann Arbor?"

"Right!" she said. "Isn't Michigan where . . ."

"Yes?"

But she, too, was stumped. Time passed. Finally she gamely said, "Who am I kidding? I don't know anything about Michigan. I've never been there and don't plan to go."

Does a region give rise to a particular kind of literature? Maybe. In Mississippi it has done so, but Michigan is so fiercely diverse in its landscapes, its economy, and its demographics that it presents anybody who wants to write about it with a kind of blank slate. You can't summarize the state easily. Emblematically, the state animal, the wolverine, is a vicious beast that lives elsewhere. The great mysterious patchwork quilt of Michigan is good news for writers, because nobody has ever written *the* Michigan novel the way Faulkner wrote the Mississippi novel, and nobody ever will. Hemingway's Michigan fiction has almost no resemblance to Harriet Arnow's, and Elmore Leonard's novels do not resemble Janet Kauffman's in any way except that both employ the English language.

When I first moved to Michigan in 1969, and then, after a time in upstate New York, back to Michigan in 1974, I thought I noticed, perhaps mistakenly, two features of the Wolverine State that struck me as peninsular in nature: an essential, isolated stoicism among many of the people I knew, accompanied by the belief that the region in which they lived was deeply significant and worthy of attention. But not everyone crossed the boundaries (as writers do—it's their business). Many worthy citizens of Ann Arbor do not care to visit the Thumb. Nobody I met in Detroit had ever been to Lake Gogebic or knew where it was, and if you mentioned the Porcupine Mountains, they would patiently explain that you had been misinformed: there were no mountains in Michigan. Grand Rapids seemed upright and Dutch Calvinist and self-contained to me, and the Saginaw Valley, where I once taught, looked like a replica of the Great Plains for sheer flatness and had been settled by Germans and Italians (like the family of Madonna Louise Ciccone, born in Bay City). The western edge of the Upper Peninsula is not in a conversation with Detroit or Benton Harbor. Ironwood does not speak the same language as Saginaw.

Michigan consists of islands, and I don't mean islands in water but islands in land, creating a strange, crazy variety with very little tying it all together except geographic proximity. Because the left hand never knows what the right hand is doing, the state accommodates all kinds of writers, like the ones in this book. They are like telegraph operators in the radio shack, describing the conditions outside, but the sheer variety of the places where they have lived has not limited their imaginations but in some sense expanded them. What I love and admire about the work of the authors in this anthology—many of them beloved friends—is the sheer brilliance of the prose, the force of their concerns, and the unpredictability of the subject matter.

When I think of the time I spent in Michigan, I tend to think in images: a nighttime blinking red light atop a radio tower seen from a car traveling over icy winter roads near Midland, the snow blue in the moonlight; the Diego Rivera murals in Detroit and the haunted vacant lots to the north; the Huron River flowing past a picnic area shaded by a giant cottonwood tree in a Metropark near Dexter; the reassembled ghost town of Fayette in the Upper Peninsula; Tahquamenon Falls and the Pictured Rocks outside of Munising; petroglyphs in the Thumb; the Mackinac Bridge's gridded roadway through which you can see the water below; the Jackson Cascades, lit up nightly and accompanied by piped-in music and the buzz of mosquitoes; music arising in the night air outside Traverse City; a conservation area behind Pioneer High School in Ann Arbor. But, no: it's hopeless. All these images and sounds are now just an inventory of what were once charged visions for me. I did my best to get them down on paper, surrounded by characters whom I had invented and who had found themselves in fictional form. Like any other author—like the writers in this anthology—I tried to make sense of what I had seen.

"Anywhere is everywhere," William Carlos Williams once said. There is not one world, ever. There are many worlds, but each one is located in a single place. I loved Michigan and endeavored for decades to dramatize the joy and desolation that I felt there. This anthology presents you with other eloquent versions of place, with an accounting of how people strive to live in the locales where fate has deposited them. To use an old phrase, I can vouch for these writers and their visions. Enjoy!

PREFACE

AEONS HAVE PASSED SINCE WE FIRST LIVED IN CAVES and warmed ourselves around small fires, listening to stories told by shamans and our elders. We listened back then because we knew if we failed to take in these stories, we could well end up dead or lost, all alone in the wilderness. Stories were told to teach people lessons about family, life, and survival. They were, and still are, a wonderfully effective way of grabbing the attention and interest of others. Stories have always had a dual function: to teach and to entertain. Storytelling, oral or written, inspires us and gives rise to invention and understanding. It is this very act of art and humanity that separates us from all other animals on the planet. We ignore stories and their rich lessons at our own peril. This is why William Carlos Williams pointed out the truth of literature and art when he wrote that "men die miserably every day for lack of what is found there."

It is still the case today that through storytelling we find our way to stay connected to each other. The stories contained in this anthology are a way of strengthening those connections. Think of them as messages sent from all over the map, stitching readers and writers together through stories that continue to honor the ancient art of the fire tale, the hunting epic, and all of the ways language feeds the blood of imagination.

The Made in Michigan Writers Series has, since its inception, sought to honor this tradition of wondrous storytelling in all of its genres and forms. It has become a keeper of new and old stories by writers connected to our state. This is the reason that we said yes to becoming curators/series editors eleven years ago when the call came. The two of us as Michigan-born-and-bred writers could not be more different from each other: Delp from Northern Michigan, speaking the coded language of the water and the tales of the land, a backwoods boy at heart; and Liebler, a champion for Detroit's gritty art and culture, his mission to channel the industrial chaos and beauty of the city through his teaching and writing.

However, this is the reason we work so well together: we understand that we share this Michigan world in our very essence, and we both strive to highlight the diverse voices of the state from north to south and east to west.

A decade after the series' humble beginnings with two volumes of poetry, the series has now published forty-five books of poetry, short fiction, and creative nonfiction, and it continues to grow and expand. Now we have called upon some old friends—and some new—to help us celebrate this ten-year milestone and our commitment to stories and Michigan literature as essential to the mind and heart as food and water are to the body. Some of the best Michigan fiction writers have found their way into this anniversary collection. Michigan writers, like all artists, are a tribe of sorts. All these fine authors have a genuine connection physically or aesthetically to the Michigan landscape. The writers in this anthology either live in Michigan currently or have lived here and still carry the influence of this iconic place in their DNA.

The title of this collection comes from Ellen Airgood's dynamic story "Bob Seger's House," in which two strangers happen to meet on the other side of the world and quell their homesickness through bonding over the urban legend of their youth: the imaginary locations of the home of iconic Michigan rocker Bob Seger. His house was always "the biggest and nicest in town," and almost every town had one. In many ways, Seger's house serves as the genuine metaphor for hard work, incredible talent, and pure (Michigan) Americana. In a figurative way, Seger's house is "the people's house," not just for Michiganders, but for everyone.

All of these stories mirror and follow the shape and shift of the human condition. Some are dark and probing, while others are deeply poignant, compelling renditions of failed marriages and lost children, some so wildly imagined that we feel ourselves transported to places we sense exist beside us, or inside of us. As you sift through this collection of stories, imagine yourself secluded somewhere in one of those ancient places where story was the highest form of communication, and that as you turn a page to read, someone is writing to tell you something to keep your heart beating. Take these stories in and use them as talismans, as directions, as honest musings and the literal chants of writers who have tried to honor such an ancient and wild tradition.

Michael Delp and M. L. Liebler

BOB SEGER'S HOUSE

Ellen Airgood

THE DRIZZLE SHE'D BEEN DRIFTING THROUGH ALL morning was one thing, but when the sky let loose with a fusillade of rain, Ruth sprinted for a lean-to that sat along the tea garden's meandering stone path. She turned her ankle on a wet flagstone, righted herself at the last moment, and sank onto the wooden bench that was the hut's only furnishing. She tucked her feet as far back as they'd go, but the bench had been built for much smaller people. Her knees were getting wet.

She sat gazing out with her bag clutched to her chest like the last salvaged belonging of a shipwreck survivor, or an immigrant. The rain clattered on the roof and the sky was like gravy, an effect she could've gotten at home for thousands fewer dollars and possibly not the sinus infection, which had slammed into her on the flight and gained momentum with each mile that slid beneath the plane's wings. Now, a week into her vacation, her skull felt like an ax had been cleaved into it. Maybe she should hail a taxi, somehow, or board a bus, and take herself to the nearest walk-in clinic.

Ruth's breath sawed at her chest; her eyes teared and stung. She sighed and reached into her pocket for a tissue. She wasn't going to look for a clinic. There was the language barrier and the culture barrier and the question of how the bill would be paid. And besides that, who knew what Japanese medicine was like? Maybe it would be something to do with dried seaweed or candied kelp, or more likely, it would so far outstrip the services she was used to that her poor midwestern, middle-aged body would go into all-systems-failure out of sheer surprise. Like she herself had, in a way, on this trip. No, what she really should do is get herself back to Narita International and book a ticket home, and never mind the cost.

The graying timbers of the shelter's support beams framed a damp, green scene. Cedars drooped; ferns dripped; a stream with an arched wooden footbridge over it wound through the miniature woods. On the street outside the garden, men and women in office clothes hurried toward their destinations, their umbrellas tugged close over their heads. Beyond that, the Sea of Japan rolled in endless waves.

Ruth shivered. What she wouldn't give for a cup of coffee. Just around a few corners there was a McDonald's—she'd spotted it yesterday while the tour bus trundled them toward Kanazawa's geisha district. But before she left home she'd resolved to drink only tea while she was here in the Land of the Rising Sun. That way, she'd told herself as she pored over guidebooks, the journey would be that much more memorable, a real change. But it turned out she didn't like Japanese tea. The taste was strange—strong and grassy—and now with the head cold she yearned for the familiar taste of McDonald's brew more than ever. Dick Phelps had laughed when Ruth voiced her desire to stop as they passed. "Might as well've stayed home in Novi." He pronounced the syllables distinctly so that it came out sounding like "No-Vie."

"Mc*Don*ald's!" His wife Maylee touched his arm; they shared a look of cozy mirth.

Ruth's skin had prickled with embarrassment, but she'd chuckled along with them, of course.

■ ■ ■

She hadn't realized the tour would be comprised almost entirely of couples. Aside from a teenager who had so far spent every moment with an iPod either plugged into his ear or briefly pulled out to hear what some adult had to say, she was the only unattached person. She had been naive. That same naïveté had led her to think that bringing an embroidered silk cloth, a hara-kiri knife, and a small leather-bound journal back to Japan was a calling, a *vocation*.

A small songbird, olive brown with pale eyebrows, hopped onto a cedar bough and gave a soft chirp. Its up-curved beak made it look like it was smiling. Ruth breathed as quietly as she could manage. By the time the bird flew away, her anger at herself had lessened, though she expected that like the tide it would in time sweep back again. Eventually she reached into her bag and withdrew the journal. The covers were soft; it was barely bigger than her hand.

She'd found it at an auction, years ago. She had just turned twelve and gotten her first pair of glasses. Her parents were off looking at a cream separator and Ruth was ambling alongside a hay wagon loaded with boxes. She inspected each one carefully through her new spectacles, as if her attention could lessen the sadness of the contents' sudden homelessness after decades of service. One held doilies, dishcloths, and a rolling pin. Another was filled with rusty screwdrivers, a broken pair of vise grips, and an old milk bottle. Yet another was crammed with coffee cups from assorted tourist destinations: the Grand Canyon, the Statue of Liberty, Gettysburg, Mount Rushmore. Then there was the Thom McAn shoe box with the journal and silk cloth and knife in it. Ruth lifted the journal out. The auctioneer's voice faded into the distance; Ruth's heart beat harder. An old man had been trailing behind her, reinspecting each box when she was done. "Ha," he said, peering over Ruth's shoulder as she stood transfixed. "Mack's Jap stuff."

Ruth looked at him sharply, frowning.

"From the war," the old man growled. "Didn't know he still had it."

When the auctioneer arrived at the hay wagon, he glanced into the Thom McAn box, then hoisted it into the air. "What we've got here, folks: a lovely old piece of silk, finely embroidered—you could give it to your mother or your girlfriend to lay across her bureau, really dress it up. And for you gents, there's a knife, a hara-kiri knife, straight from Japan. And I don't know who'll want this, but it's custom-made for somebody, a little book of hieroglyphics. That's *words* for all of you who don't know." The small crowd standing around the wagon laughed. "We got beauty here, my friends, we got history, we got mystery. What'll you give? How about starting out with a nice ten dol—"

Ruth jabbed her father's bidder number into the air.

The auctioneer's bushy eyebrows shot up, Ruth's father opened his mouth to say something, Ruth's mom put her hand out toward Ruth, but it was too late. The old man was raising Ruth's bid by a dollar and Ruth was jabbing her number into the air again. The old man glowered and raised his card and Ruth reciprocated.

It went on for a comically long time, she understood as an adult, but all she thought of then was winning.

The journal measured three inches by five, more or less. The covers were made of thin leather tanned a dull red and the pages were of rice paper. Delicate characters in faded brown ink covered every page. When she got older, Ruth always imagined a poet with his goat-hair brush and ink stone writing the words, gazing out his temple window at a round white moon. The poet might've seen a dog scratching a flea; an icy wind might've roared down from a snow-capped mountain; a bell might've rung.

■ ■ ■

And now here she was, carting Mack-the-farmer's possessions around Kanazawa along with her Japanese dictionary, which had lime-green plastic covers encased in a clear plastic sleeve as thin as a sandwich bag. Ruth pulled it out and opened it at random. *Nothing,* she read. There was a string of characters, and then English again. *Nothing plus nothing equals nothing.* Ruth snorted and riffled the pages to an earlier section of the alphabet.

Chimera, the book offered.

She clapped the covers shut. *Why* hadn't she found someone at home in Novi, which, after all, had the largest Japanese population of any city in Michigan, to translate the little journal? Or someone in Ann Arbor, at the university. Surely she was bright enough to realize *beforehand* that she had not needed to fly all the way to Japan. That had been bullheaded and foolish in a way she'd always been capable of. "Whoa there, Nellie," her mother used to say, laying a hand on Ruth's shoulder. "Settle down. Don't let the horse run away with the cart."

■ ■ ■

It was only when the professor who'd agreed to meet with her at Kanazawa University was studying the journal with pinched lips that Ruth understood what she'd done. The old farmer had been a young American man here in wartime and who knew what he had done. He might've stolen this journal. He might've taken it from a fallen soldier—

The light slap of the covers closing interrupted these slow-dawning realizations. "There is nothing special here." Mr. Nakamura was a burly man with close-cropped black hair. He looked as if he could bench press his own weight all day long without breaking a sweat. Not what Ruth had expected in a Japanese man, or a professor either, for that matter.

"But what—"

"A young girl's journal, nothing more. 'Makito Hayashi stole my red hair clip. Takeo D. is cute.'" The professor handed the book back toward Ruth over his desktop.

Ruth didn't take it. "Are you sure? Leather bound?" She pushed her bangs back. She wished she hadn't chosen this winter to grow them out. "I mean, it looks so—" She gestured helplessly. The journal looked so romantic and mysterious. So important. Maybe only important in a small way, to one person, but important nevertheless.

"My mother had a journal almost identical. Same stuff in it, too."

"The man who had it was in Japan during the war. The big war, I mean, the Second World War. Mack—Findley, I think, was the last name. He was my neighbor, that's all I know, he was old when I was growing up. He had the journal, and the knife, and this cloth—"

Ruth pulled the tissue-swaddled cloth from her bag and offered it across the desk, even though the bone-handled knife had turned out to be a reproduction made for the tourist trade, a souvenir with a blade so dull it wouldn't cut grapes, say nothing of flesh and muscle, as the professor had put it.

Professor Nakamura sighed and took the cloth. He rubbed the same thumb that had appraised the knife over the stitching, a design of flowers twining across the pale-green field of silk. "I'm not sure what you're looking for from me."

Ruth leaned forward.

"It's a runner. The kind of thing my mother kept on her bureau." He scratched the back of his skull and squinted at her.

"But where would a soldier have gotten a bureau runner and a girl's journal?"

Again it all became clear, in the light of the professor's steady gaze. A young man, lonely. A woman to take him in, if only for a night or two—a professional or no, it didn't matter. The soldier might've been in love or thought he was. Or not. She saw a man in an olive uniform slide a journal from a woman's nightstand, a childhood memento she had thought little of since she was twelve and complaining about stolen hair clips.

Ruth's face turned red. She tumbled everything back into her bag, a sky-blue cotton sack embroidered with a pattern of white circles. "I'm sorry. I—I hope I haven't caused you any offense." Confused, she riffled through the dictionary. She found only the British *offence*. Pointed at it—

"I speak English quite fluently," Professor Nakamura said. "As you may've noticed."

■ ■ ■

A horn honked at the rain-washed intersection and a wave of exhaustion washed over Ruth. Her head throbbed; her joints ached. The street with its hurrying people and splashing traffic seemed impossibly far away. The hotel, the tour bus—how could she drag herself back to any of it? It seemed more doable to just stay here in the shelter clutching her bag of illusions forever. She would become one of the garden's statues. Like them she would cause people to meditate on the nature of life.

Abruptly, Ruth set the bag aside. She would leave it in the shelter. She'd walk to McDonald's and buy the largest cup of coffee available, then return to the hotel and take a long, hot shower. She would join the talk of golf at the dinner table tonight and stop trying to make anyone interested in haiku, an aim that had never been realistic. And she did know something about golf. Her second husband had played every Saturday. In truth, walking the fairways with him had been one of the best parts of their marriage.

Ruth scooted down the bench, away from the bag. As she did, the rain seemed to lessen; the air lightened, the sky cleared. She stretched her shoulders, then arched her neck and rolled it side to side. She laced her fingers together and poked her arms straight out in front of her, almost but not quite cracking her knuckles. Then with a small sigh, she settled back to wait out the last of the rain.

At home she would clean house, finally. She would choose a few keepsakes from the farm, which sat empty except for the occasional weekend when she drove up and rattled around the house like a lone pea inside a dried-out pod, and put it on the market. She would take her mother's porcelain flour and sugar containers and a few of her dad's hand tools, and chivy her brother Joe into choosing what he wanted and even pack it up for him. Whatever remained would go to auction, or else to a dumpster.

When that was done, she would catch up her taxes for the last two years and lose ten pounds. Maybe even twenty. She would make herself feel *new*, something she'd expected the trip to do. Erroneously, she could now see, given that it was based on so much ancient history.

■ ■ ■

The tour guide had asked them all to introduce themselves, their first night in Tokyo.

John and Sal Brougham were from Houston. He had something to do with the oil industry and they were traveling in their semi-retirement. Dean and Edwina Wilkes were from Boston. He did stocks, she did law; this was a "much-needed" break for both of them. The surly teenager, Hillson, was their son. The Kilwins ran a string of luxury hotels in Florida, the Burkes owned an island off the coast of Maine, the Millers had a controlling interest in a mining company in Nevada.

They were just people, after all, is what Ruth had told herself all week, even if they did all come in matched pairs and were as rich as Croesus to boot. Some of them were quite nice. Edwina Wilkes had smiled at most of Ruth's jokes. John Brougham crinkled his eyes kindly at her when Dick Phelps made the crack about No-Vie. But really, how had she missed that these would all be married couples from an income bracket so far above her own that she couldn't see it even with a telescope?

She told herself during that first, dismaying hour in the hotel conference room that it *must not matter*. She must not be closed-minded. Married couples did not meld into some other, untranslatable species. Even extraordinarily wealthy people pulled their sweaters on one sleeve at a time.

When it was Ruth's turn, she took a deep breath to steady herself. She knew the answers to this test, after all. She smiled at everyone. "I'm Ruth Owens. I'm from Michigan, from Novi. Well, only I'm not really from there, of course." Her skin prickled when she said *of course*. There was no "of course" about it; there was no reason not to have been from Novi. She was going to mess up this un-mess-up-able offering of information and there was nothing she could do to stop it; that sled was already flying down the hill. "I grew up on a little farm—well, it wasn't really a farm anymore, my dad worked at Pine Lumber in town and my mom worked for the phone company—in the Thumb."

Ruth heard a chuckle and looked up from the point on the far wall where she'd fixed her eyes.

"The Thumb?" a woman asked. A note of incredulity laced her voice.

Ruth held her hand up like she was swearing an oath. "Michigan's shaped like a mitten—the Lower Peninsula, anyway." She jabbed at the base of her thumb. "I'm from there. That's what we do. We point at our hands." The looks on people's faces ranged from amused to blank. She plowed on. "Why am I here in Japan? I guess—a bunch of reasons. I found this journal at a farm auction when I was a kid." She held the little journal up and twisted it this way and that. "It captivated me. I spent my entire savings on the box—that was all of forty dollars, high finance—" She paused, hoping for a laugh, then coughed to fill the silence. "I spent my entire savings on the box. The contents fascinated me—they still do. A journal, a piece of silk, and a knife. I ended up having an exchange student come the next summer. Yuko. She left her dictionary." Ruth held up the dictionary, jerked it back to her lap. "She gave me a bag her mother embroidered, too." She danced the sack in the air. "We became such good friends, but we lost touch eventually. I wanted to track her down on this trip but it just seemed impossible. I suppose she got married. Well, and I did too. A few times!"

She chuckled like this was funny. Her audience gazed at her as if waiting for something they doubted would ever come.

"I ended up getting really interested in haiku—" Doggedly, Ruth flashed her own journal around the room. It had seemed momentous when she bought it at Twelve Oaks Mall, years ago. The leather cover had an oak tree embossed on the front. A rawhide thong wrapped around a silver button to close it; the pages were creamy and thick. It was nearly full of haiku she had copied from texts at the university library, where she'd gotten a card even though she wasn't an alum or a staff member. Ruth's hand trembled. She closed it tighter around the journal and the branches of the tree mumbled at her palm in a consoling way.

"Where do you work, Ruth?" the tour guide asked kindly.

"For the city government in Novi." At least she knew enough not to say the sewage-treatment plant. Though really, why shouldn't she? The job paid pretty well, the work was amenable enough, her closest friends were there. Bob down in maintenance, Chrissy who manned the camera banks, Job in tech support. There were inside jokes, a steady sense of camaraderie. They worked to find the humor in each day. And it *was* funny. Theirs was a shit job, literally. And shit jobs were necessary, a fact of life.

Ruth smiled tightly and turned toward the man on her left, who turned out to be Jason Wilkinson-Parks of Boston, a high-court judge, traveling to Japan with his wife Irena out of what sounded like idle interest. They would meet their daughter Cynthia in Italy, after.

■ ■ ■

Since that night, Ruth had slowly become a tour rebel. A loner, cutting off from the group like a stray cow in her grandfather's herd. And she felt cow-like here in Japan. Large, slow, bovine, pleasant enough but sadly not all that smart.

The rain pelted down, less insistent but still steady, on the shelter roof. Ruth pulled out the Realtor's card Joe had given her last time she saw him. She could talk to him about selling the farm right now if she was willing to fork out the money for the international call. She could change her life. She could take hold of the reins and steer it in a new direction, a *better* direction.

She was rummaging for her phone when a half dozen young people stampeded into the hut. They didn't all fit, by a long stretch. Five of the six, calling out dramatic farewells and extravagant declarations of love, moved on to the teahouse itself, a hundred feet away and not yet open for the day.

Ruth stared at the one who'd stayed. Curly red hair cascaded to her waist. She wore faded jeans, scuffed work boots, and a gray lace bustier with a long blue cardigan over it. She grinned at Ruth's inspection. "Hi," she said.

"Hello."

The girl pulled a can of Coke out of her backpack and popped the top. She took a long swig, then pushed a strand of hair off her face and wiped one corner of her mouth with the back of her wrist. "Hey, you want one of these?"

"No, thank you," Ruth said slowly. "I don't drink much pop."

"I don't usually, either, but man, it's kind of like a drink of home, right? This is all super cool, don't get me wrong, but I do not like that tea they keep offering me everywhere—*don't tell*, because that would be rude!—and besides that I'm kind of homesick. I always am, when I'm on these—when I'm traveling. And even sometimes when I'm not." She picked at the frayed knee of her jeans.

"Me too."

The girl turned her head to look at Ruth again. "Homesick?"

"Yes."

"For Michigan?"

Ruth nodded, though really it was the farm, and even more so the past, a place that didn't exist any longer, that she missed so achingly.

The girl tapped Ruth's leg with one finger. "Thought so. It was your accent, plus then you said 'pop.'"

Ruth gave her a half smile.

The girl twirled a handful of curls up into a makeshift bun and stared into the rain again. "Sorry to barge in on your quiet, by the way. You want me to go? I can catch up with the rest of my—my crew."

"You're Jane," Ruth said. "Plain Jane. And they're the Enforcers."

Plain Jane Harrison, famous in a small way, shot Ruth a perplexed look. "How'd you know that?"

Ruth shrugged. "I live outside Detroit."

"OK. But still, how?"

Some of Ruth's friends found her affection for hipster indie-rock bands odd, or anyway unlikely. But she did have it. She had a soft spot for long-haired guitar-wielding young men with shy smiles. She adored skinny girl singers with big fierce bluesy voices. A flare of pride spiked inside her. Maybe she was not so bovine after all. "I liked your last show a lot, the benefit you did downtown last fall." Ruth had ordered the vinyl, which she still had the equipment to play. The cover showed Jane and the band standing beneath the old Fox Theatre's ornate marquee in a driving rain. Even soaking wet they looked spunky and good-humored and young. Possibility poked out like porcupine quills from each of them.

"You were there?"

"No. I bought the album." *Enforce This*. Ruth smiled involuntarily.

"*Where* do you live?"

"Novi."

"You bothered to get the album but didn't bother to go to the show in the first place?"

A flush spread up Ruth's neck. "Um. Yes."

"Well—why?"

Why indeed. Ruth's flicker of interest in herself guttered out. She lifted a shoulder.

Jane's smile was gentle. "So what are you doing in Japan?"

"Nothing, really."

A minute ticked by. Jane reached for the bag Ruth had abandoned. Ruth tensed.

"This is yours?"

"No," Ruth said, less firmly than she'd meant to.

Jane pulled the tree-embossed journal out and undid the leather string from the button. The rain fell down harder again. Ruth stared out through the framing pillars at the green wood and office buildings beyond. She smelled salt in the air, which was the smell of history and of adventure.

Jane turned a page. The paper made a tissuey sound and Ruth was transported back to the farm, to that summer Yuko came, to a rainstorm that had made them both lethargic and quiet. They'd sat on their beds and followed solitary pursuits. Ruth had been reading some novel; Yuko was doing homework she'd brought across the ocean with her. There'd been grilled cheeses that night for supper. Ruth remembered how they'd giggled, making the sandwiches, after the long afternoon of quiet.

The tendrils of curls Jane hadn't twisted up into the bun shielded her face; her entire body was leaned over the poem.

"Growing up, we were so simple," Ruth suddenly said. "I went off to summer camp one year and learned about *bagels*. A revelation."

Jane looked up. Her eyes were green, and bright. "With us it was stir-fry. We bought a wok at the new supermarket out on the highway when it opened—"

"Oh, did it come as a kit, with the ring to set above your burner and the wooden skewer sticks?"

"Sure did."

"We had one of those too. I still have it. Somewhere."

A woman in a white kimono patterned with red-and-turquoise stars stepped onto the bridge. She moved serenely up the small rise and down again. "There was this house—Bob Seger's house, we called it. The fanciest place in miles, so of course it had to be his. We were sure of it. The world-famous rocker, *our neighbor*. As if. I mean, maybe he did have a place near there—I guess he grew up outside Detroit—but to be so sure just because the house was big... And it wasn't even, not really—"

Jane had grabbed Ruth's arm, and she was laughing. "I know. We had that too, Bob Seger's house. Ours was over on Snover Road."

"Ours was on M-46. White, with a gate out front—"

"Ours had columns."

"*Columns*. My stars."

Jane whooped. "I haven't heard anybody say that in way too long."

■ ■ ■

Jane hugged Ruth before she ducked out of the lean-to a few minutes later. "Come to a show sometime. We'll be at Jazz Fest this year."

"I *will*." Ruth smiled firmly.

"You're lying. Here, give me your address, I'm sending you tickets. And you send me something too, OK? The name of that haiku guy I was reading in your book there." Jane pulled a Sharpie out of her pocket. *Jane Harrison,* she wrote in spiky letters on Ruth's forearm. *9086 Muck Road, Elmer, MI. Wants haiku!* She underlined *haiku* three times.

■ ■ ■

The teahouse opened for business; the rain drummed on. The damp spread from Ruth's knees to her ankles, but this didn't seem bothersome now. She began to catalog all the words she could think of for rain: drizzle, downpour, deluge, mist, shower, sleet, torrent. A child who was wearing a red sweater and sporting a bowl cut ran in, followed by her mother, who wore a blue cardigan and a gray calf-length skirt. Ruth patted the seat next to her. "*Konnichiwa*," she said.

"Hel-lo." The woman spoke carefully, almost getting the l's. She took the child's hand and settled both of them on the bench.

Ruth opened the dictionary and the realtor's card fell out. She began to tuck it away again, but then, in a tiny motion hardly equal to the symbolic weight in it, she dropped it in the garbage can that sat in the hut's front corner. She could always get another from Joe, if she wanted. She riffled through the book and pointed to the word *rain*.

"Ah." The woman dragged her fingers through the air, wiggling her fingers, as if she was working out its tangles. "Rain. *Ame*."

"Ame."

The woman nodded. "This rain, *saiu*." She pursed her lips and rolled her eyes, mocking herself for the difficulty she was about to have, and then said, "Driz-zle."

Ruth grinned.

■ ■ ■

After the mother and child left, Ruth slung her embroidered bag over her shoulder. For some reason there was a carousel at the far edge of the garden. She would go see it. After that she'd stop at the teahouse. She didn't have to *like* green tea to drink it for another week. Also, she was going to call Professor Nakamura again. He had been very polite, after all. She would ask him to help her track down Yuko something-or-other née Kaneko. There had to be records somewhere of the children who'd traveled from Japan to Michigan in the summer of 1975 to stay with rural farm families. He could just help her find those records, that was all. It was what he owed for intimating that his mother's youthful musings about boys and hair clips had been frivolous. Ruth ducked under the eave and headed toward the carousel's faint, tinny music, her phone in her hand.

AMONG THE BEASTS

John Smolens

I AM HERE AT A COMPUTER IN THE LEARNING RESOURCES Center at the North Star Facility, the juvenile detention center in Hanley, Michigan, and at the request of my facilitator, Nolan Lyttle, MSW, PhD, I commit the following to a Word document, to what purpose I do not know, but I welcome the opportunity—not to defend myself, not to exonerate myself, not to declare my guilt or innocence, but to have my say, as they say. Besides, it's something to do. It can get pretty dull in here.

1.

So, to begin: my name is Timothy Randall Lutton, and I was born here in Michigan's Upper Peninsula seventeen years ago, on 15 March 1995. I have arrived at this point in history through what some might consider pitiful circumstances. However, the last thing I seek is pity or sympathy. Rather, it is from these circumstances that I have drawn the full extent of my strength. My greatest discovery is that I wasn't just born—I created myself. No one else deserves credit or blame, thus guilt or innocence isn't the question, despite the fact that these two opposing forces are the yin and yang that drive all judicial systems. My home, such as I've ever had one, is a small house in Menominee, about an hour's drive south from here, which looks across an untended yard at Green Bay and Door County Peninsula on the horizon. In winter, ice forms on the bay, and one of my earliest recollections is of a massive grinding sound as the floes were pushed along the shore by the wind. To my knowledge, it's the only place my mother has ever lived. She never said who my father was, and when I was growing up it was something she refused to discuss. Whoever he was, I like to think he's now found his ultimate demise, which should be perceived as the only true glory, the moment when we all witness the cosmos around us before we are forever extinguished.

2.

My mother was sometimes considered a simpleton but I know this not to be true. She was extraordinarily beautiful when young. I have seen photographs and the word "voluptuous" would not be inaccurate. She did well in school and wanted to go to college to become a teacher. Her first pregnancy—she was maybe sixteen—seems to have curtailed such hopes, though the child died in infancy. There may have been another pregnancy, or perhaps two, I'm not certain—I only know that they did not come to fruition and I have no idea whether they were terminated as a result of miscarriage or abortion. What I do know is that I was conceived in 1994 and born the following year on the Ides of March. For a time, when I was very young, we lived in the house with her mother and brother. Her mother died of pneumonia before I was old enough to attend school, and her brother Jonas studied philosophy and comparative literature at Michigan State, and was then admitted to the graduate program at Harvard. When he would return from Cambridge he would always bring me a present, some book that he thought a boy should read: terrible books about hidden treasure and children getting lost in caves, books full of hope and lies.

3.

The house was filled with my grandmother's statues of St. Francis, St. Joseph, that ridiculous Virgin, and all the rest. The palm fronds tucked behind the crucifix were moldy and smelled of decay. Often I would get up on my mother's bed and put my nose to the fronds and inhale deeply. But I unlearned religion, starting with the Day of the Dogs. A vacant lot down the street became my favorite place, the ground strewn with treasure: dented cans, broken bottles, used condoms. During the warm months winos slept in the bushes and huddled around small fires. I hid a pack of cigarettes in an Eight O'Clock Coffee can, which I kept buried under a rock. I discovered sex in that vacant lot. I saw two dogs. I saw a boy and girl down on their hands and knees. I saw two boys sucking each other off. I saw that it was all the same. We were all beasts. This was our true reward. I came to understand why Jonas would return at Christmas, and again for the summer. Nietzsche wrote, "We have unlearned something. We have become more modest in every way. We no longer derive man from the 'spirit,' from the 'god-head'; we have dropped him back among the beasts."

4.

My mother in the kitchen: not yet thirty, she smelled old. While she cut vegetables or cleaned fish, her mouth hung open and I could hear her breathe through her nose. As she worked, her breasts were often spilling out of her blouse. She took no more notice of them than of the air about her. Her skin held the scent of dish soap and stale milk and garlic and Pall Malls. On a warm evening she would sit out on the back porch and smoke cigarettes while watching the wind on the bay. When I was small there was a wooden swing, an old two-seater suspended by chains that were attached to a pair of hooks in the rafters. I often sat with her on the swing, causing those chains to creak and groan, and I would gaze distrustfully up at the rafters, fearing yet wanting the whole thing—the roof, the porch, the entire universe—to crash down upon us. My mother told me that she liked to watch the gusts move across the surface of the bay. This was the way her mind worked, like wind creating swirling patterns on Green Bay, fitful and random, with no real purpose other than the impressions they made on the water. That swing has long since fallen apart and been discarded.

5.

Nights when Jonas was home, I would lie in bed and listen for him to return from the bars. He often passed out on the living-room couch, but some nights he would enter my mother's room. I could hear the box springs beneath them, which reminded me of the dogs in the lot, how when a dog exerts itself the rib cage rolls beneath its coat. As the pace of the box springs quickened, there would come from my mother's room hoarse sounds, and I imagined that she and Jonas were in a race. Then their voices would explode, and in the calm that followed I would hear the beautiful sound of my mother crying.

6.

One day, when I was twelve, I was alone in the house. It was just before Christmas. I got a large plastic garbage bag from the kitchen and went around the house collecting the statues, the photographs, the palm fronds, the rosaries, the crucifixes. They clattered together as I walked across the yard to the water. The beach was strewn with large pieces of driftwood, whole trees with snarled, twisted roots. There was one trunk that ran from the beach out into the water, and I walked out on it and heaved the garbage bag into the bay. Back in the house I went into the crawl space in the wall behind my bed. I kept the copy of *Hustler* I'd found in the vacant lot there. I looked at the pictures of the naked women and undid my pants, staying in there until it was dark outside and I was exhausted. Over the years it seemed my mother had worked in every restaurant between Marinette, Wisconsin, and Escanaba, Michigan, and when I heard her come home that night I went down to the kitchen. She was singing and I knew she'd had a few drinks somewhere. She was happy. When I told her I had thrown all the statues into the bay, she walked about the house, speechless, but it was interesting: she looked as though she deserved this. There was acceptance in her eyes, and, of course, guilt. Only those capable of feeling guilt can really experience happiness, particularly when it's artificially induced by alcohol. She had been happy; I made her unhappy. And frightened. I told her if she brought any more religious stuff into the house I'd throw that out too.

7.

Jonas was drunk most of the time that December. Since moving to Cambridge, he dressed differently: a tweed jacket and corduroy pants, and he wore scarves even when he was in the house. And he talked with an accent now, not quite like a British homosexual. He seemed pleased that I had removed the statues. We were sitting at the kitchen table and he was drinking a bottle of beer. My mother had a fistful of salt, which she threw into the large pot of boiling water for the linguini (he corrected her when she called it spaghetti). Jonas was busy peeling the label off the bottle of beer when he asked me if I had lost my faith. I only stared back at him, and he offered an approving nod.

8.

We had cousins who lived in Marinette, just across the border in Wisconsin, and one night my mother called to say she was going to stay there because of white-out conditions and 60 mph winds off the bay. I understood what she was doing. If the weather cleared, Jonas was going to fly from Green Bay back to Cambridge in the morning and it was understood that he planned on fucking her once more before leaving. He sat in the living room drinking and I went to bed early. He came into my room soon after and opened the small door in the wall. He asked if I had been in there lately to beat off. Before I could answer, he said to take a look. I was afraid but didn't want to show it, so I took my flashlight from the nightstand and crawled through the door and there, tucked between two wall studs, was a paper bag. I brought the bag to the bed and it contained magazines that had pictures of people having sex, men with women, men with men, women with women, rooms crammed with naked bodies coupled in ways I had never imagined. He sat next to me and gently placed a hand on the back of my head. He said, "A going-away present," and left the room.

9.

The next year I grew five inches. Except for the real fatties, I weighed more than most boys in my class. I picked fights at random. My size frightened them; what baffled them was that there was no apparent reason for my hostility. More than once I would have a boy down on the ground, punching his bloody face, and he would beg me to tell him why I had chosen him. I would hit him harder and ask, "*Now do you understand?*" Eventually the boy would lie, saying he understood, just so I would stop hitting him. Teachers sent me to the principal; the principal sent me home; a man from the state came and talked to me; a psychiatrist sat with me in the school clinic; a police officer came to the house. I would not stop, I could not stop. When I was suspended I would continue, waiting for kids when school got out. When I was fifteen I was sent to another school over near Rhinelander, Wisconsin, a kind of reform school that they called boot camp because it was run by some ex-military men who believed shouting, cold showers, and physical exhaustion would cure anything. After four months they sent me home, saying I was better, but the fact was they couldn't control me either and they gave up after

I had dislocated a field instructor's shoulder. I didn't go to school that spring, but just hung around the house, walking the beach.

10.

The following fall I returned to high school. Hardly anyone spoke to me. Boys avoided looking me in the eye. Teachers were polite but wary. I didn't do any assignments but no one said anything. They just let me be. When they would work on something that didn't interest me, which was often, I would just read or look out the window. My English teacher did try to get me to talk when the class was reading *Julius Caesar*. I said I had already read it, which was true. She asked what I thought of it, and I could tell she thought she had found the key to open me up. I looked out the window and ignored her.

11.

Later that semester I wrote an essay that my English teacher found disturbing. Her word: "disturbing." The principal got involved, and ultimately people from the Department of Human Services (DHS) also found my essay disturbing, which resulted in my being sent to the North Star Facility in Hanley for "observation." This leveraged my mother into a deeper state of depression, which naturally reinforced in their minds that I needed to be placed in a "supportive environment." Jonas found some dipshit lawyer to represent us but that only led to a legal standoff, which taxed my mother's meager resources. All this because of an essay I wrote for an English class. I could beat the crap out of kids and the school would deal with it, but write a paper deemed disturbing and you get the State of Michigan on your case. The essay assignment was to describe a "process"; it could be anything, and in class we had small-group sessions so we might "brainstorm ideas," which led to students developing papers that described how to cook a hamburger, how to change a tire, how to twirl a baton, how to comb your hair. We were given the option of conducting research or basing our essay on personal experience. Needless to say, the subjects listed above were based on the personal experience of the students, some of whose personal experience did not include writing a single cohesive, grammatically correct paragraph in their sorry lives. My essay was based on information I found on the Internet, in the school library, and in some of Jonas's books. Here's the paper (for which I never received a grade):

Process Assignment: Punishment for High Treason

The punishment known as being drawn and quartered was first employed in England in 1241, when the method was used on a convicted pirate named William Maurice. Commonly perceived as one of the most sadistic forms of execution, the British government reserved this execution for cases of "high treason": acts of rebellion toward the government, spying on behalf of the enemy, or attempts upon the life of royalty. There were also, particularly during the 1500s, over one hundred executions of men found guilty of "spiritual treason," which were seditious acts toward the established state religion. Though there have been exceptions, drawing and quartering was reserved for men, whereas females found guilty of similar offenses against church or state were more likely to be burned at the stake.

The term "drawn and quartered" is really a misnomer. It would be more accurate (and in many historical documents is stated as such) to call the execution "hanging, drawing, and quartering." Though there have been numerous variations throughout history, traditionally this execution began with the victim first being hanged by the neck, though not in a fashion that resulted in immediate death caused by a broken vertebra. Thus the victim, whose hands were usually tied behind the back, was first stripped naked, and then hanged so that strangulation began. The victim was not pushed off or dropped from some considerable height (which would often result in a sudden and lethal breaking of the neck); rather, the victim was gently hoisted up by the neck, just high enough that only the toes touched the ground. The victim's "dance" was an integral part of this procedure (such executions were usually conducted before vast crowds and were intended to be both entertaining and instructive). Before the victim expired (the dance often lasted more than five minutes), he was lowered to the ground and his "privy members" were cut off. Next, his abdomen was slit open and his intestines were pulled out, piled before the victim, and set on fire. Then, in most cases, he was decapitated. There are numerous accounts in medieval documents that claim that if the procedure was performed properly the victim would still be conscious enough to witness the burning of his intestines.

Finally, the body was "quartered," or cut into pieces—often, but not necessarily always, four sections. At times the limbs were severed with a saw or a sword, but there were also instances where each limb was tied to a horse, each of which then ran in different directions, thus tearing the body apart. The severed body was usually put on public display. Often the parts were first boiled in water to retard decomposition, and then the heads were erected on pikes in public places such as the London Bridge. In certain cases, the king would mandate that the body parts be distributed to various regions of the country, as a warning to any other plotters who might be considering violence and rebellion against the crown.

For more than six hundred years the punishment known as being drawn and quartered was employed as a lawful deterrent to acts of high treason, and it was not until 1870 that language pertaining to this form of punishment was removed from England's Forfeiture Act.

12.

The following fall I returned to school, repeating sophomore year. The only thing worse than sophomore year is sophomore year the second time around. I was sixteen and weighed over two hundred pounds, and everyone avoided me. Except there was a girl named Leanne, who had spiked hair and a silver nose stud. She did things with boys for money. We met in the lot down the block. It was October, not long before Halloween, and the air smelled of burning leaves. I asked her how much and she said for me nothing. I told her I'd rather jerk off for free and left. For weeks I would go by her locker and slide a folded twenty-dollar bill through one of the air vents in the metal door, and next time she would see me she would return it. She would wrap the money in a note, insisting that for me it was not for sale. Sometimes I found tapes of music in my locker (how she got the combination, I don't know). She listened to heavy metal mostly, but then she also liked certain pieces by Mozart, particularly his *Requiem.* She said she would not wash until I touched her. Though her hair color changed every week or so, she wore the same jeans, T-shirt, and leather jacket day after day. She sat two desks in front of me in homeroom and eventually I could smell her. Once she turned around (the desk between us was empty, having been abandoned days earlier) and stared at me. Her tongue and left nostril glinted silver. She said she didn't believe in compromise but in this case she would accept a ten-dollar honorarium. After school we walked down to the vacant lot. When I gave her the money, she tore it up into small pieces and ate it.

13.

Sometimes we would go to her house when her mother was at work. Sometimes we would go to the vacant lot. She knew a guy named Derek who could get us coke and pills, and to pay for it I told boys I would beat them up. When that wasn't enough we robbed a few places in towns farther north in the UP: Crystal Falls, Iron Mountain, and once all the way up to Marquette. We hit gas stations and corner stores that sold bread and milk. We were never caught and we never made more than four hundred dollars. One night, as we were driving back to Menominee, Leanne told me she'd decided to commit suicide. She asked me if I would be there for her, if we could fuck as she died. I told her I might just go with her too. She said that was unacceptable. This was something she wanted to do on her own. She wanted somebody (me) to bear witness. She wanted somebody to remember it. If I died too, everything would be completely lost. People would just think it was some *tragic teenage-love suicide.* There would be no one to know the real beauty and purity of it. I had to admit she had a point.

14.

There was the question of practice. While fucking me she would have a knife and pretend to slit her wrists. Once she drew the dull edge of the knife across her throat. Another time, when I tried to help by putting my hand on hers, she said, "No, you can't be a part of this. This can't be murder. This has to be my suicide. It's the only thing that is completely mine." She wouldn't speak to me for days. Until finally I realized that again she was right. She said that suicide was the only truth, the only honest act. All else was cowardice, weakness, cynicism, and blind faith. The only way to defeat this life, its pain and hardship, was to leave it, without fear, on your own terms. Then you were untouchable. Then you were all-powerful. We began to make plans.

15.

We debated the need for pain. That it is required in this life goes without question. Whether it was necessary to her suicide, we couldn't be sure. She believed that a painful death would be more beautiful, more significant. It would allow her to achieve some greater perfection. But then she was something of a purist. And a perfectionist, so that naturally she worried about the final moments before she died. The last thing she wanted was to lose her nerve and resist her death. She didn't want to be one of those people, so often depicted in movies, pleading, begging for their life to be spared. She didn't want some survival mechanism to kick in, causing her at the last possible moment to do anything to stay alive. She definitely did not want to shit her pants. Yet an element of fear was essential. To go quietly, to simply slip into endless sleep, without some physical sensation of dying, she believed would be a cop-out. So it was determined that there would have to be some kind of pain, self-inflicted. But what kind became the problem. As in everything, Leanne took a methodical approach. She experimented with blades, knives, razors, tools. She practiced slicing her flesh. Rows of scars lined her thighs, which were always concealed by pants. To develop a greater tolerance for pain she inserted needles into herself. She decided that she didn't want to die screaming. Writhing, however, had a certain appeal. She suspected that someone who writhed in pain would be so far gone they would welcome death. To ensure that she would remain silent, she decided that she should have her mouth taped. She said there was certain to be a point where she might lose control and her body would react to its demise. So as an experiment we fucked with her mouth taped closed. Breathing only through her nose was difficult. She wondered if she might actually suffocate during an orgasm, an idea that intrigued her, for a lack of oxygen (usually through strangulation) is known to enhance the orgasm. If she taped both her nose and mouth, it might cause silent writhing, and, as she said, she might go off with one incredible bang. But this method would be bloodless, and that distressed her. Without blood, she feared that the act of suicide wouldn't be *inflicted* enough.

16.

Jonas returned from Cambridge to spend the summer in Menominee. His transformation was complete; he no longer looked like, sounded like, or acted like he came from the northern Midwest. He was consumed by his dissertation, which discussed primarily Byron, de Sade, Schopenhauer, Nietzsche, and Camus. His room was filled with stacks of books and I read most of them. I was most intrigued by H. L. Mencken's translation of Nietzsche's *The Antichrist.* It was written just as Nietzsche was ascending into absolute madness. The voice is so direct and unequivocal. It's pure music.

17.

One night while we were in the vacant lot, Leanne mistakenly opened a vein in her forearm with a piece of broken glass. She said she wasn't ready yet, and I got her to the hospital emergency room. A doctor stitched her up, and he was skeptical when Leanne explained that she had fallen and cut her wrist. This created problems at home for Leanne. She lived with her mother and there were visits by the DHS. They eventually concluded that Leanne might be taken away from her mother. That word "observation" was used. Leanne considered leaving the country. She wanted me to run away with her. We discussed whether we should flee to Mexico or Canada. Crossing either border would be difficult because neither of us had a passport.

18.

Jonas no longer showed any interest in my mother. She had gained weight over the previous winter, and during the summer, which was particularly hot and humid, her clothes seemed constantly soaked with sweat. She was severely depressed in her quiet way and often acted like a true simpleton. Though it was summer, she was having trouble finding waitressing shifts in the restaurants along the Lake Michigan shore. Evenings she would sit out on the porch steps smoking and slapping at mosquitoes. A lot of nights she stayed with our cousins over in Marinette.

19.

One night I called Leanne and her mother said she was gone. Her mother wasn't entirely sober, as usual, and she said the authorities from the DHS had come to take Leanne to a juvenile facility. But the way her mother said "She's gone" made me wonder if Leanne had managed to run away. At that time a man named Kenny was living with her mother and he got on the phone, not sounding exactly sober either, and told me not to call the house again, and if I did I'd have to deal with him. I told him I'd be right over and hung up. When I got to the house, maybe a half dozen blocks away, Kenny was standing on the front porch with a golf driver in his hands. He was balding and the way the hair on the sides of his head shot straight up he might have been standing in a powerful updraft of air, making me wonder if some alien force was about to suck him off the face of the earth. He wore boxer shorts and a V-neck T-shirt, with brown corduroy slippers on his feet. His legs were scrawny and red, looking like they'd been parboiled. When I approached the porch steps, he said, "You get off on beating up those little assholes at school, but all they need's a good number-one wood." He extended the club head toward my face. "This here's my Ping." I retreated to the sidewalk, where the pavement was broken up, and found a piece of concrete that weighed a little more than a baseball. Behind Kenny, Leanne's mother appeared inside the screen door. I heard the sirens coming from the direction of downtown and the way she stared out at me I knew that she had already made the call. I dropped the piece of concrete and began walking back toward my house. A police cruiser pulled over beside me and we talked in the heat for a minute, but somehow I gave them the impression that they should be dealing with a domestic disturbance involving a couple of drunks. The cops told me to go home and raced down to Leanne's house.

20.

For several weeks I heard nothing, knew nothing. I called various state agencies trying to locate Leanne. If she was confined in some facility, it might lead to her committing suicide by herself. When I'd first been at North Star, one of the "issues" that got a lot of airtime in counseling sessions was what I call the Big A, abandonment. Since I've been back here, Nolan Lyttle, MSW, PhD, has asked in various ways how I felt after Leanne disappeared—if I felt abandoned. In his own sly but not very subtle way, he has tried to link her abandonment to the fact that I don't know who my father is, and to the fact that my mother was not in the house much last summer after Jonas returned from Cambridge. I'm not buying into Nolan Lyttle's notions about the Big A. I've never given two shits about who my father is, and my mother has been MIA pretty much since I tossed her religious statues into the bay.

21.

In August, less than a month ago, I received a letter from Leanne. The return address was a post-office box in Oakland, California. The one-page letter was written on lined notepaper in her small, tight script, using virtually no capitals except when she WANTED TO MAKE A POINT:

> *dear tim, this has been the most extraordinary journey. when it was clear that those agents of the STATE were about to nab me i had no choice but to run. i hitched rides across the country (the hardest part was getting from menominee to marinette—go figure). along the way i encountered so many people steeped in AMERICAN WEIRDNESS that i really wished i had a passport or some means of getting across the border to canada or mexico. when i arrived here (i am not hint-hint actually IN OAKLAND but arranged to have this letter mailed from there) i was very close to taking my own life, with or without a witness. i'd been robbed in nebraska, raped by two truckers in the cab of an 18-wheeler parked in a utah truck stop, and forced to solicit when i first arrived in californ-I-A. weary of life on the streets i went into a shelter for women run by an organization that you would despise for its religious affiliations. but this turned out to be the reason for my journey i truly believe that. i have been introduced to THE LIGHT and all my pain and despair has been replaced by LOVE and JOY in HIS PRESENCE. i know what you're thinking but i am not bullshitting you. i have found PEACE and so can you dear tim if only you'll open your heart. you can always write to me at this address, and please find it in your heart to contribute to HIS WORK. In the past we welcomed death but now I pray that you find your way to being the WITNESS TO LIFE.*
>
> *may you dwell with me in HIS LIGHT,*
> *leanne*

If you were Nolan Lyttle, MSW, PhD, who will take notes while reading this, you might say that my abandonment issues kicked in at this point.

22.

The evidence (I am told by my court-appointed attorney, as much a dipshit as the previous one) is all over the first floor of my mother's house. After I procured the necessary equipment, my biggest concern was where the rope could be suspended from, until I realized that on the back porch there were the two hooks in the ceiling rafters, used at one time to hang the wooden swing. Getting him to the porch and under the rope and block pulley proved to be the greatest challenge. After he'd passed out in the living room, which he did almost every night, I dragged him out to the porch. As I pulled him across the kitchen linoleum, he was alert enough to ask where we were going and I said he could use some fresh air. He agreed and within seconds he began to snore, until he realized that the irritation about his throat was caused by a noose. By then it was too late. I hauled him up just so he could do the dance, tiptoeing on the porch floor. After I tied the rope off on the railing, I proceeded with the process, which was conducted in a proper fashion. One for the history books.

23.

My story went viral. The right-wing blogosphere lit up and a state representative in Louisiana told his constituents that if they were serious about reducing the crime rate they would support his bill, which would make the punishment known as being drawn and quartered the penalty for heinous crimes. I was the lead story on CNN, Fox, and MSNBC. I think my mother liked the attention. When she came to visit me, she wore a dress and even some makeup. On TV she looked a bit of her voluptuous, youthful self as my attorney hustled her past the camera crews outside of North Star. She did respond to one reporter's question, saying that the reason for her son's actions was to protect his mother. This resulted in speculation in the media that Jonas was my father, a notion that my mother steadfastly denied. During an interview on TV she said couldn't recall the name of the man who had been my father—she only remembered that it happened in a car after she finished her shift at Lucky's Lounge in Escanaba, which had gone out of business years ago. Reporters delved into Jonas's activities in Cambridge and, wielding their favorite word, *allegedly,* suggested that he had a long history of predatory behavior. Not that I was exonerated. If the news angle on the story wasn't exactly sympathetic toward my actions, at least some bloggers asserted that, considering the circumstances, they were understandable. My mother received several marriage proposals, the most promising from an Oklahoma dairy farmer who'd recently sold his land to an oil company and moved to the Cayman Islands. But these didn't pan out, and once the story faded from the TV news cycle she began to show up at North Star looking the worse for wear and not a little medicated. Her tear ducts seemed to have run dry, her hollow gaze reminding me of the evenings when she used to gaze out at the wind patterns on the bay. Yesterday, when she and my attorney visited, I could tell from their body language that the state's prosecuting attorney had succeeded in convincing the court that I should be tried as an adult. It was in that moment that it happened, that it came to me, and I reached across the table and took my mother's hand and asked her if she would pray to Jesus with me, the way we did when I was a small boy.

LAY OF THE LAND

Janet Kauffman

BABIES ARE BORN HERE AND LET LOOSE. IT HAPPENS IN various places, in lowlands where you don't expect to see animals, not even cats, or where if you do see them, they're bulky as grade-schoolers with wide faces and combed yellow hair. Out in farm country especially, where you don't expect to see trees or even stumps of trees, but where if you see them, they're shamelessly inhabited, wired and roofed, and inside the plate-glass windows you see large sofas and tall lamps.

A baby in that sort of place walks off.

There she is, crossing a field.

A baby is conceived and born into the world. Mother and father are not entirely extraneous. But the baby enters her first room and before she has anything to say on the matter, the sun falls across her body, or light falls from a lamp whose firing power, generated from coal, traces all the way back to leaf, and sun on leaf.

And so from the moment of cutting loose, the baby is weathered, not fathered or mothered. Let the father and mother, fully attired, do what they will, the baby has feet and arrangements of toes pressing against the variable textures of the ground. She has armpits accommodating air, whether still or blowy.

It is interesting to see how the weight of her legs shifts, the awkwardness of her crossing furrows. She learned not long ago how to cross one leg under the other and grab onto cloth, or branch-works, or onto the side of a sand hill, and pull herself up. Already she knows what to do with her shoulders when the unevenness of the ground rocks her. She rocks back. A graph of the points of the top of her head, as she meanders, would be a graph of topography, the lay of the land, and its relative give at the weight of each step.

This is a sandy field, and it is hot. It is probably summer, or she wouldn't yearn, as babies yearn in that weather, to walk off in every direction. Of course it is not ambition. She doesn't know east from west. She hasn't asked for directions to the nearest community college. She is, in fact, too low to the ground to see over the lowest hill and count the roofs of Valley Country Estates, its conglomeration of thirty-five roofs.

She is out for nothing but pleasure, and the answers to unvoiced bodily questions concerning wind direction, sun and shade, colors of this and that, relative humidity, tastes, light and dark. She knows already of discomfort and pain: thorns, cuts, chills. What she's learned from these matters is hard to say. She goes on. She expects more of that kind of thing, that's about how it looks. She is not deterred. She is not, apparently, frightened. She has seen birds and they seem very simple to her.

No wonder this baby has kept herself going for three days. She is almost out of range. She has not thought once to enter a backyard. She keeps at a distance, within hedgerows, low in the ditches, on the shadowy side of brush. She follows those intermittent, leftover bits of wild growth, the tangle comparable to her own purposelessness, and abandonment.

She is a rangy, leathery baby, three days out.

A baby is easy to track. To start with. But out of familiar territory, the ways she chooses to go may be so erratic, involving so much backtracking and looping about, that the tracker cannot count on patterns within the species to guess where a baby might turn up next. Not many babies are tracked beyond the first miles. And dogs, befrienders of babies always, lick the toes and fingers when they come upon a baby, and leave her to her play.

At the edge of a sandy field, the baby finds herself in an interesting place. The ground slopes off abruptly—she will have to slide feetfirst. But beyond that is a gradual tilt toward a marshland, its wide expanse of water and toppled straw-colored grasses. The place is a flat-bottomed bowl, a no-place.

She slides halfway down, holding onto the stalks of switchgrass to steady herself. She stops when she hits the lull and the heat—that line where the bowl's edges block off the wind. She turns her head, sorts out the noises: insects, frogs, birds. Overhead streaming of air.

She leans into warm sand, newly dug, the debris from a fox hole, a groundhog hole, just up the slope. It is soft, beachy sand. And she sleeps.

There is no need to worry. It's the middle of the day, the safest hour for a baby in the wild. She's lucky not to be at the corner of Main and Church, where a baby about her weight has just been thrown into the air by a Ford Ranger; lucky not to be under the third roof in Valley Country Estates where—what you'd expect—a baby is thrashed by a 38" Wrangler belt, wielded by her mother. Some babies are sleeping in their cribs, that's true, and some are eating peas and carrots. Even so, they are babies at risk.

In the wild, or at least the out-of-the-way, a baby sleeps profoundly. If there is danger, or death, it is no anomaly. It is simply there, for all species, equally. Could it be their democratic nature that drives these babies out? The reason they refuse pillows, and pack nothing?

Probably not. They haven't talked enough, haven't got far enough past the nouns. Sun. Rock. Bird.

Tree. Wolf. Sky.

■ ■ ■

When the baby wakes, she recognizes it is a wolf beside her. It is not a fox. It has blue wolf eyes.

And it paces, it will not sit down. The wolf walks around the baby. When any one of its feet hits the sand, there's a spit of dust. The fur on the paw flares out, muffles any sound. Circling, the wolf comes to terms with the baby. There she is. She stands up. She walks as best she can in the deep sand. They mirror each other: they walk, they halt. The baby does not think to smile. The wolf has a mouth that is shadow. And the baby holds her tongue in shadow, too. She does not have teeth. Does the wolf have teeth?

Likely. Very likely.

And yet it is not until evening that she sees how the whole of the wolf body works in the capture and feasting on rabbit, for instance, and how the tongue draws in water out of the swamp. The baby, scooping up water, becomes aware of her own muscled arms, the intricate fingering. She recognizes how, without plan, she swallows and chews at mulberries. How she can throw them away.

The wolf circles and settles down under a shelf of wild grape whose vines have overtaken a tree and arched the lowest branches. In the same place, some feet away, the baby heaps up leaves and maneuvers under them, her cover. It is possible the wolf has wandered from its haunts. Why else would these two link themselves without suspicion and watch over each other's sleep—the wolf, perhaps a baby, too, awake from midnight to dawn; the baby alert from dawn to noon.

At noon, they take off. We can guess where. Fables are what we recall. Or something quite different. The baby, for instance, when she is able, grows hair on her body. It is not fur, but still, she is never mistaken for Miss Arkansas. And the wolf—he eventually stands, when he must, and trims off a bit of fur. They live a long time on their own. They sit around; they fabricate musical instruments out of dried mud and reeds. They are sick, and wounded, more often—or is it less often?—than adolescents in Valley Country Estates.

They have chance, inevitable contacts with farmers, surveyors, the Army Corps of Engineers. And as they grow larger, the territory they inhabit diminishes, that's how it seems. They consider the advantages of permanent shelter, and there—that's the turnabout point.

They walk into town and enroll in a literacy program.

Before long, they are both employed, paying taxes, and enjoying the fruits of their labor. For vacations, they choose the national parks, where their tax money does what they like, and where they feel peculiarly at home. They never figure it out, but even in town where there is painted plaster and a wall of particle board, they make love. They roll themselves around. Belly to belly, belly to back, they aren't very particular about the light, or the dark that falls into the room.

You might say they're home free. You might say the mat of hair on their bellies is a thing of the past. You might say that.

THE CHURCH OF THE FELLOWSHIP OF SOMETHING

Thisbe Nissen

GINNY MAAKESTAD WAS IN THE MIDDLE STALL OF OUR LADY of the Prairie's ladies' room, struggling blindly to unwrap and insert a tampon without reducing her wedding dress to something out of *Carrie*, when the tornado sirens commenced their purgatorial tugboat wail. The dress had been sewn in its entirety by the groom's sister, Eula Yoder, on a new Singer 2662 that Eula had purchased at the Highway 1 Walmart with money she earned cleaning the Iowa City home of the bride's parents, Phillipa and Michael Maakestad. The Singer took up residence in Ginny's old bedroom at the Maakestads', as Eula still lived on her dead parents' farm and the Yoders had neither believed in, nor relied upon, electricity. It was Silas (Eula's brother, Ginny's betrothed) who ferried his sister those forty miles round-trip (which was eighty miles for him, as he lived in town, and had for some years now, in a condo, full amenities, rent-to-own) every other Wednesday and thus enabled her budding career as a housecleaner and matrimonial seamstress. During its creation the dress had suffered at least two tulle-shredding attacks by what was suspected to be either a mouse or a vole, and one near-fatal encounter with a bottle of acetone nail-polish remover that spilled across the front hem of the dress, prematurely aging the taffeta to a crisp fawn-colored paper that crumbled to the touch and had to be shorn off entirely, reducing Ginny's wedding dress to "tea-length," which was both odd-looking and unfortunate, for the bride's razor-scarred ankles were not her best, nor her favorite, feature. *Fortunately*, Ginny was heavily medicated.

The skirts of this wedding dress—tea-length, tiered, trained, and apparently somehow bustle-able—were at the moment being held up by the bride's mother (Phillipa Maakestad) on one side and Linda, the maid of honor, on the other. Phillipa and Linda were perched, respectively, on the toilet seats of the first and third bathroom stalls, heads and arms sticking up over the dividers like pranksters waiting to strike, clutching fistfuls of tulle like toilet-paper bombs. The bride—in stall #2, eight pounds shy of a hundred, panty hose at her knees—looked like she'd been caught by the blast of a subterranean volcano tunneled up through the plumbing from beneath the prairie. It was in this precarious configuration that the bridal trio was discovered by a heavily made-up soprano soloist from the choir who came crashing into the ladies' room and slammed the door behind her. "There's a twister!" she cried. "We've got to get to the bomb room!"

"The *bomb room*?" snapped the maid of honor from her stall #3 toilet-seat pedestal. "Who are you: *Dr. Strangelove*?" Linda was a former junkie who weighed over two hundred pounds and was known neither for her tact nor her gentility, though she'd been corralled, on this special day, into a dress made from a not-insubstantial quantity of satin yardage, and was bearing it stoically—among a host of other traditional wedding-party indignities—like a hair shirt woven in Statue of Liberty green.

"What*ever* you *call* it," said the soloist.

"Who *are* you?" Linda said back.

"I don't matter," said the soloist, who then seemed so pleasantly shocked by this assertion that she was compelled to try it out again: "I don't matter!"

"Yes you do," came a small, insistent voice from stall #2. "Of course you do."

Outside, the wind hurled something against the frosted bathroom window. It thudded, stuck there a moment, then whipped off again, like a swimmer flip turning at the edge of a pool.

"Ginny, honey," said the bride's mother from her perch on toilet #1, "have you got it?"

Linda was craning over to peer into Ginny's stall. "She's got it *in*," she announced. "Just don't *touch* anything, Gin. Your hands are a bloody mess."

"Jesus Christ," sighed the bride's mother. "You couldn't give in this once—your *wedding* day—and get the applicator ones?"

"It's unconscionably wasteful," Ginny said. "Besides all that *bleach*." She reached for the toilet paper, mounted on a SAV-U-MOR non-rotating dispenser, and pawed at the roll, her fingers sticky with blood.

"They don't make the organic ones with applicators?" her mother pressed. "That seems rather—" It was difficult to converse over the drone of the tornado siren.

"They *do*," Ginny whined. "They were *out*." She held her hands as far from her person as possible, picking at her fingers like a child covered in glue, or paint, or cookie dough.

"*Stop* that, Gin! Look at the mess you're—" Phillipa Maakestad lifted her attention from her daughter on the toilet seat below and addressed the soloist: "Could you—could you please wet down some paper towels for her?" She jerked her chin toward the bay of sinks on which two bouquets rested, and then to the towel dispenser. The singer didn't budge. "Could you please?" Phillipa said again, this time indicating with her chin toward her bloody-fingered daughter in the stall below, concurrently seeming to realize that the woman could not *see* Ginny inside the stall and had no idea what was going on behind door #2. "She's . . ." Phillipa lifted her own hands above the stall divider so the woman could see what she held. "Her *hands*," she explained. "She needs to clean her hands."

And though the soloist looked like she'd just been asked to *wipe* the girl, she strode obediently to the sink and moistened a wad of brown towels until they looked like grocery bags left out in the rain. Then she turned back toward the stall, only to be momentarily confounded by the fact of the door, as though it had just materialized between herself and the bloodied bride. She stood blankly as if awaiting direction.

"Gin," Phillipa said into the stall. "Can you . . . ?" but it was clear that Ginny could not reach the lock from where she sat. Phillipa turned back to the soloist. "Can you put them under, reach them under the door to her?"

"*Down* on my—?"

"Well come and hold *this* then," Linda interrupted. "And *I'll* hand her the fucking towels, for Chrissake!" At which point the soloist, cowed, looked down to inspect the cleanliness of the church's bathroom floor, apparently found it not unacceptable, and lifted her choir robe with one hand as she sank slowly to one knee, like a lover in proposal. She steadied herself with a shoulder against the frame of the stall and reached the towel wad under the door. Ginny grabbed it—"Thanks"—and began to pinch at it ineffectually. When she was done, she held out the defiled lump as though she expected it to be removed via the same means it had arrived.

"Put it in the trash, Gin," said her mother from above. "Right there, on the wall, beside the paper."

Ginny located the bin, on whose aluminum lid someone had appropriately, if not particularly tastefully, scratched the words *Blessed Be The Bleeding*. She peered inside as though checking for mail, then deposited the soiled towels and clapped the lid shut. The tornado siren moaned on.

In the mirror the soloist swabbed a clot of mascara from beneath her right eye and wiped the smudge on her choir robe like it was a cooking apron. Then she spun toward the stalls, her tone bolstered with a new authority: "I've got to ask you all to come down to the bomb shelter immediately." The frosted-glass window shuddered in corroboration.

Phillipa adjusted her hold on Ginny's skirts. "Can you stand and get your hose up?"

The bride hitched up her stockings as directed, Linda and Phillipa swaying above her like puppeteers. Then, Ginny undid the door lock expectantly, as though it were her beloved awaiting, and not just some lady from the choir, but as she moved to cross the stall's threshold Phillipa cried, "Ginny—stop!" and they froze, as it seemed to dawn on all four of them at once that if Ginny took one more step Linda and Phillipa would be forced to either let go of the skirts or fall off their toilet perches or both.

There was a moment of relative silence, the tornado siren white noise in the air. No one seemed to know how to proceed. It was finally the soloist who sprang to action. "I'll come in," she cried. "I'll get behind, hold the dress from behind!" She looked up to Phillipa, then to Linda. "I'll take it from you. Below." She turned to face the mirrors to demonstrate, lifting her arms over her head like she was making to land an airplane right there in the ladies' room. Then she doubled back, shimmying sideways past Ginny and into the stall. Pausing, she seemed to consider the advisability of flushing the toilet, decided against it, and moved to part the tulle, like a canopy of mosquito netting, and duck beneath Ginny's bridal trains, lifting her hands above her to catch the skirts as they settled. She was able to follow Ginny out of the stall, the dress tented safely over her, like the back half of the inevitable two-man sheep costume in Our Lady of the Prairie's Christmas pageant.

■ ■ ■

The sky had gone the color of split-pea soup. Outside the ladies' room the siren's drone was a physical presence. Phillipa held the door as the procession filed through, the soloist holding Ginny's skirts, Linda bringing up the rear, both bouquets clutched to her satin stomach. As she let the bathroom door swing closed, Phillipa stood suddenly taskless, and for a moment it seemed she might well bend down and lift the hem of the singer's robe so they could travel as a great train of billowing white.

At the far end of the hall—beneath an exit sign onto which someone had snaked a magic-marker S between the I and the T—a junior pastor in a black robe several sizes too large held open the stairwell door, his robe flapping around him as though billowed by a pair of enormous hidden wings. This junior pastor was a sylph of a man, elfin in stature, with attached earlobes, very blue eyes, and a chin so pointy it almost looked like Plasticine, all of which lent him an air of great mischief, as though he might be ready to throw off his cloak and reveal some extravagant peacock-blue Mardi Gras costume, all spangles, plumes, and tranny glam. Behind him, to the right of the doorframe, a pinwheel of sinister triangles, yellow on black, marked the route to the relative safety of a World War II–era fallout shelter, although the exuberant flair with which the junior pastor beckoned the bridal party (and their ad hoc, soprano fourth) toward the stairs created the impression that what actually lay at the foot of those stairs was more like the entrance to a very hip, underground S&M club.

The bridal party, Linda now in the lead, made their way into the stairwell, and the black-flapping junior pastor followed, closing the door behind himself. At the bottom of the flight was a tiny vestibule that Linda nearly filled entirely. A door on the left opened to the outside, where a wheelchair ramp spouted off like a toboggan run. Lightning flashed through a porthole window; the sky turned the color of roasting eggplant.

A second door opened onto a dark, down-sloping ramp. "We call it 'the catacombs'!" the junior pastor called enthusiastically, still only halfway down the stairs behind the bride's mother, the soloist, and the rear half of the bride and her train. His voice echoed out like a fun-house ghoul.

From the vestibule below, Linda peered down the fallout-shelter ramp. "Fuck," she said, and then paused as though waiting to hear what kind of echo might resound. "We're going to fuck the shit out of these dresses in there," she said, turning back to her compatriots, which was when she seemed to realize the utter inappropriateness of her language, which she acknowledged with a further "Oh fuck," then silently vowed to try not to speak another word until Ginny was done and married.

"We *all need* to get to the shelter," the soloist lobbied. She still held Ginny's train, which she lifted in both hands for emphasis, her fingers clenched as though she might begin to wring the tulle in desperation.

Ginny said, as a matter of fact: "This dress can't take any more ruining."

"I refuse," said the mother of the bride, "to die as an Iowa tornado casualty." Then added, "In a church!"

"Well," said the junior pastor, who, if he was insulted, gave no such indication, "then let's get ourselves to the shelter."

Down in the vestibule Linda turned her back to Ginny, gesturing something with her bouquet that Ginny did not clearly understand. "Un*button* me," Linda snapped. Ginny obliged and helped Linda step free of the dress. Ginny's maid of honor was not an immodest woman, but she'd already shrugged off the entire confection of the wedding as patently absurd, and numbed herself down with a few strong shots before she'd boarded the ship that was her dress and prepared to walk down the aisle in support of the ninety-two-pound bride whom she credited as her personal savior, which was on account of Ginny's unflagging devotion as much as it was out of gratitude for the not one but *two* occasions on which it was Ginny who found Linda, called 911, and performed the CPR she'd learned in high school until EMTs arrived with a defibrillator. For Linda, *wearing* that dress and *removing* the dress were equally ridiculous propositions, and she stripped down to her slip with no more than a second's deliberation, stepped out of that oxidized-green refrigerator box, and began bunching it up so she might pass it most efficiently up the stairs. "Hang it on the banister," she called to Phillipa. Then she took Ginny by the shoulders and spun her around as far as she'd go, her skirts and train twisting around her like a stowed umbrella. The soloist, still tenaciously keeping the train from the floor, tripped down a few steps, tugged by that leash of ivory veiling.

With incongruously nimble fingers and an almost magical dexterity, Linda unfastened thirty-six pea-sized, satin-covered buttons from their looping as if they were so many snaps, then helped the bride step from her tempest of tulle, which the increasingly fastidious soloist swooped fervently up, her estimation of the bridal gown seeming to have inexplicably risen to par with the American flag. The dress was passed up the stairs and hung delicately on the railing beside Linda's, their bouquets set down on a step like a pair of extravagant bedroom slippers or elaborately coifed lapdogs. Then, led by the maid of honor, in a full slip befitting a geriatric nun, the party resumed its descent.

■ ■ ■

Our Lady's bomb shelter was as long as a bowling lane and only a few times as wide. It was lined with wooden benches, which did not provide enough seating for the forty-odd people now assembled therein. At the far end of the bunker sat a child's playpen gone blue-gray and ochre with mildew, so thickly draped in cobwebs it had become a silvered angora nest in which a tenement of small creatures had assumed habitation, some now deceased. Beside the playpen stood a three-foot-tall Fisher-Price kitchen, a slab of plastic sirloin thawing on the alert-orange counter beside a play sink that seemed now to serve dually as a grave pit and outhouse for resident mice.

Wedding guests, clergy, and choir filled the shelter. Elderly sat along the benches; the more spry crowded the center aisle like rush-hour subway riders, their stances wide and sturdy as though they expected the ground beneath them to shift at any moment. A cheer rose as the bridal party entered, and it echoed through the underground chamber.

The expectant groom cut a path to his bride-to-be as if drawn by magnet, and no one tried to stop him, collectively forgetting, in the hubbub, that bride and groom were to be kept from such prenuptial consort. The only person who had not forgotten was, in fact, the groom himself, but the prohibition had been explained to him as a taboo against glimpsing the bride's gown before she came down the aisle, and since it was readily apparent that Ginny was wearing no gown, nor any dress at all, Silas saw no conflict in rushing to her scantily clad side. Silas Yoder was a small man by most standards, yet stood confidently taller than Ginny, who had managed to ingest little more than blue Trident and Diet Sunkist between 1986 and 1994, so silencing her pubescence and stunting her growth that she had, even upon reintegration to the living and eating population, never crested the five-foot mark nor tipped the doctor's scale far enough to require even a hundred-pound poise on the coarse-adjustment beam. Silas shed his tuxedo jacket and eased it over Ginny's frame, thereby completing a look that had gone from bridal to *Desperately Seeking Susan* in a matter of minutes. She wore a white satin bustier and a long tutu of crinoline, and in the oversize topcoat with its wilting pink boutonniere Ginny Maakestad might well have been dressed for a Madonna concert twenty years earlier, dancing among the preteens in precocious paeans of renewal to a virginity they hadn't yet lost.

"I'd about die for an Advil," Ginny said, kneading at her cramping abdomen like she was wishing for the first time in her life that there was something more there to grab onto.

Silas thought a moment, then clamped a work-worn hand to the back of Ginny's knobby neck and steered her through the bustling bomb shelter toward Linda, who'd made it to the far end near the mossy playpen where she was hovering in her pumps—a girdled vision in white—over her friend and NA sponsor, Randall, who squatted on the ground by a filthy Sit'n Spin.

"It's always the junkies they come to for drugs!" Randall said. "Hey, by the way, you know, I got whaddya call it . . . Online, some Church of the Brotherhood of something."

"Ordained," Linda said.

"Yeah, by the Church of the Fellowship of something or other."

"Your grandma's got my purse," Linda said, and they craned to search down the length of the benches for Bernadette Maakestad.

"I could marry you two right down here underground," Randall said. "Legal as a priest, swear to God." He held up three fingers. "Virginia Maakestad and Silas Yoder, by the power vestered in me by the state of cyberspace, I now pronounce you . . ."

Bernadette Maakestad sat in the church-owned wheelchair she'd requested for the trip down to the shelter, though she was not actually physically infirm save for a measure of deafness that was, arguably, more practically useful than it was medically diagnosable. Upon her lap, buffered by the arms of the wheelchair, Grandma Maakestad had amassed an impressive collection of handbags, evening bags, and dress clutches in everything from scarlet patent leather to something that looked like the pelt of a marsupial. She'd either been designated the unofficial bag check of the underground party, or was in the process of carrying out a strangely overt purse-snatching scheme. It took some minutes to figure out which bag was Linda's, and then to convince Grandma Maakestad to release it into Silas's custody, and for Linda to unearth from it a cache of Advil she had complicatedly interred in a swaddle of plastic sacks and rubber bands that lent the over-the-counter anti-inflammatory a darker contraband mystique. Though Linda stood just a few feet from Ginny, she handed the tiny Saran-wrapped bundle to Silas, who presented the nest of miniature mauve-colored eggs to his bride like an offering of delicate hors d'oeuvres.

Ginny peered into his hand, her own poised above like she couldn't decide which pill to choose. Silas remained like a little butler until at last she pinched one up and popped it into her mouth, then snatched up another few and crammed them in as if to stow them away in her cheeks for leaner times. Then she held up a hand to receive the glass of water she seemed to assume would appear, by the way. When, unsurprisingly, it did not, Silas and Linda both began to cast their glances about in search of a remedy. But it was Randall—who was now improbably seated *on* the ancient Sit'n Spin—who reached a stealthy hand into the front panel of his jacket and removed a sizeable tin-colored flask.

Ginny removed the cap thoughtfully and took a whiff of its contents before swigging. She shuddered, swallowed hard, and shuddered again, clearing the burn from her throat with the dry phlegmy hack of a cat with a hair ball. Silas gave her back a thump, gentle but not without potency. Silas's uncannily intuitive sense of Ginny's needs was a subject of great interest, particularly to Phillipa, who had never felt herself to be as adept a nursemaid to her daughter and could not decide whether Silas's proficiency stemmed purely from love, or from some innate, healing Amish-ness, the notion of which both mystified and repelled her.

"Keep off the junk." Randall's voice was a TV announcer's. "Embrace your inner alcoholic." He accepted the return of his flask and took a swig himself before stowing it back inside his coat. "Sure you don't want me to marry you all right now?" he asked again, earnestly hunched into the Sit'n Spin.

Silas looked mildly alarmed, but Ginny just smiled her chipmunk smile, head swaying lazily as if in time to some sultry song piped in from outside to her ears, and hers alone.

■ ■ ■

The unquestionably ingenious Eula Yoder appeared to have fashioned herself a sort of jumpsuit of industrial-strength trash bags: a neck slit and armholes in one made a smock, legholes turned another into a pair of plastic bloomers, the whole ensemble cinched at the waist with a Hefty sash. She'd become a walking garment bag for the bridesmaid's dress she wore. Eula had been shunned by her own Amish community for such deviant indulgences as her sewing machine, her Yahoo account, her mild obsession with *Witness* (and not-so-mild obsession with Kelly McGillis), and for the cruise she'd taken the previous winter, which had, in fact, been some sort of a Mennonite historical cruise, and though Mennonite wasn't Amish, it wasn't like she'd sailed away on *The Love Boat,* or if it had been a love boat it was a *Mennonite* Love Boat, the exact nature of which was still a matter of some speculation, though there was only so far such speculation could go before one's thoughts turned decidedly unorthodox and patently unchristian. Eula had not been exiled or ostracized, but she was actively ignored in the marketplace and excluded from the marriageable pool. Presently though, she was finding herself wholeheartedly embraced by the bomb-shelter congregation, for with typical foresight she had brought the roll of trash bags down to the fallout shelter and was now distributing them among the wedding guests and clergy as makeshift seat covers, picnic blankets, and protective garb. Two girls had opened the seams on one bag and sat cross-legged facing each other singing "*Oh little playmate, come out and play with me . . .*" clapping and snapping and slapping their palms together in choreographed ritual. One mother had simply stuck her young son into a trash bag feetfirst and held him on her lap, his head and arms poking out the top like carrot greens too tall for the grocery bag.

A small crowd had gathered beneath one of the kerosene camping lanterns that had conceded to ignite, straining like seedlings toward a taxi-yellow shower radio blackening with mold like an overripe banana, struggling to hear the emergency weather broadcast.

The flutist—a music major from the university who'd been hired to play a rendition of "Let Hope and Sorrow Now Unite" for the recessional—turned to the man next to her: "Is it the whole state?" she asked.

The man (who was actually the father of the bride) faced the young musician, his eyes clouded with far more sadness and confusion than a stint in the storm cellar seemed to warrant, and said, "Sounds like it touched down over in Story City, so they've had us all on watch—Story County, Marshall County, Tama, Poweshiek, Johnson. And now it's touched in the Amanas so they've upped it to a warning as far east as Illinois."

"Until when, did they say?" The flutist, who also played jazz clarinet, had another gig that evening with her quintet on one of the riverboat casinos up near Dubuque.

"Five forty-five?" he answered. He sounded like a soldier who'd seen enough bloodshed to know things could always be far worse than one imagined. He eyed Eula's roll of Hefty bags, then panned the shelter as though plotting where he might lay a few down and close his eyes.

"What time is it now?" asked the flutist.

The bride's father checked his watch again, as though it might have changed dramatically in the seconds since he'd last looked. "Five fifteen."

It was unclear whether or not the flutist recognized Michael Maakestad as the father of the bride. He'd had a haircut, a shave, and approximately eighteen minutes of sleep since the rehearsal the previous afternoon. He looked unwell, as though an unshakable shame had crept over him in the night, burgled its way in during those few defenseless minutes when he'd abandoned his insomniac vigil and fatefully allowed himself to doze. To marry off one's troubled only child to a lapsed-Amish carpenter seven years her junior was not proving to carry the relief he'd anticipated. That his own thirty-two-year marriage to Phillipa was on the verge of collapse did not inspire confidence, and the treaty they'd managed to broker between them to make it through the wedding as the to-all-appearances-happy parents of the bride (which had involved, the night before, a variety of spanking that he thought would help diffuse his cuckolded hurt and anger but so far had not) was proving to feel less like the Geneva convention and more like a crooked arms deal. It was all Michael Maakestad could do to follow the weather reports, for which, if he'd been able to think more clearly, he might have realized he was quite grateful.

■ ■ ■

The bride lifted one foot and then the other, inspecting the soles for dirt, then checked again once she was done, as though she expected their state of cleanliness to change spontaneously, or fearful that she might have missed something on last glance. "What are we *doing* here?" she said.

Silas spoke patiently. "It's a tornado warning, Gin. We have to."

And then, as though Silas had said something else entirely, Ginny shook her head and spoke in the voice an adult might use to calm a crying child. She took Silas's hand in hers and rested her head on his thin shoulder. "It'd've meant a great deal to your parents," she recited drowsily. "May they rest..." Silas affectionately patted the salon tendrils that cascaded from Ginny's updo. His bride closed her eyes.

And then, as if on cue, from the far end of the shelter rose the dusky call of the flute in a melody only the children seemed to recognize. The "Oh Little Playmate" girls leapt from their garbage bag shrieking "Ariel! Ariel!" in breathless ecstasy and followed the piper's infectious mermaid-movie song.

The mildewed-yellow waterproof radio hiccuped loud burps of static until it lost its station entirely and someone thought to turn the volume down. A crack of lightning and thunder exploded with such violence that it seemed to come from the very earth around them, under which they'd sought protection. There were gasps, then a hush, then the muffled cries of a child trying to bury its head into the illusory safety of a parent's body. And then the flutist resumed her song.

The power of the wind was surely tremendous aboveground, as even from beneath the congregants could hear the slam and barrage, feel the relentless death-bent pummel whip around and through the church above them as if to rip it from the ground and send it sailing off to Oz. It seemed impossible that the shelter would protect them from the determined ferocity bearing down, and no one would have been particularly surprised if even the earth below and around them began to tremble and quake, sending the white-robed soloist tumbling over, feet in the air like a slapstick cartoon, and lifting from the sole of her crepe-soled shoe a tiny whorl of bloodied toilet tissue, sending it swirling into the air, caught in the twister of the Sit'n Spin, knocking Randall to the floor, shedding its dust and cobwebs to reveal the blue-and-yellow spirals stickered crookedly on its seat twenty years before, the dust and cobwebs catching up in their whirl a hundred Hefty bags, a dervish dance of black plastic joined by the billowing black robes of the junior pastor, flapping, and lifting from the wheelchair lap of Bernadette Maakestad a great sandstorm of pocketbooks, airborne and determined, it might seem, to fly back to their rightful owners like homing pigeons. Up the ramp the wind would rush, up through the stairwell, ripping the bride's gown from the banister where it hung to send it dancing up the steps, followed in quick pursuit by the enormous green ghost of the maid of honor bent on saving the wedding, the two of them trailed by their bouquets, breaking apart in the wind, a spray of petals tossed by invisible flower girls. Up through the church hall they'd fly, past the bomb-shelter sign threatening to pinwheel right off the wall like a sinister boomerang. In the ladies' room three bowls of toilet water—two clear, one pink—would eddy into whirlpools, and in the chapel the bride's veil might alight from the pew on which it lay, catch briefly on the T of Jesus's cross, sweep across the altar and hover a moment in respect by the memorial bouquet for Obadiah and Orah Yoder, killed just a year before in a horrific whorl of horsehair and collard greens and blood and steel because the SUV driver never even saw their buggy as he crested the hill by the Yoders' farm, and as the veil lurched upward, lightning flashing prisms through the stained-glass cupola of the nave, outside the new spring tulips in the parishioners' garden would be stripped to their skinny new-green stems, petals of orange and purple and yellow and red quivering through the air like firecracker flares and tails and star shells, until they slapped, wet, and stuck against the broken windows and mangled sliding door of Randall's old Chevy Caravan, crushed beneath the willow that had earlier offered plentiful shade, its split, splintered trunk now pointed accusingly into the premature night saying *you did this,* its other half torn and felled to the ground, splayed there and gasping up to ask *why,* the sky clearing, wind dying, debris settling, the day's second dawn brightening to say *because.*

THE SILVER SAXOPHONE, MASKS OF PAIN, AND THE PEOPLE IN THE HILLS

Gordon Henry

THE DAY I REALIZED HOW POOR I WAS, WAS THE DAY I SAW my grandmothers fighting in the yard. Grandmother Judy Standing Grand had just landed a weighty right hook into the mouth of Grandmother Alvina Good Spoken. As the blood dribbled out of the old woman's mouth with spewed denture and spumed curses, I knew I was thirteen-sixteenths skin, which is what blood always reminds me of, my own skin, degrees, thirteen-sixteenths equals seven-eighths ancient Good Spoken and three-fourths Osanomish.

It had been a good fight, though a bit uneven since Grandmother Standing Grand loomed large over all people and had always used her loomyness presence to intimidate everyone until they backed off or went forward foolishly or onward drunkenly enough to call for an ass kicking. Believe me, I know. Before I took up hoops old Standing Grand had kicked my butt more than a few times. But the fight, which had once been like the weather, predictably rainy, had taken another turn and now was like the seasons, almost climactic.

Good Spoken instinctively remembered the drunken sluggings of her dead husband and she was fighting back, postimpact, postcontact, postconsciously imitating the technique of her husband batterer and his brain-injured progenies Archie and Louis, who both lost in the semifinals of the state Golden Gloves, in gee what year was it? Grandma Good Spoken followed the bloody hook with a breathtaking body shot, dropping Standing Grand to her knees. I turned away then and went inside the Standing Grand house to get another beer. My cousin Luke sat there in the kitchen, still sobbing at the table, his picture of his father in front of him, a flat face, glossed by the bulb of light above us. Luke was crying about the land, about drinking too much and setting fire to his father's Jimi Hendrix records.

"Jesus," I said, "will you quit crying, Luke? You been like this for months."

"It's not a good day to be Indian," he said. "My father's dead and my uncle lost his job on the tribal fishing boat."

"Let's go for a drive," I said. "I got some mushrooms in the glove box. We'll suck them up and go find the people up in the hills."

When we got into the front seat, I took the mushrooms out of the glove box. Luke popped a couple of beers and we sat there for a while chewing the mushrooms and washing them down with the Rolling Rocks.

"Where'd you get these 'shrooms?" Luke asked.

"My cousin, Michael—he's an ethnobotany student at the U. He's been researching ceremonial fungi and fire-starting brackets. He gave these to me last Christmas. Where'd you get the Rolling Rock?"

"You ever tried them before? Out of your grandmother's refrigerator."

"Yeah, but I've been conserving. I eat a little every time my relatives fight. I found out it makes their cuts and bruises more colorful. But this is really bad with my grandmothers, so I'm taking as much as I can."

"What are they fighting about?"

"Who knows," I said. "Grandkids, missing lard, habitual anger, bingo strategies. It's Saturday, let's drive."

Some Indian cars only work in reverse, some only work in the morning, and some only work to get you lost. My uncle Buick said it's because Indian cars are tired of being beat up, owned first by white men, until they abuse them almost to death, or just after the last five-year payment is a ten-year memory. I don't know about all that, but my uncle passed the car on to me, complete with an empty pack of Lucky Strikes between the front seat belts and a pair of Pampers, with a hole blown through them, on the backseat floor. He said, "Careful, when you drive it. The mirrors tell more than the view through the windshield. If you can, drive only with the mirrors and side windows. That crack in the windshield will fool you. You look into it, you'll be like a fly in a spider's web and you'll lose your sense of the road." Yes, that took some gettin' used to, but by the time I went in the car with Luke to go look for the people in the hills, I used the mirrors and side windows like my own eyes and the windshield like my subconscious. (It was there all the time, but I didn't know if I was payin' attention to it or not.)

After an hour or so we came down the incline on old smelt road, miles from the reservation, near a suburb of Big Traverse.

Luke said, "See that."

"What," I said.

"That," he said, pointing to the side of the road, "that big car over there in the ditch."

I broke from my view in the rearview mirror and turned to the passenger side. Beyond Luke's bristle-cut head, I saw the car, its chrome lip nudged into the ditch dirt and rain runoff, like our dog Lightning nudged into a smell of Uncle coming home from netting on the bay.

I pulled over onto the shoulder, just in front of the big Electra. Luke and I got out, walked back to the car, and peered into the driver-side window. There was no one. I opened the back door and looked in. Again, no one.

"Luke," I said, "what's this?"

I dragged a black box across the backseat and out the door and set it on the ground between us. It was beginning to rain hard again and in my mind I saw my grandmothers fighting.

"I don't know," Luke said. "Open it up."

I flipped up the brass latches and lifted the lid. Inside, surrounded by a deep-red velvet interior, in the bell-and-horn-shaped curves and crevasses of the case, sat a disassembled silver saxophone.

"Wow," Luke squealed. Then, he lifted the instrument out piece by piece and put the sax together. He walked around to the front of the car and jumped onto the hood. The red light of our old Impala glossed across the hood and Luke as he playfully put his lips to the mouthpiece and blew. He mocked a musician's expression, contorting his face into a mask of pain, like ecstasy, as a low blue note sounded from the dark hollow of the sax bell. Luke held the note for a long time, and raindrops fell into the darkness of the horn and beaded on the gleaming silver of the instrument's curves and lines, in the spaces between the stops. As Luke rocked and bent in performance, some of the raindrops slipped off the instrument and floated to earth, in shining full orbs of deep reflected worlds that extended in weight and gravity as each fell. I moved closer and stared into each drop as it fell. I looked deeply into each drop then and I saw stars, a bit of some lost moon, a few dark clouds, crystallizations and fractals, and I knew that each raindrop was itself a vibration, calling out and entering the earth, to move its particular place on the earth with the energy and flow of its own transitory and mattered vibrations. I felt the vibrations from where I stood on the earth. I stared for a long time like that, then I felt and heard my own tears talking to me in a swishing muddied river of memory streaming out, down my face. I bent over and sobbed and spontaneously spoke that tearful remembrance:

hey, hey we walk the edge
beerhouses, broken mirrors and lives,
glasses, plastics, waste, a history of
blood and hunger, a memory
of white bread and deep dishes
of boiled yellow potatoes

hey, hey one brother dead in war
one sister alive and still fighting
her desperate husband
a child sleeping in the car
a child sleeping under the table
in the beerhouse
in the cracked mirrors
beneath the game heads
one sister alive and still fighting
saying "buy me another one"

Luke slipped and fell off the car then, clutching the sax, laughing where he landed. I walked around the car, looked down at him, and saw footprints in the mud. The prints started from the passenger side of the car and moved down the ditch into the grass on the hillside. There, a path of parted, trampled grass ran up the hillside. I went and shut off the Impala. It cut out in a cough, like my emphysemic father had, ten years before. I turned away and we took that path up the hill.

We crested the hill and saw a smoldering fire of weak flame and thick smoke. The rain had let up a bit and I remembered my grandmothers. Their fight was probably over by now, maybe one of them lay punched out, or maybe my uncle Buick came home and tied them both to chairs. That's what he did when they fought. He'd put them in chairs. Then, he'd open a Bible and read from whatever page he opened. I didn't understand it, to me bibliomancy was an art, not a cure or a punishment, and it never seemed to work for my grandmothers. They kept doing the same things over and over again, fighting and cooking, advising and enabling, giving their last twenty dollars to the toothless drunks they called sons.

When we got closer to the fire we saw the sweat lodge, a canvas, tarpaulin turtle in the dark. We saw a sweater on all fours just going in. Luke and I ran up and stripped to our shorts. He covered the saxophone with his shirt and pants and left it there, outside the lodge. We crawled in behind the last sweater. We sat near the door, Luke right next to the door, me next to him. There were five others already inside.

The Domestic Animal Sweat

Of course it was dark inside, but when the doorkeeper passed the heated grandfathers inside I saw some of the shapes and features of the other sweaters in the stone glow. The sweat leader was an old man with thin gray hair and a glowing face, cracked of hard living. He prayed rapidly in our language, then downshifted to English and prayed for a long time, laughing hard and long after he spoke of suffering and misery, and sobbing when he turned to joking after the first door opening. The old man passed the water bucket to the sweater on his left and I realized Luke and I and the old man were the only natives inside the lodge. The first sweater began to speak. Then things turned strange.

The First Suburban Sweater— The Hamster Channel

First I'd like to thank our grandfather Beartail for leading us here in the sweat. I'd like to thank him for coming here to the suburbs to support us suburban sweaters. I'd also like to thank the Creator for touching the minds of our Big Traverse subdivision association for allowing us to use the vacant lots at the end of this cul-de-sac as a place for our lodge. This is really important to us and we're thankful that we could work these things out. Also, we all know why we're here tonight. We have come to pray for the animals, the domestic animals in our subdivision. There's been a rash of deaths among our beloved here lately and we're here to pray for those who have passed on and for the safety and care of those still living. In the past two weeks, we've lost two cats to cancer, a long-haired dachshund to kidney disease, and a blue heeler to pneumonia. We've also lost an Armenian parakeet, a hamster, an angelfish, an Irish setter, a boxer, and a mutt. Creator, what can you say? Sure, one of them was taken by that careless school-bus driver and one looked like a suicide, but the others are mysteries. That leaves two animals in the subdivision. Myself, I believe it's chemical, environmental, polyvinyl chloride, the same siding up and down the subdivision. I know it's hard to prove, but until now, my family hasn't lost an animal for years and we have natural cedar siding. And you know, the strange thing is our animals are trying to tell us something, especially those of us in the lodge here. The dead animals have been coming to us in dreams, or visiting us in image gaps, between web screens at work. More recently, some of us have channeled our animals. Last night at dinner I spoke to my daughter of things only a hamster could think of. So that's what I'm doing here. I'm going to call on the spirit of that hamster to speak through me and I'd like you all to do the same with your dead domestic friends. Call on them, let them speak through you so we can cleanse this subdivision, bring back healing relationships, and maybe they'll help us to see why this pattern of death has swelled up among us at this time.

I'd like to give thanks for the big silver wheel. That thing gave me a lot of exercise, broke up the days of boredom while everyone was gone. After a while I really came to appreciate that wheel and the morning sunshine coming through the window and gleaming off those metal bars. It even got so I could tell the passage of the day by the places where the sun shone on the wheel and where the sun bands fell between spoke shadows on the good cedar earth, and I want to give thanks for the cedar chips, the good smell of that cover in my home there. That made the days easier as well. I'd also like to give thanks for the big hands that reached down and touched me over the year I lived. Those big fingers of lettuce and the way the hands reached down and set that little Chinese teacup of water there in the corner where I used to drink. Yes, I was truly blessed and I felt loved. I felt it in the big faces looking down and in the smaller faces peering in through the glass every evening before the lights went out. There's a lot to give thanks for I know, and there's a lot I don't know, I know. And that's part of it. I know you all want to know why I passed on, why so many of us are dying, but I can't tell you that. The Creator will leave it to another to reveal to you. I will say this though: You have to learn to laugh with your animals, not at them. The approximate size and weight of your animal should be dealt with the same approximate weight and degree of humor. And yes, you should keep talking to us, but go a little lighter on the special voices, especially the high voices. Remember we hear and feel at different frequencies, so look into the frequency and vibration of your animal voices and see if they match up with the optimum communication frequency of your animal. This is all spiritual information I am giving you, so look into these things. I say this with respect. I hope you all understand this. I'd like to pass the bucket.

The Parakeet Channel

I too would like to give thanks—for all my relatives, domestic and wild. For the bamboo cage and the trapeze before the mirror, for the grinding stone for my beak, for all the water and good seeds that sustained me, for those good prayers of my hamster relative. That thing he said about the voices was really great. I know I vibrate at different frequencies and if we think about it we can see evidence of that in my reactions to music. A Mozart CD makes me sing. A jazz-fusion number makes me want to push my head between the bamboo bars. That reminds me. I'd like to give thanks for all the times the big hands opened my cage and let me fly in those bigger spaces of their home. It was great. I liked the different landings, the curtain rods, the tables, the top of the bookcase, the heads, the shoulders. (Except for that one time when I landed on the shoulder of that kid. There was loud music, a lot of big bodies, smoke, and colored lights. That time when that kid blew smoke into my face and spit beer into my beak. That was not good.) With that I pray that you keep in mind our limitations. I know because the big hands take care of us and house us, that they expect us to live according to their beliefs and tastes, but we have limitations. Yes, I can talk. I give thanks for that gift of speaking, but I can't say everything and I have to hear it at least a few times before I can catch on. So don't expect too much too fast. I know some of you big hands are really intelligent, but that doesn't mean you can get me or any of my budgie relatives to recite the Psalms or the prologue to "The Pardoner's Tale." And have some imagination. Lay off the hellos, hey beautifuls, the quoth the raven, the nevermores. Think about what's inside us all: the hunger, the desire, the quest for a meaningful life. With that said, Creator, don't let too many of the big hands leave us alone, as single budgies in a single cage. Bring us some partners, give us the opportunity to be among our own. Two on a trapeze is better than another in the mirror. I say that without trying to sound ungrateful. But imagine a life without a partner, a friend. With that I'd like to sing a song to close my prayers.

The Parakeet Song

If I am one alone
let me be
with another
Let the big hand
come to hold me
up to sun
to hold me up
to sun
let me be with
another.

The Pet Turtle Channel

This is good. We don't get to speak very often, you know. So first let me give thanks for this opportunity. I'd also like to thank old man Beartail for being here, for coming all the way from the reservation to lead this sweat. There aren't that many old ones who will do this, you know. There are a lot of false leaders out there, spiritual charlatans. But let me give thanks for my ancestors who have passed on and for those living ancient ones who are entering their second and third centuries of life. Tell them to stay deep and not to surface unless it's absolutely necessary. I wish I could have lived half that long, half that long, I don't know, the way things are going around here, I don't expect many of us will ever live that long again. I'd also like to give thanks for my place in the home of Mary and Jack and the kids, Dylan and Chelsea. Thanks for that beautiful terrarium they set up for me, for the stone island Chelsea painted with flowers and cattails. Also, if any of you people see Dylan tell him I forgive him for engraving the American flag on my shell. Though I couldn't see it, I could feel it, and yes, it hurt for a while, but eventually I came out of my shell. Thanks also for the times they let me roam outside, into the garden, along the wall where the shade cooled me and let my blood sing cool even in summer. Thanks too for the bathtub moments. You know, it was great sliding around in there, with the water, the boats, and the plastic fish. Also, I want to pray for all my relatives who will try to cross the road and for those who won't make it. Please give those drivers some compassion and tell them to at least try to swerve when they see us on the road. Yes, it's been a good life, the big hands were generous and I am grateful. Now the spirits told me to tell you about the deaths here. About why the animals have died and are dying here. This land where this subdivision is built was a battlefield a long time ago. A lot of animals died here—dogs, horses, rodents—and a lot of people died too. Each animal type likes a certain space, you know. For instance, a dog will avoid a vortex and a cat will sleep in one, but this whole place is a spiritual vortex and the animals are taking on the energy of the vortex and dying to warn the big hands that you can't put a subdivision just anywhere. The only way you can save the animals that are left is to get them out of here. Maybe take them to a shelter, where hopefully someone from another place of better energy will take them, or maybe just let them go, so they can find their own space, through their deeper knowledge of earth energies. I'll sprinkle the grandfathers then, and again, I give thanks and I pass the bucket to my relative here.

The Yellow Dog Channel

Greetings. My name is Solstice, and I too am thankful for this opportunity. I appreciate all the good words that have been spoken here and I know that this is good. I'd like to pray for my masters, for those who gave me shelter, for those who fed me, for those who stroked my back and scratched my hindquarters and spoke kindly to me as they looked into my eyes. This has been a good life and there are so many things to give thanks for: the children, Alex and Gerald; the old man, who was a great teacher, though he often used inappropriate punishment—newspapers, spray bottles, fits of screaming—but I know he was trying to make it better for us all to live together. And I wasn't always a quick learner. I know I jumped too often and snatched a few things that the old woman had prepared for others, and I know I snapped at a few visitors, even when I recognized them, just to show I was on guard. But these things take time and in spite of all that I got a lot of love and attention and that's more than I can say for a lot of my relatives. I'd also like to give thanks for the gifts I've been given: the good sense of hearing, the ability to smell. Those two things alone were worth life as a setter. I remember times when I could hear a cat in the grass at night, or when I could smell a strange mutt on a blade of urined grass. Sure, those gifts drove me to do things and go places I shouldn't have, but the sense and the instinct were worth the mistakes in judgment. As for the dying, the spirit speaking through the turtle was right, but I would like to add a few things. There's a lot of poison around here. I've licked it in the rain and smelled it in the morning fog rolling up the hills from Big Traverse. More than that, I could feel it in the lethargy of the children and in the seeping of water in my food mix. But what can we do. The masters don't seem to notice the signs and they all go on as if one pure scent is the same as poison. Still, I have to hope and I pray for better senses among our masters and for all living beings. Thanks, I pass the water.

Luke—The Anger Channel

When the water got to Luke, all his sadness and anger poured forth.

What's the matter with you people? As soon as he spoke old man Beartail laughed and he continued cackling at Luke's every word. Why are you trying to steal our ways, with your petty concerns and your selfishness. This is a sham, your words are a bunch of hokey, white-man, touchy-feely, new-age shaman shit. You white people couldn't channel a duck if you had Looney Tunes cable and your name was Daffy. You couldn't empathize with anyone else even if you were schizophrenic. Why don't you all get a life. Quit calling on our elders, quit taking advantage of our spiritual leaders . . . quit whining about your suburban tragedies and get some backbone. Take your animal voices into your own churches and give them to the priest in the confessional. Bless me Father, I am an Irish setter and I crapped in my master's shoes; bless me Father, I'm a hamster and I'm suffering from glass-house syndrome; bless me Father, I'm a budgie and I say "asshole" under my breath every time a suburban kid says "Polly want to be an upwardly mobile cracker?"; bless me Father, I'm a miniature turtle and I want to play snapper on the gin-and-tonic blossom of that dick who thinks I'm a chess piece for his spoiled kid. You don't need your animals' spirits to give you messages. It's all right there in front of you, in your subdivisible ignorance, in the chem-lawn competitions and the noxious barbecues and the cell-phone communications from your tribal-named SUVs. Tell it to your own spiritual leaders, in your own churches, in your own church bazaars, in your sorry excuse for concern for anyone other than your sorry subdivision selves. I tell you people, wake up, you got life, live it, break out of your denial and look at who you are.

Good Spoken's Prayer

When Luke was out of steam he passed the bucket to me. The stone grandfathers were almost cold. The sweat ran real then. I was no longer observing. I felt spirits watching, observing me. I prayed from a small flame in a fractured indigenous heart. I prayed for the planets, the magnetic flow and biding of elder sun, the material world, the gaseous wraiths and shimmers, the dense-matter people, the inhabitants of mists above, the beings of flight, their blue wings, their morning calls from hidden limbs, or brief passages through sky. I honored the keepers of the vegetal villages, the makers of heal all and pearly everlasting, the tobacco dwellers, the red-willow elders, the strawberry grandmothers, the weeping sisters of squash, corn, and bean, the brothers and great uncles of syllabary shapes in oak, maple, elm, and ash. I gave thanks for the insect transformations, for the communities of bug peoples. I talked of the light-struck memegwasay. I remembered the little people, the point makers, greasy man, little hairy ininni. I prayed for the hunted as providers and as the wisdom behind traps and survival weapons. I saw into the center of the heart flame and watched part of it lick back into smoke. I didn't know where words came from. I remembered saying that the stars' names were wrong. That the wide star roads held the names of us all and all who came before. I spoke of the dead senses of humans, of the atrophied regions of brain and vision, of the lost genes in the replication of dead moments of lust and the phoniness of our manufactured desires. I was not angry, but sorrowful. I sang the song of my dead father, recalling him barely breathing in the hospital where granddaughters sang in fours, three verses about going home. I asked for forgiveness for the anger, for the shame that leads us to worthless, worthlessness. I called on memories of diviners I'd never known. I resequenced dream transmissions, talked of vibrations penetrating us as receivers and of the resonance of voices between doorways and dark nights from which we never returned. I told the stories of self-betrayal and stunned the stone hissing quiet with some tears I had been carrying for so long I forgot where it was I should have left them. I was drawing closer to this sorrow. I felt a spirit on my tongue walking out with my voice, ready to deliver a word of love. Then I heard Beartail. His laughing shadow contrary to the voice, and all I said was "all my relatives, all relatives, relatives, particle, wave vibration, all caught in nets, all my relations, all life, skanda, orenda, all streams, all dreams, must be finally it seems, all my relations." I fell forward and lost myself in a spiraling darkness, like sleep, but beyond.

Little Boy in the Clouds—Good Spoken's Sweat Dream

White mist spins, rolls, and thins, whirls rapidly from tissue wisp, to
thick cloud, full billow and bellow, shaded blue tint underneath by
darkness from the earth, up higher, beyond the white faces in profile,
tinted metallic red gold shines over globed edges above rounded animal
backs, the unnameable emergences of spheres and the hills beyond
which there will be no horizon. Laughing comes lightning, someone

approaches dancing in the distance, wrapped in white cloth from the waist down, still laughing as in a moment's breath he stands before you, whatever you are in this world that you've come to. He carries a small bow and invisible arrow that turns into song, as song is his aim.

I will tell you of the gift of water
I will make you think of the days
In the life of a glacier
Of deep measures of earth
Where surface is unknown
Where animals and vegetation
Shimmer bright as suns
In all spectral bands
In light of their own making.

I will tell you of the gift of water
Of less than a vial's worth, after three
Days of absolute thirst calling
As if an eaglechild
Grandfather, Grandfather
The sound keening
Through a bone between your lips

I will tell you of the gift of water
And still you will forget me
even as you hand a cup to a child
as they come panting to you
burning after hours out in summer sun.

Then the cloud boy goes dancing back to cloud back, disappearing as if part of a field of mist and vapor, of the place between fluidity and form where that is held together.

The rain had stopped when I came out of the sweat. The suburban sweaters had already gathered their things and were gone. Old man Beartail sat on a lawn chair smoking a cigar, a baseball cap reading *pow wow of love* set slightly crooked on his head. Gray braids hung behind his ears beneath the back of his cap. Luke held up his soaked shirt, picked up his drenched pants, and pointed.

"It's gone," he said.

"What's gone."

"My instrument. Fucking white thieves."

"It wasn't yours in the first place," I said. "The car wasn't yours, so the saxophone belonged . . ."

"We've been invited to a feast, my boys," Beartail said. "They told me to tell you to come along."

Luke looked at the old man. "I ain't feasting with those bastards."

Beartail howled, a deep laugh, from a core of elder bemusement. "Listen," he said.

Then we heard it. A wail straining faintly through the subdivision hills in the wet night. Luke turned toward the sound. I looked up the road from the cul-de-sac into the thick of the subdivision. We followed the sound of the sax to a clean, well-lit executive home up the road. Beartail trailed behind us, limping a bit, leaning on a red cane with a carved eagle top and a rubber bottom. The saxophone grew louder as we approached. When we got to the door of the house where the saxophone came from, the old man rang the bell.

"A few of my favorite things," Beartail chuckled as a thin redheaded woman opened the door.

"Come in," she said. "The food is ready. We've been waiting for you."

Inside was all lightness, the order of an eclectic suburban taste of things, a fireplace, a few generations of faces in well-framed photos on the mantle above. Interethnic art sat dispersed throughout the room, next to the photos, on end tables, on walls: an African thumb piano, a Chamorro fetish, a bodhran, an array of Oaxacan figurines, one a multicolored ceramic bovine divinity transporting little natives hanging on its back and sides with fruit and pots, a sand painting, baskets, pottery. On the coffee table, an oversize picture book lay open to a dervish dance, next to an abalone shell full of copal. Beyond, above the dining-room table, above the feast, a chandelier tinkled minute, minute refractions, coruscating in the muted Coltrane grooves, between conversations of about ten people.

Good sweat. Yes, good sweat. Powerful. The elder was amazing. Amazing, He didn't even feel the heat. I've been in hotter. Once near Sacramento. Did you see the spirits. I forgot to sing the song, the one that came to me in a dream . . .

The redhead spoke to us again as we approached the table. "Welcome, thanks for coming," she said. "Everyone said the sweat was great. Come, come eat something." She turned to Beartail. "Grandfather, can you say a prayer before we start?"

Beartail removed his baseball cap and stood before the table. The redhead's husband, a guy sporting LL Bean all over, went out of the room and Coltrane spiraled away. When he returned, the suburbans, five men and five women and me and Luke turned our attention to Beartail. "Get me a plate," he said. "Put a little of everything, a little of all the food on it." The redhead took a small plate and moved around the table, carefully spooning small portions of mashed potatoes, stuffing, corn, squash, turkey, ham, and beef onto the plate. She handed the plate to Beartail. He took the plate in one hand, held tobacco in the other, and held both up, above his head in front of him. "Hmmm . . . made in Mexico," he said. "The message on the bottom told me to say that." Then he prayed. "Thanks for this holy food. Thanks for the spirits who brought us this food and for the hands that prepared this food in this way. Thanks for the spirit that brought us here and thanks for the one who brought us this sweat. With this we remember our ancestors; we honor their living and we feed them in their passing and beyond to the other side. Thanks also for this good day. For grandfather sun who rose to remind us of our place here on this earth and for that cleansing rain that came with the gift of water. As we go on let us respect each other and all life under this good and beautiful creation." Beartail held the plate out to Luke. "Take this outside and put it down on a stone with this tobacco." Luke took the plate and went out through the front door.

As I went to the table to get a plate, I saw Luke, beyond the dining-room window, walking into the lit breadth of an exterior light. I watched him go away from the house and disappear into the dark. When he came back into the light he no longer had the plate. He came up to the deck at the back of the house, and as I shoveled mashed potatoes onto my plate, I saw him stop and turn back toward the darkness, pointing out into the darkness. He waved for me to come out. I went to the sliding glass door of the kitchen. Luke was already moving away in the direction he had pointed. I saw him turn and run beyond the play of light, out away from the house, up into the hills behind the subdivision. I set my plate down and went out through the sliding glass door.

"Look," he said.

"What? I don't see anything."

"The light," he said. "The light."

Then I saw a trace, a speck of golden light, moving back and forth, rising higher into the hills beyond the subdivision. Luke and I ran toward it. The wind had picked up and wound creak and rustle through the trees. We came up higher into the tree-thickened hill and saw the light, a sphere, moving more slowly now, through the trees, to disappear behind the trees. Luke pressed forward, moving up the hill ahead of me. I stopped and rested a bit, trying to keep Luke in my sight in the dark, following him following that faint light. As I rested against a white birch I heard a whoosh inside of it. I looked at the tree and saw into its interior, saw interior skins, the true depth of knots. I saw the cells of the tree. Each cell sparkled and glowed in pulsing light of various colors, each color a different cellular makeup, a different being, breathing through the whoosh, the deep interior exhalation of the tree. Then I realized all the trees were breathing in this way. It reminded me of my other cousin, Two Dogs, and his experience with DMT.

Then I heard Luke. "Look at the little son a bitch," he said. "He's got the sax." I raced up the hill to where Luke stood. There was a little guy there, standing holding the sax. He was about three feet tall, with dark, greasy hair. He was shined up with grease, it seemed, like a Vaselined boxer, naked to his waist, and he wore an animal-hide breechcloth.

"Hey, little man," Luke said, "who are you?"

Ah bah day diddle wah nah wah nah, train, rain wah blay, wah nah blay wheet, tah wheet.

These are not words, I thought. The little man communicated this to me directly and to Luke too, it seemed.

"Give me the sax," Luke called out.

Zootway, way, yant, tee, diddle, tee diddle, it wah, wah is, toowheet not tootooway yant toowheetyours. The music is not yours. The music is not yours, the little man sent wordlessly back.

Luke ran at the little man then, but when he got to the place where the greasy little guy stood, he was already gone, through the tree, a bouncing golden light. Luke ran after him again. I was tired of that game so I sat in the wet grass and rolled a smoke. Then I walked over to the spot where the little man had stood and I offered some tobacco.

I stood there in that place for a while and prayed. After two more smokes, Luke showed up carrying the sax.

"How'd you get it," I said.

"I ran him down. We wrestled for a while. He's a strong little son a bitch. We both got tired. I gave him a Marlboro, he gave me the sax."

Luke and I went back to the house then. As we came through the front door, he cradled the saxophone, purring scat vocable scales while gazing intently at the horn, me right behind, following, while thinking of the quickest way back to the Impala. There was no quick way. One of the sweaters, a woman who sounded like the parakeet channel, actually asked Luke if he played. The way back to the car got away from us then. Luke said nothing but he jumped on the coffee table, struck a few bad accidentals with his silver Nikes on the African thumb piano, knocked over a wooden fertility god of some sort. He looked at the parakeet woman and then at Double L and said, as he stood on the table: "Bean, my man, yes, I have some facility with this."

Then he said it again.

"Yes, I have some facility with this."

He said it again, and again and again and again, over and over. Then, he put the saxophone to his lips and he blew out notes in the same meter as:

"Yes, I have some facility with this."

Bah, bah beep blay beebeebeebe bah blay.

From there he entered different zones of the language of that phrase, he rode the back of a musical sunfish, wiggling beyond phonemes through tonemes through syntactical sonatactical fissures, in subtle undercurrents, through waving aquatic weeds, of dissonant lexical diversions, inversions, excursions, back into the original phrase and then back out. He played that into a night of snow, thick-textured flakes, some turning descensions, some sliding down against some unseen night surface, some dropping onto backs of shadows of people on a road to a lit funeral church; he played that phrase slowly at first, then he picked it up, the snow fell faster, and the church was full and then in a coal-fired surge the train left that station, the church was gone, a hundred skin memories were headed out for relocation, rapidly moving faces, sun-glazed in glass, note for note, train window by train window by train window, Amtrak to Santa Fe boxcar to **angel loves chief** graffiti boxcar, rust empty and coal full, flat and empty. Everything blew by fast then. I could not follow memory that way. I caught a glimpse of the picture of a circle of Mevlana, in the open *Dances of the World* book on the coffee table. I looked hard at the picture. I looked up at Luke, then at the picture of the dervishes, I looked at Luke, then at the picture, then at Luke, the picture, Luke, the picture, Luke, picture. I felt a tap on my shoulder. I turned. Old man Beartail said:

"Don't

try

to

seeeverything

at

Once."

I heard Luke slowing down then blowing soft, soft, a few low breathy puffs, a couple of rapid pepper shots then softer yet; the saxophone gave way to old man Beartail's voice.

"Once," he said—as soon as he said "once," all the people in the room, the sweaters and the feasters, gathered around the old man. A couple of women lotused on the floor, on a Persian throw, and focused on the wise old skin. Double L Bean sat on the arm of the sofa next to Beartail. Another guy moved in and sat on the end of the coffee table. In no time they had the old guy surrounded. "Once," he said, again when everyone was settled, "there was nothing between us and the Creator. There was no need for pipes, drums, rattles, sweats, dance arbors, nothing, no instruments for contacting the Creator. We had a direct line, we didn't even have to make a sound, the line was that clear, that pure. And we too, we could hear things, from way beyond, from beyond these hills, in the trunks of trees, in the fluttered departure of birds from their places in tall grass. There were these lines, these things we knew, as we know by gesture and walk our own relatives. But something happened. Some people would say that someone got hurt, or that someone interfered with another's messages to the Creator. Someone else said a bird landed awkwardly somewhere, or maybe some spirit grew jealousy out of the time we spent with the Creator. I don't know, but the line was lost, it was cut and we started talking and when we started talking we got further from the line and our story turned to words. We made ways with words but a few among us then still had a line, though it wasn't as pure and wasn't as constant, it wasn't easily called anymore. So those few among us dreamed, or some of the dead who remembered contact that way had pity on us and visited us in spirit to help us find ways to get that old kind of contact back. This, what I'm telling you, I know this because I've known a few people who still have this contact, this line." Beartail paused then and looked hard at me, then harder yet and steadier at Luke. "And they say we can still find that," he said.

"Let's go," Luke said. "Maybe things have finally quieted down back home." As Luke and I left, I looked back and saw the old man still talking. He looked tired, drained and alone, as if the words he spoke to the suburban sweaters were wringing him out to dry.

When we got back to our car the Electra was gone. The saxophone case flung open and empty in the middle of the road. Luke took the saxophone apart piece by piece and put all the parts back in the case, except for the mouthpiece.

"I'm keeping this," he said. "I'm not talking anymore. I've got my own mouthpiece to speak for me." Then he stuck the black fixture between his lips and laughed. I tried to grab it but he bit down hard. The fight was on then.

I tackled him on the road and we wrestled, rolling into the ditch, into rain runoff and mud. I punched him in the gut and heard two hisses of "asshole" as we rolled to the ground, as he hung on, biting down on the mouthpiece. I felt his desperation in our fight. He fought from a deeper impulse, as if a little man inside drove him, twisted his grief to anger, his sad loss to random thrusts of a heart, casting out through wild limbs. I heard him growl with the energy of loss. I got on top of Luke, pulled his head back with one hand, and yanked the sax piece from his mouth. He bit my hand. I slugged him hard in the face. I rolled away, stood, and ran parallel to the road, Luke cursing behind me, and then I threw the mouthpiece into the tall grass. I stood there then and turned, knowing Luke was coming. A thin rain began to fall. We squared off, circled each other. Luke's fist came from the hills and the dark. I took it with a movement of head, a turn of jaw, and responded with my best right cross. Luke buckled to the road and I kicked him twice in the ribs. He groaned, drew his knees to fetal. I kicked him twice more, once to stop him from groaning, once to start him up again. I walked over to the car, got in, turned the ignition, and called to Luke.

"Get in," I said.

Luke staggered over, a drunken beaten shadow. He got in. He reached into the backseat and grabbed a Rolling Rock.

"Give me one," I said.

"Last one."

Then I backed the car up, pulled onto the road, and heard the crunch of the saxophone case beneath the car. I stopped the car immediately and backed up and drove forward and backed up, over the case and the instrument, again and again. I imagined squeezing the instrument into the earth, flattening it out sound by sound, back to its mineral origins where it would eventually become ground with everything else that would eventually die on that road.

When we got back to Grandmother Standing Grand's, Luke went back to the picture on the kitchen table. He picked it up, walked over to the counter, opened a drawer, and rummaged around until he drew out a scissors. He cut his father's head out of the photo, got some tape from the same drawer, and walked into the living room. I followed. Grandmother was tied up in a chair there, her head in a nod of sleep, in front of a television, set on the evangelical channel. A violet bruise pulsed on her cheekbone and a shiny knot stretched her skin into a tight bubble over her right eyebrow. Jack Van Impe spouted vitriol, something about prophecy, the Middle East, the Antichrist, welfare, homosexuality, and the second burning Bush in the White House.

I felt weary, beaten up myself, so I went to my room where Luke had gone. He had taken his father's photo head and taped it onto Jimi Hendrix's body on the poster over my bed. This somehow made things right for Luke, even in the disproportion of the merged images. I could see it in Luke's face, feel it in a lost tension about the way he carried himself. I could also feel the mushrooms wearing off, so I lay down. Luke lay down next to me. I heard him sobbing and I could feel him shivering through the sheets and the star blanket as we both lay faceup staring at the ceiling. The wind blew cool through some crack in our HUD house and sang through the broken fences, the poor fit of doors, the road to the BIA school, the clinic, the Catholic cemetery, the bush-hidden trachoma cemetery of death by epidemic, the ball-field chicken wire, and the Episcopal church. Then the wind sang the names of our village and beyond, Mary, then Betty, Beartail, then redheaded strangers, it sang right through us, ran away through rez trees, until it got so far away and then turned around on some dark highway, to come back again later to find us and lick our warm covered skin until we woke from the strangeness of our own lives, these fixed minds, these wandering bodies, stopped in spaces where we were never home, this time under the government-made roof.

FRIEND

Laura Kasischke

A PERSON WHO HAS NEVER BEEN THE CAUSE OF ANOTHER person's death cannot understand the plight, which becomes the life, of the person who has. For instance:

What is it like, you might ask yourself, to disappear into the fitting room with your white gown, trying it on for the first time, your wedding a few months away, your mother waiting for you outside, and to observe yourself in the three-way mirror (the lace across your waist, the little pearls seeded in a V at your chest, the hidden zipper up your back, the train you will drag frothing behind you down the aisle) and to feel, really to feel, that what you are seeing in that moment in that three-way mirror is your past/present/future.

To look straight ahead and see that, in the present, you are a grown woman trying on a wedding gown.

To glance to your left and see that the future is right there, too, and, in it, you will be a bride, a wife, maybe even a mother.

To turn your head to look behind you in the third, last, mirror, and to see that—

And to see that, in the past, you were a girl—

A girl who brought to an end another girl's life?

■ ■ ■

Let her name be Girl, because she never got to grow up. She stayed a girl (Girl) in every way, and will never change her girlish ways. Until the bitter end of her life she liked to talk in a high singsong voice, like so many young girls. It was annoying. There were other girls, plenty of them, who couldn't have stood to be Girl's friend, who (pardon the expression) would not have been caught dead with her.

She smelled bad, too—a little like the dirty dog her family had, a little like cheap fabric-softener sheets. Let everyone else remember her as an angel, smelling of lilies (at the funeral, they acted as if Girl had descended from heaven to die), but you haven't forgotten that she smelled like laundry chemicals and her dog, which spent its days chained up, eating its own shit in her backyard.

Hygiene meant nothing to Girl, and now it never will.

In truth, if it hadn't been for you, Girl would never even have combed her hair or shaved her legs. But luckily, or unluckily, Girl would adopt any habit you had, and do anything you said.

■ ■ ■

And there you are in your wedding dress, fourteen years older than she'll ever be. You look away from the mirror, down at your bare feet on the dressing-room carpet, and hear your mother call from the other side of the door, "Well? Honey? How do you like it?"

"It's—"

You're about to say, "Perfect," but when you look back into the mirror, there she is—

There she is—

Girl, eyes all bugged out, face blue.

"Honey?"

■ ■ ■

Still, somehow, your life just goes on and on. You get a divorce a few years after the marriage, your mother dies, you move as far away from that town as you can get on the same continent, you have a pretty decent job in an office where they let you keep to yourself and do your job. You have sixty-two Facebook friends, mostly from college, people you wouldn't necessarily have thought of as friends back then. When Girl's clueless mother friends you on the same day your ex-husband (remarried, six-month-old baby) friends you, you realize that Facebook is like a kind of afterlife: everyone's together again, without bodies, and no hard feelings.

You spend a lot of time on the Internet.

■ ■ ■

There are nights you might have a dream in which Girl is perfectly alive and says in the voice of an adult (so real you can smell her breath, which, after all these years underground is very sweet), "I forgive you. It had to happen. It wasn't your fault."

You sleep a little longer the next morning, so full of the incredible relief, the sweet-sick smell of her, the breeze blowing over you (you're always at the seashore with her, always walking barefoot on the beach) that you don't notice the thing up ahead of you in your dream.

At first, it just looks like shadows on the shore, maybe a rowboat. You keep walking. You and Girl don't need to talk. She's in a better place, and you're there with her (although, unlike her, at the end of all this you're going to get to leave), and the sea is full of silvery wrinkles, very calm, and all that salt-sweet breeze, and you keep walking, and suddenly it heaves—

It heaves up—

It heaves up the Thing—

Which is a mass of dead Girl. Eyes bugged out. Rope around her neck. Something has hoisted her up off the sand (something black and many-handed) and it's swinging, swinging, swinging her around in the air.

■ ■ ■

"Betsy?" (That's your name, although you prefer Elizabeth now. Still, you must seem like a Betsy because it's what you always end up being called.) "I'm thinking of heading out of the office early. I have some personal time coming. Want to join me for a drink?"

All these years, you've carefully avoided having friends in real life, but Young Woman is fun to work with. She's a few years younger than you are. She has an odd and exciting sense of fashion—buttons in strange places, one earring with a feather and one with a key, a scarf scattered with peace signs and pinned to the lapel of her vintage mink with a rhinestone skull and crossbones.

Sometimes she makes you laugh so hard with just the raising of an eyebrow that you have to leave the room to compose yourself.

"OK," you say to her, surprised to hear the word come out of your mouth.

■ ■ ■

A drink turns into drinks. The music in the bar (they call it a pub, but it's a bar) is loud, but you think she just told you that she's had sex with every boss in every office she's ever worked in.

"And I'm (not?) proud of it!"

You nod.

Now, she's married, but she's fucking Mr. Svalina. (Is that what she just told you?) You ask her to repeat this surprising bit of information several times, to be sure that's what she's just told you. She has to toss back a shot of tequila before she can say it again, bursts out laughing, sweeps her hair away from her face. "I'm fucking the boss again!" You let your mouth hang open dramatically for a few seconds, and then you both start laughing so hard that everyone at the bar turns to look at your corner table.

Luckily, they're all drunk, too—men, and horny, and not annoyed.

But, Jesus. Svalina? He's got to be thirty years older than she is!

"I'm so sorry," Young Woman says. "I'm so sorry. I shouldn't burden *you* with this. It's *my* cross to bear. But you *can* keep a secret, can't you?"

"Oh my God, yes," you say to her, and genuinely mean it. "Oh my God," you say. "Keeping secrets is my specialty." (Drunk, slurring the words.)

She asks you why, are you fucking him, too, and you both start laughing again, and the waiter doesn't ask, just slams down a couple more shots of tequila.

"Well," you say, "no, but I have a cross to bear, too."

You look away. Coy. Trying to intrigue her, you suppose. In your life, always a little drunk, you've told a few acquaintances, a couple of roommates, and your ex-husband that you have this secret, this cross to bear, a guilty conscience because—

Because you were awful to a girl in middle school and (coincidentally, tragically) that girl died.

"Holy shit. You're fucking Everson?!"

This time it's sincerely hard to catch your breath. Everson! He has two rows of eyebrows over each eye! You cross your legs fast and recall how, once, Girl wet her pants at a slumber party laughing so hard about something so dumb no one else was even laughing. All the other girls ran from the room, squealing, along with you. *Gross! Oh my God! I'm gonna barf!* You feel a spasm in your bladder and feel panicked for a second, but then Young Woman (who from now on will be referred to as Friend) puts her hand on top of your hand, and leans toward you, and it seems to you that she's speaking very quietly. (But, really, she has to be shouting, doesn't she? They didn't turn the music down just for this.) Tell me, she says. Tell me the whole story.

■ ■ ■

You have no intention of telling her, or anyone (ever), the *whole story*, but you're happy to tell her part of the story. It's quite a story. And because you live a pretty solitary life you wouldn't mind the attention. It's not unfamiliar, this attention. Even at Girl's funeral, people came up to you. Just like this. Touching you, saying how hard this must be for you. Even Girl's mother, who is now your Facebook friend. You start the way you always start, with the saddest, truest part—

"I had this friend," you say. "I was thirteen. She was, too. She was a follower. Really needy. I was her only friend."

Friend nods. Go on.

"We hung out a lot. Probably too much. I wasn't very nice to her. I know it's every kid's excuse, but my parents were getting a divorce. Actually, they got back together after everything happened, but at the time my dad was moving across town, and I was pissed, I guess, although I never thought about my parents' divorce."

Yeah, but of course you were angry. Who wouldn't be? Dad leaving. Little kid . . . Little kids always shove that stuff into their subconscious, act it out instead.

(You pretend to consider this, take comfort in it—although it's everyone's first impulse to tell you this. She might as well be reading from a script.)

"Well," you go on, "for whatever reason I was always telling this friend all the time what to do, and something about how she'd just do it made me even more angry. She'd jump into a pool with her clothes on, or close her eyes and run across the street. I mean, not that I told her to do this. She'd just—"

That's not normal. Friend shakes her head. That wasn't you, that was *her.*

"I've thought of that," you say. "And, let me tell you, I've paid a lot of money to a few different therapists to tell me that."

Friend laughs ruefully, knowingly. She's been in therapy, too. She tells you about one therapist with a lisp, mimics him. He grabbed her breasts. She had to sue him. She won, and took a three-week trip to Puerto Rico with the money. You laugh about the incompetence of therapists for a while and then she turns the story back to you, and hers becomes a hushed, sad laugh. Tell me more, she says.

■ ■ ■

And you're happy to tell her more. Not the whole thing, of course, but a little more. Maybe even a little more than you've told the others. She's got a hand to her chest, and she's waiting, as if she's scared of what you're about to tell her next.

Not scared of what happened, you think. She's not scared *of* you, she's scared *for* you.

"So"—you clear your throat, you go on—"my friend told me she always had this fantasy that she would kill herself, that it would really get back at everyone, really get everybody's attention."

Friend nods. You sigh, look at the ceiling. It's plaster, yellow, cracking.

"And instead of doing any of the things you're supposed to do"—self-deprecating head shake, hands to the cracked ceiling—"like tell a trusted adult, I just kept this information to myself."

You're not sure, but you think there might be tears in the pink guttery ducts of your eyes. Something feels wet there, anyway. Friend seizes, and then caresses, your hand.

Yes, there must be tears. Her hand is sweet. Her hand is smooth and warm. She is really with you, completely present, not like your ghostly Facebook friends. She's right here, on the edge of her seat. A special listener. A listener with a gift. A real audience.

But her rapture, true as it is, is also not entirely unexpected. People feel so bad for you feeling so bad about this. You've seen it on them, in their eyes. Watched it transform their faces from putty into stone, back into putty. You've *smelled* it on them, and it smelled the way you imagine a rubber plant might smell—clammy, and absolute, like a deep trust in something completely insincere.

And such empathy, why not?

They can so easily imagine themselves in your shoes!

How many people have had friends they tried to ignore, or whose neediness they took advantage of, or whose deaths they secretly wished for, or whose warning signs they were pretty happy not to notice?

There but for—

So, here, the story is about to stop. Yes. Its climax is this moment of semi-truth. This is where you ended the story when you shared it with your college roommate, your ex-husband, your therapists (both One and Two, never even getting this far with Three). This is story enough. This is plenty of guilt for any thirteen-year-old girl to have borne across the forthcoming years.

But Friend won't let go of your hand.

Tell me, Friend says. Just tell me, Friend says.

■ ■ ■

Can she tell, somehow, that there is more?

"Well," you equivocate. "Well."

Well, you explain, here you were, and you knew Girl wanted to die, or *said* she wanted to die, and, just think, you didn't tell a soul!

(Really, it's no more of the story, it's just a bit of stalling and editorial, and, just as you'd expect her to, Friend says, *But you were a child yourself, you had no way of knowing, you have to accept that this wasn't your fault, you couldn't have changed anything, you can't cause another person's suicide, and if her own parents didn't know what was going on, and they were adults, living with her blah blah blah.*)

It's slightly disappointing, her response. You've heard all this before. The roommates, the therapists, the ex-husband. If what you'd told them had actually been true they might have been giving you good advice (although, in truth, none of them could have known what it was like over at Girl's house—her mother asleep on the couch, her father storming around, sniffing the coffee cups, muttering) . . . But this wasn't even the beginning of the story.

After her commonplace advice, Friend says the thing anyone might say, the thing everyone *has* said: Yes, but you didn't *want* your friend to die.

You pretend to let that sink in. You stare into your empty shot glass. You pretend to consider it.

Then, you look from the shot glass to the cracked yellow ceiling again, breathe in, deeply, as if sharing a very dark secret—

"Well," you tell her then, " . . . maybe I did."

Friend looks at you sadly. Such sadness. It's bottomless. It's black. There's a ship on it, and on the ship is a bed with soiled sheets and an old man breathing his last breath.

"Yes," you say (bravely). "I think maybe I wanted her to die."

■ ■ ■

Friend shakes and shakes and shakes her head. She's wearing those earrings—the feather and the key—and they begin to waft around furiously in her black hair.

No, she says.

"Yes."

You place tremendous emphasis on the word, as if only now, placing it down between you, have you realized the incredible weight of it. You say the word as if you've never said it aloud until now. You focus your eyes just over her shoulder, as if you can't bear to look into her eyes, as if taking your own evil in, as if it were in the air beyond her, hovering and incomprehensible.

This is the *yes* that always inspires the *explosion* of compassion. One of your therapists leapt to her feet, seized you in her arms. One of your roommates burst out crying. Often you have thought that it was this *yes* that was the moment when your ex-husband decided that you were brave and kind enough to marry. (His mistake—how could he have anticipated your coldness?) Another of the therapists told you that you no longer needed therapy, that being able to say that word proved that you were a hundred times healthier than the average human being.

So, you've said it again, and here you are anticipating what comes next: the exclamation, the embrace, the—

So you're surprised to hear her say, *Did you say yes?*

Not as if you've shocked her, but as if just checking to see if she heard you right.

So, "Yes," you say, again—

But this time it lacks all profundity, and Friend says nothing. Friend remains completely silent across the table for what seems like a very long time, and then she sort of snorts it back at you. Yes?

■ ■ ■

You freeze. You try not to look at her. You try to keep your eyes on the spot just beyond her shoulder, and now you can't even blink. Your eyes are going dry. In your peripheral vision, she doesn't seem to be moving at all. Is she looking at you? Is she smiling? Finally, you can't help it, you have to take a peek at her, so you look at her forehead, not her eyes, while taking in as much of her face as you can.

(Is it possible that there's no expression on her face at all?)

You try to read what you can there without betraying that you are reading, still avoiding the eyes—

The eyes would be a terrible mistake—

But then you can't help that either, and you are looking at her eyes. They are remarkable eyes. You thought so the first time you met her, introduced by Svalina. There's a thin ink-black strand around each of her pale-blue irises. Uncanny, really, so intense. You can sort of see why Svalina would risk everything to sleep with her. She snorts, it seems, again, and says, Well (sounding, actually, a little distracted, maybe even impatient, or, worse, bored)—

Well, even if you did want her to die, so what? God, if every time I wished someone dead, someone died . . .

And then she's flagging down the waiter, as if she's done with this conversation, as if she thinks she's heard the whole story, and she's thoroughly disappointed.

"But, maybe," you say (and try to catch her eye now, and can't), "maybe my wanting to see her die inspired her to kill herself. She was a show-off. I was her only friend."

The music seems suddenly cranked up again. It's the Boss. You hate these old guys. Their raspy tunelessness. Their bleeding billionaire hearts. Their sentimental lyrics. The waiter slaps another couple of shots down in front of both of you. Friend picks up her little glass, and then, startlingly, slides over to your side of the table.

She pulls her chair right next to yours. You can smell her hair. Long, black, shiny. Sage?

She puts her hand on the back of your head, and brings the little glass to your lips, tips it, smiles at you from the corner of your eye as you swallow. She picks up the other glass then, and pours the tequila into her own mouth, and then takes your face in her two hands and pulls your face to hers, leans in, spills the tequila from her mouth into yours.

A cheer goes up from the guys at the bar, who have turned all the way around in the barstools, raising their beer bottles in the direction of the kiss.

Friend laughs, kisses your cheeks, says, Ignore them. You needed that more than I did. You haven't finished your story.

■ ■ ■

Although, even at the time, as she's staring into your eyes, you realize it's probably just that you're shit-faced, not that Friend is reading your mind, you still have the feeling that she's seeing the whole thing taking place in there, in that little corner of your brain—

Some cortex or thalamus or whatever it is, some little gaseous cloud of memory and truth tucked away somewhere inside you, that place where Girl lives—

That she's pulling it out of you, the memory of it, the way a magician might pluck a coin from behind your ear or draw a long silk scarf out of some orifice you didn't know you had. She's looking into your eyes, and, it seems, looking straight at it—

She can see it—

The way you and Girl locked Girl's bedroom door, and how you were saying to her, You owe it to your fucking mother, I mean, what is this, passed out every day on the couch, and your dad down there sniffing the coffee cups?

"You think so, too?!" Girl said, as if it relieved and alarmed and amazed her that anyone could be thinking what she'd been thinking, that anyone could so completely read her mind (which wasn't really that hard for you since every time she went to the bathroom and left you alone in her bedroom you read her stupid diary).

Of course, you tell her, putting a hand on her shoulder. And think how freaked out everybody will be at school. Like, Peter Maniscalco.

(She'd had a crush on Peter since fifth grade, and he had no idea she was alive until she died, and then totally freaked at her funeral—about all that you were a hundred percent right.)

And Leanne? Jesus, she'll puke her guts out when she thinks about how bad she treated you—

You paused. You let that sink in. You could see it sinking in to Girl as she looked around her room—although she was also probably thinking about how she was going to miss a lot of this, too. She had a poster of Tom Cruise (blech) on the wall over her bed, and about ten thousand pictures she'd cut out of magazines: country estates and little cabins in the woods and flower gardens in England, like maybe she was going to have such things someday.

Now, she was realizing, she could forget all that. She was only halfway through *Gone with the Wind.* (I mean, she'd seen the movie so she knew how it would turn out, but still . . .) She might have been thinking of that awful dog, too, and wondering who would feed him when she was dead.

Still, Leanne.

That might have been the clincher.

Leanne called her Piss Pants and Zit Head.

Leanne would go crazy when they gathered everyone at the school gymnasium to tell them Girl was dead. Leanne *did.*

"How will I do it?" Girl asked you, and you told her calmly, simply, that you'd brought a piece of rope with you from your father's shed.

(Once, he'd said to you, *That's hangman's rope.* You still have no idea why he said that. But you'd looked up noose tying on the Internet, and he was right. It was exactly the right kind of rope, and happened to be just the right length and width.)

You opened her closet door to show Girl how sturdy the pole in there was. You shoved her ugly dresses and stinky sweaters out of the way and held on with both hands, let your legs swing around under you. You didn't have a lot of upper-body strength at that point (pre-gym) so you couldn't hang on very long, but long enough to prove that it wasn't going to give way under the weight of a girl—

Or Girl.

And she wasn't even five feet tall. Once she got herself up there, Girl's feet would be at least four inches off the ground.

You'd seen it done on TV—

A stool, kicked or pulled out of the way, and then the plunge.

■ ■ ■

The guys at the bar are gone. Friend watched them as they were leaving, looking disappointed. One of them blew her a kiss, and she smirked, licked her lips, looked back at you, and said, wearily, as if bracing herself for more of your dull story, going through the motions now that the male audience had gone, So, OK, you actively encouraged her. You helped her do it. It's not the first time. You're not the only person who's ever done something like that, you know—

As if she's heard this story before.

You feel the tears spring hot into your eyes as if by some chemical process—some amino acid mixed in a test tube with a few powdery grains of truth.

You say, "But, God, what kind of a person would do such a thing?"

You, she says.

She's looking at you fully again. The bartender and the waiter are whispering over by the cash register, nodding in your direction. This was all fun and games when it was just two drunk women fooling around. Now, one of them is sobbing, and it's you.

Friend has fished a cigarette out of her purse, but she isn't lighting it. She says, Just tell me. Just tell me what happened and get it out, get it over with.

You can barely catch your breath. Over your shoulder you see the waiter and the bartender (everyone else has emptied out of the place) forcefully turn away, their gazes fixed on the television where some game you've never seen played before is being played. Sticks. Knee socks. Referees making wild motions in the air. Fans waving the flag of some country you feel quite certain you'd never find on a map. Friend looks from your face to the backs of your hands, as if observing them from a great distance, a great height, from inside that ceiling crack, as you're spilling tears all over them, aware of how stupid and ugly you must look. All this hysteria. It's got to be for something. There has to be some part of this story she'd never guess—

Yes.

Yes.

So—

She starts to fish around in her purse (for a match?), and then glances behind her, at the door, as if she's thinking of leaving, going out there to smoke, and you feel what you could only have described, later, as panic, that you've bored and disappointed her, and—

And—

Then—

For the first time in your life, you tell the story—

■ ■ ■

You go ahead and tell her the whole story—

How you had to tie the noose six or seven times before you got it right (thanks again to the Internet and its five billion pieces of holy gossip, information, and advice), and then how Girl, lower lip quivering, let you slip it over her head without even a whimper, still looking around her tacky room the whole time, telling it good-bye.

How, after you pulled the little stool from her vanity out from under her (*hunkh*—that was the last word Girl said), you slammed the door shut and didn't open it again for a very, very long time.

■ ■ ■

And then you closed it again, slipped by her mother (still passed out on the couch), and went home. When the phone rang in the middle of the night and your mother told you what had happened, you burst out crying, or at least you tried, and although your mother never asked you another word about it when you claimed you hadn't seen Girl at all that day, and that you'd never had the slimmest, had the vaguest, had the slightest—

Your mother always gave you a fish eye when Girl's name, Girl's suicide, any suicide was mentioned for the rest of your mother's life, so that it was almost a relief when she died.

Friend stands up as you are telling her about the funeral (almost oblivious to Friend now that the details are returning to you, and finally, you're saying all of them out loud) and about the ugly white dress they'd stuffed Girl into, and how—

Friend walks straight over to the cash register.

(Is she paying your tab?)

And, then, without bothering to come back for her coat, she walks straight out the door.

By the time you get out there too, she's gone, and you're standing outside the bar in the rain.

It's a long, wet walk home.

In the morning, Friend is at her desk. She smirks a little when you stop by to say hello, to give her the coat she left behind at the pub, to thank her for—

She waves you away. Here comes Svalina. He's got a pile of forms with him, and a pen in his mouth, and he doesn't look at you as he passes by, but you can smell his cologne (like whatever might be extracted from the gland of a mole or a mink during the height of summer) and Friend turns away, staring deeply into her computer screen, waiting for you to leave.

When you don't (because you suddenly can't move), she looks back at you, and the computer screen is still reflected on her face:

Staticky light, an impression of terrible depths and surprises.

And the noises of the office surge around you. Coughing. Sputtering. Someone's printer galloping through reams of paper, shuttling them onto a tray one by one, while someone else is shredding just such paper in another corner of the office, and someone is laughing, forced and thin, about something that must not be very funny.

■ ■ ■

In a few days, Friend's blog will have been read by more people than you have ever met or known or passed on the street or imagined in your life. Other bloggers will call it *viral*—

A million members of a choir, the choir loft on fire, the music burning up on their keyboards, in their basements, in their offices and coffee shops and studio apartments. All singing a song, the same song, a song about your blood—

Calling for it, crying for it, desiring to spill, to spill it, to spill your anonymous blood—

Which is only anonymous until one bright detective housewife with some extra time on her hands manages to find your name, your office phone number, your Facebook wall, your previous employer, your college roommates, ex-husband, neighbors—

And the mother of Girl, who'd always suspected, and who's sobered up since her daughter's suicide—

But all you know at this moment, standing beside her desk, is that Friend is looking you in the eye, and you see yourself in there, upside-down and haggard and lonely and stupidly gasping and sobbing (again) at the same time.

And you look around at this ugly workplace, all these cubicles and this carpeting and the stupid slogans thumbtacked to every inch of vacant space, and realize for the first time that you really liked it, that you maybe even loved it—

The place, the persona, the future, the past—

What it was, and what it meant to you, and that—

That it's over—

That it's gone—

That it's all gone now—

Now that you have been led to your closet, and handed your noose.

THE CLEAN, WELL-LIGHTED AFTERLIFE OF ERNEST HEMINGWAY

Michael Delp

"The world breaks everyone and afterward many are strong in the broken places."

—*A Farewell to Arms*

I'VE LIVED UP HERE FOR WELL OVER 135 YEARS AND EVERYone knows me. I walk the streets and it's as if I were in the same category as Keats or Balzac, both of whom live somewhere in the neighborhood, but I just have not had the inclination to ascertain their whereabouts. I spend most of my days sitting in the same place, purely agitated over the very notion of punctuation. A comma here or a semicolon there. . . . It takes hours and hours to decide, and then I'm too exhausted to get up and make myself more visible. Oh, there are so many of the anointed ones up here, it would take too long to name them. They go back too far to mention. I've heard Nijinsky lives down by the coast but have never set eyes on him. But there are days when I pass Whitman's or Van Gogh's villas and oh so many more. And I know for sure that some of the miscreants from the past life are up here, Isadora Duncan and that crazy Russian Yesenin only two examples of the worst.

I revel in this place: the weather, the food, and as much wine as we care to drink. We are close to being gods here, or at least we are told that by The One, "the High Mucky" who lives up highest on the Hill. I've made a few friends but balked a couple of decades ago when they wanted me to move in with James Fenimore Cooper. I never cared much for his writing. Tedious. Barbaric, in a way, and nothing of the decadent French life I had grown to love before I died.

Last week when I walked into my villa, I knew full well that Tennyson, my neighbor to the east, had stormed out of his place in a rage, and I worried who might show up to become the new resident. So whom did I see sitting on a bed as I walked past Tennyson's place? Hemingway. All dressed to the nines in hunting attire and still carrying a shotgun which I was positive, given the notion of how he did himself in, they would not, under any circumstance, let him have. I nodded, he nodded, and I sat down at my garret window, dipped my pen into the frog well, and wrote this in my journal:

> "I shall wonder if this suicidal melancholic can exist next to one of his kind for very long."

■ ■ ■

That first week as neighbors was pressing, to say the least. He pounded and shrieked, bellowed and actually shot holes into his ceiling. After he calmed down a bit I entered and introduced myself, and he immediately perked up. We became instant friends, taking our meals together and engaging in rousing, sometimes almost physical debates about sentences and language and women. He was a large bull of a man, and today at dinner, I knew it was the beginning of a dark journey.

Today he wore his beret. Yesterday it was the pith helmet. He's only got two hats left because he wore out his bush hat drinking water. He insisted that he always have a tub of ice-cold spring water next to the dining table to dip the hat in, which he had carried all the way from Kenya. He'd curl the brim, dip it in, and bring the wet felt to his lips. He knew everyone was watching. But today, it's the beret.

When he's writing, I can hear his muffled grumbling and shuffling as he paces the room for a long time. Then, it goes dead silent for hours. I know his villa is just like mine, about twelve by twelve meters. Of course, we all have our own belongings in our places. But last week, when I stopped by unannounced for a visit, I noticed that one of the corners of his bed had been moved. He wasn't in, so I poked around under his papers, looked under his bed, even opened his huge armoire, which he claimed had been sent over by Louis the XIV as a house-warming present. Hemingway even claimed that Louis, all one and a half meters of him, had been there when it was delivered by six gigantic, beautiful women. And there it was, hidden behind his clothes in the armoire: a secret door into the wall.

So, when I find myself poking through this hidden door, I look into a huge, mist-filled, freezing room. It's long and lit high overhead every six meters by mercury-vapor lights, and it's hazy in there, like the Rue Morgue.

So, I inquire, Hemingway, you in there?

No answer. Then I see him, walking toward me out of the haze. He's wearing a butcher's apron and he's carrying something on a meat hook. When he gets about three meters away, he just stops and stares at me.

Don't bother me, he says. I'm working.

Working?, I say. Looks to me like you're up to something you shouldn't be up to.

He huffs and turns away, his arm backhanding the air. For a minute I think he might be cutting up some kind of exotic meat like emu or elk, which the Muck sometimes sends in from Idaho. There's blood on the apron.

I'm right behind you, I say. He looks back over his shoulder and merely grunts.

When I get close enough to see what's going on through the wet mist in the air, I see that he's not carrying meat at all. It was not a flank steak or a full side of pork ribs. But he did have an iron meat hook in his hands, and dangling from it was a word. Honest to God, honest to the High Muck who put us here and keeps us happy, he was carrying a word. He had the word "Michigan" hanging off a meat hook and he was carrying it back to an even larger, colder section of the room.

Then, I started seeing hundreds of words hanging in the thick air. Everywhere you could see: words. All type and manner of words, right down to what must have been hundreds and hundreds of "ands" and a million commas and periods on smaller hooks.

I started in with a question, but he cut me off. He straightened out his beret and puffed out his chest like he was on the bow of the *Pilar* or something and then lifted the word "Michigan" off the hook and slammed it down on a huge butcher-block table. Then he reached over his head, grabbed the word "Up," and did the same thing. I turned in a slow circle and as far as I could see in the hazy cold I saw words: "Macomber," "Bells," "Kilimanjaro". . . every word from every single piece of writing that ever leaked out of his troubled head, I suppose. I wasn't sure, but I surely did not want to admit that I had not read all of his novels, much less all of his stories. Like most people up here, I half read a few of them and then got bored. Some of the newer residents, like Mailer, who claimed to have read all of them, would spend hours barking at us about hero codes and symbols and then someone else—I think it was Fitzgerald—remarked that Hemingway once wore dresses as a child and that his mother called him "little summer girl." The list of his detractors was long, indeed. Cooper had a mutual disregard for him and it was all Capote could do not to become completely apoplectic at the mention of his name. He did have several brilliant defenders, including a new resident, Hunter S. Thompson, who, because he was so incredibly unstable, lived in his own gated villa. Thompson once came over and rammed his way into our little discussion group and threatened to ransack all of us, and then left as fast as he had entered.

Yet here I was, this fellow's closest neighbor, and I hated his work. It was all stylized to me . . . all those drawn-out descriptions and extended sentences spending precious time telling me about African breezes and sweating canteens and how the wind felt all the time. It took everything I had as a writer myself to get through the one about the old man and the ocean.

Hemingway looked confused—that bewildered, electroshock look. He poked the words on the table a few times and then tried to rearrange them into a sentence, only he could not get it right. "Michigan In Up" one read, or "Michigan Up In."

I can't quite get this today, he rasped.

I looked at his face. One eye was half-shut. His beard was scraggly. He looked tired and irritable; he swept all of the words off the table and onto the floor and gave them a kick.

I'm done for today, he bellowed. Christ, Flaubert, I'm not you. I can't spend a whole day on such tiny things, like that night you still brag about, how you spent hours changing a comma to a period and then back again. Jesus.

He was deeply angry and he was no one to irritate even more. I've seen him put on sixteen-ounce gloves and storm down the street and head for Fitzgerald's place for no reason other than waxing nostalgic.

Let's go outside, I said.

Let's get a beer, he said and pulled off his bloody apron.

It was warm outside. We drank our beers on the front step, and from where we were sitting I looked down the rows of the other villas, strung out as far as you could see. Neither of us mingled much. We'd nod at some of the others who sat on their porches as we walked past on our daily turns toward the chess park, which we never used. On these walks, every day at about the same moment, Hemingway would stop, usually in front of Faulkner's place—who, by the way, never came outside—and he would start in about the Hill.

You know, he would say, I used to live up there.

I know, I said. Like a god, you claimed.

Well, I was close to a god, he said back.

Tell me again, I would always say, why did you decide to come back here to live at the base of the Hill, instead of up there above the cloud line?

It was my wing shooting, he said. None of them there liked that I could shoot better than any of them, or fish or hunt. None of them knew how. I mean, you'd think Edison or even Einstein could handle a fly rod, but no deal, he scoffed. But they're up there. All brains, he said. No brawn. So, I left. Besides, Edison was one sick bastard, even if he has turned himself around, wiring up elephants all over the country just to prove he knew something about electricity. At least the animals I killed had a chance.

Now, sitting with him, I summoned the courage and asked about the secret room and the words.

The words, I said, how did you get them?

The High Muck sent them down—had them sent at his personal request. These days, I'd rather fish and hunt. I thought I might be able to pound out a few more stories. Then he grinned, that half-of-a-face grin that told you he'd lost interest in everything he'd written.

We sat and drank our beers, remarking now and again how lovely it was . . . only lush hills and street after street of those who died and came here to work again using their art as a kind of sustenance, a place where the creators of the world could make as they saw fit, free of want, but ever full of desire. To be sure, there were stories of some, like Pollock and Nijinsky, who could start fires with desire alone, lighting up the night with the fireworks of their internal cauldrons. I loved that aspect of desire as much as I loved the place itself. Desire somehow made visible, as if it had walked out of the spirit and become flesh again.

When he wasn't "writing," as he still called it, spending hours in his cold-storage room chopping up words, Hemingway was painting. We spent a good deal of time sipping wine on our way through discussions about the painters who all lived in an enclave three blocks over. I knew that when Picasso came by Hemingway's every day to enter into yet another more distant room tucked into the Hill, that the Muck had encouraged the visitation. The room was massive, the size of a coliseum, and the ceiling was all glass, open to an endlessly bluebird-blue sky. There were billowing silk curtains a hundred feet in the air that Hemingway could manipulate from the floor, and sometimes he just stopped painting and stood there, watching them, moving them like kites or white birds. Then he would go back to painting.

Hemingway and Picasso were not instant friends. Hemingway loved Picasso's eyes and his wild gestures, and lusted after all the women who were constantly around him, as if they seeped up out of the ground like water. So, Picasso would come by in the mornings, bring one or two women in with him, and sit on a bench and neck with them while across the way, Hemingway would paint like the madman he was. Occasionally, Hemingway would look back to observe and then turn ever more frenzied, into his work, as if Pollock, who almost never left the painters' compound, had taken up residence inside him.

Hemingway had chosen to paint a mural of the scope and size of *Guernica*. It was a huge, brawling canvas of Hemingway's life. He left nothing out. Even in the four remote corners, which he could reach only with scaffolding and a wire harness, Hemingway had painted the vestiges of his life on earth: bulls and African hunting scenes, Cuba and Fidel Castro, boats and guns and naked women on balconies, and wine bottles, war scenes, whole expanses of ocean. When your eyes swept over it, your gaze always came to rest on the business end of a double-barreled Purdey, only it was tiny in scale, incredibly insignificant in comparison to every other object in the piece. If you saw Hemingway strapped into his painting harness, high up toward the sky window, you would have thought Icarus was moving across the canvas with a magic brush. Hemingway was proud of the shotgun depiction, he told me, buoyed by the notion that he had chosen to almost paint it out, as though it did not matter, because he had found himself in this wondrous place where the Muck was known to be forgiving.

Hemingway's biggest regret, he once told me, was that he knew Geronimo still lived on top and he wanted to just pack up and go back, just to sit beside him. And Twain was there wild-haired and filled with stories he never stopped telling. The others on top had often wondered if he would choose to come back, but there was always a detractor or two, as if they were trying to blackball an undesirable. It was rumored that the worst of them was Shakespeare, but he was softening, it was told, after he found out that Hemingway had devoured his work in one bout of rereading late in his life. Besides, if you ask me, Hemingway was the embodiment of all of Shakespeare's best characters: Falstaff, Lear, Prince Hal, and the combined hearts of Laertes and Hamlet. To be sure, he was no Polonius, and I hoped the Bard had seen it too.

All this is true. He came to love Picasso and share his women from time to time. But it was Chagall who made Hemingway into what he called an "honest" painter. All those dream animals floating in midair seemed to come out of Hemingway's dreams. I know because every morning, Hemingway would regale me with his dreams. I used to write them in a journal, but one day he caught me and made me burn them, on the spot, right in front of him.

He often sat with Chagall on the porch, and Chagall would gesture toward the sky and it would immediately fill with images from his paintings, birds and men in top hats and women in gossamer gowns.

Occasionally, at night, Hemingway and Chagall would get the Muck to come by and drive the roads in a classic, sky-blue, 1934 Voisin C Roadster. We rode far beyond where anyone lived, and as he drove, the Muck would ask us where we wanted to go and instantly that landscape would unroll under the tires. I found out later that the Muck loved our conversations, always trying to pin us down on theological issues, but mostly, Hemingway would lose his focus and Chagall would be gesturing as he always did, the sky turning into shapes of fleshy creatures instead of clouds, and Hemingway, lost in it all, trying to makes sense of the road ever changing, and the Muck speaking in tongues. I usually just took it all in, and on occasion would offer comment on a particular form of cloud, say, or would bring up the exact word to describe a feeling. And once, on a particularly long evening, the Muck let Hemingway drive and the Muck sat in the back with me, positing and probing, saying over and over again he had been so fascinated with my sense of "le mot juste." And

I knew Hemingway was listening intently when both the Muck and I arrived at an equilibrium of thought when we agreed that, yes, in fact, it was time well spent, always seeking that perfect word. And leaning in, the Muck admitted to me that one of his favorite phrases in all of my work, quoting it loudly so all of us could hear, was "human speech is like a cracked kettle on which we tap crude rhythms for bears to dance to, while we long to make music that will melt the stars." And at the exact saying of it, we looked into the sky and the very stars began melting. I was pleased beyond all pleasure at his rendition of it, and the melting stars suddenly reformed and on the side of the road, bears danced all the way back home.

The next morning there was no answer to at least four loud knocks, so I slipped inside Hemingway's villa and was met with an eerie sense of his absence. There was a cacophony coming from nearby, as if the varied notes of wind and falling water had come together into one rolling wave of a larger presence. On top of that, I could not scent Hemingway, though I usually could from a distance . . . all musky as if he had mixed spit and dirt with some kind of grassy perfume, the ever-present odor of those grand Cuban cigars beneath it all. I looked through the crack in the door to his painting studio and a brilliant glare, almost as liquid as water, poured out of the room. I could hear the sound of water. River water moving over river rocks. When I looked deeper in, I saw Hemingway far off.

He was standing in a river, and he was painting his way deeper into the Hill. There was an overwhelming sun and a wildly blue sky in this gigantic mural. Clouds in all manner of animal shapes drifted through the air. As he painted they moved away from him. He bent and painted water and trout and pines.

I could barely hear over the river noise, but I knew he was weeping. He turned his head toward me and dipped it toward the paint can and as he dipped his tears mixed with the paint. He dipped and painted and as he painted he wept even more. But he was laughing and weeping at the same time. He said later that the Muck had encouraged him to paint a dream, and that's what he was doing, painting his way back to where he knew he could recover what he'd left behind. Somewhere in that time of painting, Hemingway said he had run into someone he thought looked like Nick Adams, or maybe it had been one of his younger selves, all geared up with a fly rod, headed for the Upper Peninsula.

Now, at night I can hear the sound of water surging behind his wall, and I know Hemingway is in there, painting himself loose, wading upstream in all that wild blue light and water, and I can hear, faintly, the sound of a fly line moving through air, and sometimes I hear other voices too, that old raspy crackle of Twain reciting from *Huck Finn*, and believe this or not, I heard the Muck himself back there, casting over huge rainbow trout, which were, in fact, literal rainbows melded into the bodies of fish.

That was aeons ago. Hemingway painted his way upstream, deeper and deeper into the Hill. That desire had flamed up in him as it had in others, a full manifestation of artistic combustion alive in his entire body. Once a week now, he waves me into the Voisin and we take only the back roads and behind us, in the backseat, the Muck and Shakespeare ride in full recitation, the road lined with every character from every book that ever lived in the heart of every reader.

NOT REALLY

Michael Byers

WHEN AMY BEASLEY MEETS CHARLES PELLETIER AT MICROsoft in the late 1990s he is a sandy-haired software developer with a big laugh and downslanting eyes and a broad face on which the skin appears stretched as though to dry. He is thirty-two. He wears red flannel shirts, khakis, and is married to a painter named Monica Millikin. Charles and Monica have a child together, a baby girl, named Jane.

Amy picks all these facts up within a week of beginning work. It is her first job here in Seattle, and for the first few days all the halls look the same to her and she loses her way in the beige-and-green corridors, coming out onto a stairway or a bright glass wall overlooking a stretch of pine woods where she least expects it—where she has expected something else. She and Charles meet when she pokes her head in asking for directions, feeling she is possibly in the wrong building.

"No, you're right down there," he answers, "about forty feet, by the giant gray pencil."

"The giant pencil!" she exclaims softly, a joke on herself. "I need a GPS."

He grins his apish, unashamed grin, all huge front teeth. It is an interesting, sort of brutal face, on the verge of strange. He lunges backward in his chair and shows the little device in a black belt-holster, attached to him like a medical appliance. "Like this," he says.

"I'm Amy Beasley," she tells him.

Amy Beasley herself is married—newly married—to a young assistant professor of classics at the University of Washington: Paul Lake. She and Paul live in a big house on Capitol Hill, very definitely too much house for them, but the Lakes have money, especially Paul's mother. (Paul's parents are long divorced.) When Amy and Paul moved back to Seattle from Chicago, where Paul had finished his PhD, Mrs. Lake offered to buy the house for them outright, but Amy and Paul, fresh from being elsewhere, and on their own, and uneasy about taking so large a gift in the first place (while arguing to themselves that it was, after all, practical, given the tax laws), instead arranged for Mrs. Lake to pay only about three-fifths of the price, in cash. The rest she and Paul have taken on as a mortgage. Now they conduct long married conversations with one another in the enormous wainscoted living room. They are pleased but embarrassed by their house. There is no denying, of course, that Mrs. Lake had the money to spend. "We're being realistic . . ." Paul offers.

"The money is there," she agrees, "and it's going to be yours someday—"

"*Ours*—"

"So we should really be grownup about it."

These conversations have the air of an argument with an invisible party, or multiple parties: their friends, Amy's own not-rich family, some other, perhaps more principled version of themselves. They have no children yet. The old house is beautiful, with lemon-yellow walls and stained glass on the broad oak landing and a feeling, upstairs, of a great complicated space to be occupied. The bedroom closets feature built-in cupboards and drawers, with porcelain knobs worn smooth and gorgeous with age and use, doors that open onto little secret places behind the walls, like a dream house, or a house in a storybook.

On the flip side, Mrs. Lake is often hard to get along with, and Amy is uneasy being indebted to her.

So it is a good thing she likes her job. She enjoys working for a living, putting herself right with the world in the way a desk, an office, can do. She takes the bus to work across the floating bridge. She writes readable, intelligible content for internal and external sites, explaining how to make various software suites work together, information that she harvests from sloppy heaps of turgid developer manuals. The pay is all right—she is officially a contractor, with an hourly wage, a small percentage of which goes to the placement company that found her the job. She has this modicum of freedom, not to be so seriously committed to the place. And she makes friends quickly. Soon Charles invites her, and Paul, to dinner. "Hooray!" she replies, quietly, through Charles' doorway.

"Friday?" Charles asks.

"I think so." She is nodding, and has to add: "Let me just check with Paul. Sometimes he forgets to tell me things."

Paul is game. While recognizing the cliché, he is finding most of the other professors excruciating company. "They stand and tell you things," he fumes at night in his underpants, ironing his next day's shirt, "that you *have* to already know about, being a participant in that world—so it's either, A, they don't know you know these things, which means they're clueless condescending *buttheads*, or, B, they know you know these things but want to tell you anyway!" He shakes the iron like a weapon. "Because they're arrogant goddamned didactic douchebags!"

It is a tremendous coup for Paul to have landed this very good job in his home town, but to say as much would be to suggest that it might have been possible for something else to have happened. They are still that young, that they will let such a thing go unmentioned, unrecognized.

"You just have to walk away, finally," he spits. "You just—turn and go. Because these guys have no radar for normal human interaction. At *all*."

She tells him, "I want friends. Somebody to talk to who's not related to you."

"Well, I do too," he answers, peaceably.

She is still getting used to this—that her husband can have these passions and not be somehow angry with her, too, by accidental overlap. (This is what would happen with her father. But she has put all that away, behind her.) Paul is blond where she is dark, boyish in figure but his shoulders often hunched as though expecting a blow from behind. "Every marriage is a mystery," is one of his pronouncements. Usually he says this after meeting another couple, abrasive or otherwise difficult. But how does anyone live with anyone else? Paul's idea is that people moderate their youthful fire, the disgust they feel for anyone who doesn't measure up. Because no one measures up. Himself included, he will admit. Meaning, also, her.

Also, "Everyone is crazy," he will say, another pronouncement.

Charles and Monica live in the south end of the city, past Paul's old high school and down into Rainier Valley. It is a neighborhood on the edge of being dangerous. Most of the houses have bars on the windows. This is still just before everything really booms, so the area is mostly black and

Vietnamese. Five years later it will be mostly white. But five years from now Charles and Monica will be elsewhere themselves.

Paul parks their Honda in front of the house. It is a small white stucco with a long, fenced-in yard. Inside, Charles introduces his wife Monica to them, and Amy introduces them to Paul. There are some comical diagonal handshakes. Charles repeats their names: Charles Pelletier and Monica Millikin. He says, "We're the Pellikens!"

Actually, sometimes they do call themselves the Pelicans—a joke. Monica says they briefly considered changing their names. "My mom would have shit herself, though," she mutters.

Charles laughs, hugely. "Can you imagine!"

"The name thing—we thought about hyphens—" Monica waves vaguely, including in her gesture the kitchen, the entryway, and the baby, blond, big-headed, who sits in a high chair in the middle of the living room, staring in their direction. "But that just pushes the name question off another decade, like the national debt or something."

"And this is Jane," says Charles.

"Hi Jane," Amy calls.

It is a strange place to put a baby, out of the way in the middle of nowhere, the way you would put a lamp somewhere when you're cleaning. Amy waits for someone to say something about it, but no one does. Well, it is strange, but the house is small. She feels its size immediately. Not jumbled or messy, but everything at arm's reach. Two little dogs run underfoot. "Havanese," Charles explains. "They're very low-allergen dogs."

They are fuzzy, friendly, wiggly brown things, named Mimi and Zack.

Through a doorway is a kitchen too small for even a tiny table, also a narrow living room at the end of which sits a desk, recognizable as Charles' because of all the gadgetry. Elsewhere, everywhere, tacked up on the walls, are small painted squares. Amy realizes these are Monica's paintings, and she is relieved to find that she likes them. They each contain a little strange lined figure, sometimes off-center—an odd hybrid shape, part human, part coat hanger, dark black against a background of dark blue, emphatic orange, forest green.

"Like Paul Klee," says Paul, "but not so psycho."

"Right!" Monica laughs, which means she catches Paul's apologetic note, the undertone that means, *Don't take me seriously.* For Monica having understood this about her husband, Amy instantly likes her. (This undertone is one of the things she first really noticed about Paul, this sort of anxious humility, in contrast to his difficult mother, and as a counterweight to the fact of his really very accomplished family.) She is also proud of her husband, impressed, abashed, for his having the name Paul Klee so readily at hand.

The house smells good. Something complicated and filling is cooking. The oven is on, the stovetop crowded with pots. Monica says, "What do you want to drink? We have beer, wine, we've got mojitos."

When Amy admits she has never heard of a mojito, Monica swoons in mock despair and hands over her own glass. "You poor thing." She is almost pretty: blond, sturdy. A good match for the big bones of Charles. "Charles makes them," she says. "I just drink them."

"Cheers," Charles says. "To new friends."

They are a little embarrassed, all of them, to be so eager and delighted with one another.

Dinner is osso buco, so good Amy feels tremors of pleasure go through her. She has to resist plunging her face into the broad clay dish. She has never had it before, and it is obviously a dish that takes long planning. Charles and Monica have wanted to make a good impression, which puts her at ease. The wine is good, too.

Baby Jane sits in her high chair at the table, rocking a little. Her eyes are heavy and her stare is vacant.

There is something wrong with Jane, Amy understands, very belatedly.

Halfway through dinner, Jane begins to squawk. Monica pushes back her chair and goes to the baby, pulls her out of the high chair, carries her away into a back bedroom, down a hall, where they stay for a while, twenty minutes or so. In the midst of this obviously important, child-related absence, Amy finds herself feeling rather sophisticated, grown-up. Something is happening down the hall, but she doesn't need to ask about it. In fact—maybe it is the wine, the rum, and there is more wine, or whiskey (the men each have some)—she doesn't quite trust herself to ask about Jane, because she has had too much to drink.

When Monica comes back she announces, with satisfaction, "Asleep!"

"Asleep," she repeats. So maybe this is all it was, then, bedtime.

But afterward, in the car, she says, "I think there's something wrong with Jane."

Paul looks at her sideways.

"They wouldn't just put her in the middle of the living room like that. And she's almost a year old, that's not how a year-old baby looks. Or acts."

"I didn't notice."

"They didn't *talk* to her. They hardly even talked *about* her."

Paul shrugs. "Maybe," is all he will concede.

But she is certain. The next Monday, at work, where the rules of social intimacy are more flexible than elsewhere—you can have a fairly intimate conversation hanging on someone's doorjamb for five minutes, you can talk about your parents, for example, safely there in the droning undangerous halls, far from their silly treacheries, you have proven yourself, after all, as an adult, by being here, nothing can harm you—she asks Charles. Not directly. Instead she says, "Thank you for having us over." And then, "It's nice to actually make *friends*."

Charles hears the question anyway and serves up his giant, fence-biting grin. "We like you guys too. It's been hard, making real friends, with Jane."

She nods, in what she hopes is an understanding way.

"She's disabled," Charles tells her. "Retarded."

"It's not Down's."

"No-oo. Nobody really knows what it is. But she's pretty profoundly, you know, retarded. We're not even sure how much she can really see. Or hear. *Some*," he offers. His face registers a plain distress. Not a crisis, but something much larger, a life-defining effort. He twirls a mechanical pencil over his thick finger. "Anyway, it's hard to get out much."

She has nothing to offer in return. "It must be hard."

Charles rallies, pulls his rolling chair up beneath him again. "Well, there's a parents' group we're in, some of them have it harder than we do. Some of them—!" He breaks off with a gruff, deprecating wave. "War stories," he says.

Without children of her own, she has nothing suitable to present to Charles in trade for this confidence—in return, somehow, for the situation he and Monica are in. It is stupid even to think this way, of course. She can only respond to him from the general pool of empathy that she uses for everyone drastically unlike her: old men, the horribly injured, people in Bangladesh. This is not good enough, and she wishes she could do better. And of course Charles knows this about her, because it is true of almost everyone, and he does not hold it against her. Possibly he holds it against people in general, but not her, in particular.

After this, she leans against Charles' doorjamb to talk every day, sometimes more than once. She has always made friends easily. She is pretty, and thoughtful, usually quick to smile (not as much with Paul as with other people, as she worries he will think she's trivial, and Paul is so harsh sometimes, so quick to judge, on the other hand he has his own family's expectations of him to contend with, for which she does not envy him). But with Charles it's easy. She invites Charles and Monica (and Jane of course!) to dinner, in preparation for which she sweeps the porch and the foyer and runs a vacuum over the rugs and at the Pike Place Market buys thirty dollars' worth of freesia, Paul's favorite. Paul will do the cooking but she assembles the flowers and does the shopping.

It is not until their new friends are almost there that she realizes what a liability the house is, what an unexpected obstacle. She is ashamed for thinking it, ashamed also for not having recognized it sooner. But she is right. "This is your *house*?" Charles asks, incredulous, creeping through the foyer, as if expecting the box beams to pounce on him. "You're a—*professor*? And you're a web writer?"

What is there to say? It doesn't need to be said, does it? Of course they have had help. But neither of them can say it.

Instead, brightly, witlessly, Amy says, "Yep!"

But they must know—everyone knows more about things than they let on. They will consider whether it is Paul or Amy who is the source of the money, and they will know right away that it is Paul—the family, so long in this town, the accomplishment that surrounds him (his father a doctor, his brother a lawyer, his grandparents on his mother's side both legislators in Olympia, it is where they met, in the halls of the statehouse). They will consider what Paul, then, has seen in Amy.

They will measure her, and what they will decide—well, she doesn't know. (There is so much she doesn't tell people.) They will also judge Paul, of course, depending on what they have decided about her.

Yep.

She could kill herself for such a flip, helpless statement. Not suicide, but *murder*—she has an urge to *murder* herself.

Instead, she does what she must, she shows their new friends the house. They are beginning to work on it—themselves, not wanting to spend money. Paul points out the webby ceiling, the hamhanded job the former owner (a doctor) made of his own renovations, which Paul has been undoing with the claw end of a hammer, pulling out clumsy window-seats made of cheap two-by-fours to reveal the old beaded wainscoting behind (piles of bent nails are in the corners where he has halfheartedly swept them). He fingers the gaps in the plaster, he swings open the door of a back bedroom where he has been heat-gunning paint off the woodwork—there are also cans of paint thinner here, and paint-stripper—

"The hazards room," Paul mutters, and swings it closed again. There is a flat, damp smell to the air in there, because they keep the windows open.

Charles and Monica exclaim again and again. The house gives the sensation of going on forever, a *fractal house,* Paul called it once, in which the details are themselves detailed—the hall linen closet whose built-in cupboards each have a brass knob, which when turned produce a heavy, satisfying click, to release the spring-loaded cupboard, inside of which is a row of brass hooks, each of which—well, on and on. It would be rude not to show it all, so they show it all. The tour ends on the third floor deck, overlooking the city and Puget Sound.

"Holy crap," says Charles, shielding his eyes against the sunset.

"The deck leaks," Paul says. "That's why the ceiling's falling down below, right *here.*" He toes the faulty spot.

He, too, is uneasy.

A ferry is making its way onto the mirror-bright Sound. The Space Needle stands on its spindly legs, red light winking on its spire.

It is beautiful, she knows, but what of it? Does it make her happy?

She hears herself on the phone sometimes, to college friends: "So, we're happy," she will say. Paul too.

What she really means is, Well, there's no reason not to be, is there? She does not want to be ungrateful. Maybe she's just greedy. She wants to have all this, and she wants to deserve it, too. But nobody deserves it—their luck, their present position.

Get over yourself, is the other part of this. Shut the hell up. Imagine if your life were like Charles and Monica's. Enjoy your good fortune while you have it.

Downstairs in the kitchen they sit at the table (a pretty modern cherry-wood from Mrs. Lake's basement) and eat the salami and cheese and olives. Paul gets up to tend the dinner—risotto, which he makes often, from his own chicken stock, asparagus which he will slide under the broiler with olive oil and sea salt, salad. He leans in to the pot, stirring, while he drinks from a short tumbler of red wine. He is limber, happy, playing the host. He is just learning this role, but it suits him.

They are talking about families, and Amy offers up Paul's for discussion. "*His* family is very strange. The strangest family I know."

Her husband grins, accepting the topic. "Yes! Schizophrenics, manic-depressives, crazy cousins all over the place."

"Tell them about the one in New Haven."

"My—" he pauses to figure it—"mother's uncle's son, whoever that adds up to, a cousin, I guess? Had, or *has*, I think, this giant apartment in New Haven, and he's one of these *accumulators*. So, he's maybe forty-five years old or so, and his apartment is just insanely full of furniture. Seven armchairs in one room. Six sofas. You know," he waves the wooden spoon, "eleven tables."

Paul has never been to this apartment, never met this person, and every time he tells the story the numbers change. But the story is basically true. She listens every time with a hungry prurience for all of it, the abundance, the neglect, the leisure and status, the sadness.

"Also, he's got one of those parquet floors, right, a zillion little pieces of wood, and one day he decides he's going to refinish the floor, so he pries up each individual piece of parquet—" Paul mimes it—"and sands it down, and seals it with polyurethane, and puts it back. And he does the whole apartment, *one piece at a time!*" He flourishes. "For example."

"How does he do that with all the furniture in the way?" Monica asks.

But that is not the point, the point is the craziness, how lucky Paul is to have escaped it. "Patience, I guess."

"What does he do for a living?"

"Nothing, as far as I know. Draws disability." Paul, balked by Monica's questions, subsides. There is a sense that the Pellikens are not impressed. Still, the list: the schizophrenic cousin who tore out all his plumbing; the paranoid grandmother who mistreated her daughter, Mrs. Lake, so ferociously; the now-dead uncle once featured as a character in an erotic Japanese novel.

Monica says, surrendering, "Okay, your family *is* pretty strange."

Paul, grateful, says, "And that's just my *mother's* side."

"Oh, no!"

"No, actually, my dad's side is normal. He's remarried, actually, to—she's the chief of genetic counseling, you know, for pediatric genetic disorders, at

Swedish Hospital?" He glances away. "I don't know what you guys are thinking about, for, with, but—"

Monica is chewing. "Oh my god," she says, "your stepmother is Gabby Dieterman."

"Yeah!"

"We've been trying to get in to see her forever. She's just totally busy. I mean we're on her schedule but it's not for like another couple months! That's—that's incredible."

"She travels. So." He is still unsure. "You want to see her?"

"Well, yeah!"

He reaches for the phone. A minute later he is talking to his stepmother. He stands up, walks a little way into the dark living room. Then he comes back, hands the phone to Monica, who stands, grateful.

"How about that," he says. He has done something unmistakably good, and he knows it. And his expression—relief. She is so glad to see it—that he has got *this* right, at least. He can give himself some credit.

But in fact it is not totally, unmistakably right. The next time Paul and Amy visit his father and Gabby, Gabby speaks to them in the kitchen: "I don't really like to talk to patients at home like that. Even if they are your friends."

"Oh!" he says. "I'm sorry."

"It's all right. Patients call me all the time anyway. But I try to keep those things straight. Otherwise—" She is a tall, graying blond with funky half-glasses on the tip of her nose. "I'd be on the phone eleven hours a day."

"Thank you for talking with them."

"You're welcome. They're very conscientious parents, it sounds like. They sent me all their records and this *stack* of documentation." She sees Paul about to apologize again and says, "I looked through it already, because I was curious, you know, and it only took me about half an hour. Jane, is that the girl's name?"

"They are good parents," Paul says.

"Well." A grievance remains. "It sounds like she's not really human. I'm sorry to put it that way, but she's really not. The question is how long will she live."

"How long?" Amy asks.

"Probably around twenty years." Gabby is bluff, matter-of-fact, a professional. Either the result of her work or a reason she is so good at it. "She's just got so much wrong with her. Fifty years ago she'd have been put in a home and let die."

This is such a terrible thing to say that Amy recoils. Gabby sees it and says, "It's just the truth." She does not want to come across as wicked—the wicked stepmother! And she is a doctor, and she knows far more than she will ever say about certain things. And facing Paul and Amy she must feel a certain impatience. They know so little.

And in fact, she does manage to see the Pellikens sooner than she might have otherwise. A few weeks later there is a cancellation. So Charles and Monica and Jane go to Swedish Hospital and up to the eighth floor, in the genetics wing, for a morning-long session involving blood being drawn and a family history taken. But Dr. Gabby Dieterman knows almost at once that Jane's condition is not something hereditary. Instead it is a random mutation. Amy hears the name and repeats it to Paul, but neither of them can remember it. They only hear the term once, and it feels bad to ask to hear it again, once they have forgotten it. It is something complicated and multi-parted, like Klingler-Katsura-Something-Something-Deficiency Syndrome, and the name is not important, really, or so they tell themselves. The important thing is, Charles and Monica aren't carrying something—they were only very unlucky.

How do Charles and Monica stand it? Amy wonders aloud.

"I don't know," Paul says. "People are tough."

This becomes another one of his pronouncements.

Not long after, feeling it is time, or that they have no reason *not* to, Paul suggests they try for a baby.

It would be good, they think, to exert a little positive influence on the world, on Paul's family, even. It is possible to steer the ship a little one way or another. After a generation or two those adjustments can add up. This is how they think of it.

She takes herself off the pill. For a few weeks they use condoms as it is believed better not to get pregnant during the time when she is readjusting to her natural cycling. They try on what they think is the right day, but two weeks later she knows she is about to get her period. They try again the following month, and again she feels the familiar heaviness in her abdomen. They had not imagined that they would have any trouble. They are still so young. They have looked with pity, contempt, on those couples who, having waited too long, are forced to extreme measures.

"Maybe it was all the heat-gunning," Paul says.

He gets rid of the chemicals, and sweeps up that room, and mops it carefully, until the house is fresh and clean and uncontaminated.

They try for four months, six, eight. This becomes a period of their lives—the time when they couldn't get pregnant.

During this time, she keeps a careful record of her "core temperature," as the books call it, and keeps charts of her ovulatory cycle. There is something called egg white discharge. She documents when this occurs. There are a few months during which they see doctors to seek the cause of things. Paul's sperm have average motility. She is ovulating regularly.

What's wrong, then?

The doctor shrugs. "Nothing," she says. "It'll happen."

But she cannot help consider other possibilities.

If her mother had been more caring with her.

Or if she did not have the sexual history she herself has. It is possible she has done some damage to herself. The terrible time after she left home at sixteen, certainly making very bad decisions about things, picking up men.

Altogether there is a great deal in her past she does not like to think about. She has not thought about these things much, not for a long time. Because she decided, some time ago, that those things were all behind her, they have been out of her mind.

She is capable of this kind of willfulness.

Paul knows only a few minimal things, things whose omission would amount, as she accounted it, to deception: that she was once raped. And that her father used to hit her.

Also, that she was in a mental hospital for some months. She does not quite know how long, she has never tried to put it together, so ashamed, and everything else in her life—

When Paul asked about this, early during their time together, she told him she didn't know how long she was confined. He couldn't credit it.

"But can't you figure it out?" He was genuinely puzzled. "I mean—months, really?"

She thinks that now she could piece the facts together, probably. She knew it had been after she made it to college, free of most of the worst, a scholarship student, seemingly on her way, but then her mind had become unreliable for the first time, she had been doing things that seemed to be the actions of another person entirely, she does not care to remember the list. Not sleeping for a week at a time, finding herself in places without remembering how she arrived there. Coming to, as it were, in someone's car, not knowing the driver or their destination, once a big man at the wheel. Once on a bus.

All those things in the past now. And if she begins to think about them now, she is not sure she'll be able to stop.

The growling presence of Charles, his size, his air of restrained danger, rings a very distant, very deep note in her.

If she were to have an affair, she thinks, it would be with someone like Charles. Not Charles himself, maybe, but he is not out of the question. The violence contained in him—urgency, anyway. He would not be gentle with her. He would take his own pleasure first. His body sounds that far note in hers.

It is fine to think these things, but she will never tell anyone.

And anyway, Charles is out of bounds. Not because he is a friend, but because of Jane. Jane makes him too complex a creature for her. This is what she tells herself.

Then, as the doctors promise, she ends up pregnant after all. And at just about the same time, Monica becomes pregnant again too, across town, in their little house. She and Monica have almost exactly the same due date. In summer, Amy has her baby, a girl. They name her Margaret, and call her Peg. Two weeks later Monica has hers, a boy. The boy is normal, and has Charles' broad, open face. They name him Michel, call him Mike.

A month later, the Towers are attacked, and for a while, it seems nothing will be the same ever again. Paul stands in front of their bookshelves, hands on his hips. "None of this *applies*," he says.

At any rate, things do begin to change the year after.

Charles and Monica, who have been talking idly about leaving Seattle for some time, suddenly decide they're going to move to San Francisco, where Charles is going to work at the corporate offices of Pottery Barn, on their website, bringing the online business end up to speed. (This is still early enough that people are more likely to research something online and go buy it in person, rather than the other way around.)

Next, Paul has a run of interesting and unexpected success. Two papers of his on Peloponnesian coinage appear in very good places a month apart. Then a colleague of his, Vlad Draco (who despite his hilarious name is from

Connecticut and rowed crew at Brown), suggests he repurpose some of them for a more general audience, and introduces him via email to an old crew buddy of his who now works at *GQ*. Sitting in a t-shirt in the old paint room he puts together an article about hunting coins in old Sparta (nothing he ever did, but about which he has read a good deal).

"I could get used to this," he grins. The check he gets is almost three months' salary. "Talk about a lucky break."

From then on, every few months, he puts together a short article of this kind, nearly always with the same result: some sleepless nights, a paycheck, and a small and wholly unexpected touch of glamour and even something like celebrity in their lives. And the money matters, because of course she has quit her job. At eighteen months Peg is a decent sleeper. She has Amy's blond waves, lighter and curlier, and when she stands she extends her spine like a released spring. In her little canvas Robeez she skiffs all over the house, clambers up and down its broad staircases, and with her mother sets up temporary encampments in a high, distant attic room. They call one of these blanketed nests the Away Cave—a room on the third floor, with a single north-facing window, the room is the quietest in the house.

She is a stubborn, willful, easily amused little girl. She will sit for hours in her mother's lap and be read to, her green blanket heaped in her lap, Big Kitty at hand.

Motherhood is, as everyone said it would be, an experience unimaginable from the outside. Nothing prepares you. She is shocked by the waves of devotion, the stupid fascination with Peg's hair and olive-shaded skin and brown eyes, and by the utter, wearying boredom of it, the tiny laundry and the messes and the meals. And also unimaginable, the shameful feeling that she could simply do this for the next ten years and no one would think she was inadequate. She finds herself seduced by such an idea, feels herself leaning toward it as though it were a broad bed. But then, in ten, twenty years, who would she be?

Imagine feeling all this but knowing your daughter barely knew you, could hardly hear or see, would likely die at twenty.

This gives her a sweeping sense of doom evaded.

She takes Peg to some music classes, sits in the circles with the other mothers, she strolls around their neighborhood, walks to the grocery store. But it's hard to make friends once you have a little kid, and they are in the wrong neighborhood for it (doctors in their sixties, dot-com millionaires barely out of college).

She misses Charles.

When she mentions this to Paul he says, "I haven't had a friend in fifteen years."

"But you don't care," she says.

"No," he admits.

"Plus, you get to go to work and see people. I never see anyone."

She even tries to befriend Paul's stepmother, Gabby Dieterman, invites her out to lunch near Gabby's office. They have fun, because Gabby is bright, friendly, serious, funny, but she's just too busy to be friends with. Plus, there would be a question of loyalty, eventually, which they both sense. She hugs Amy, her big parka crinkling, then gets on her bicycle and pedals away.

Maybe the house is part of the problem. Because of it, they have not been able to take their own situation seriously; they have not been able to afford to take anything seriously, as to do so would mean acknowledging who they are, what they are—really, what they have agreed to. They have taken more than their share. So they have not made any real friends, and failed to become really close with Charles and Monica, or with anyone, really. They have not had the credibility, at least to themselves, to do so.

But no. Amy knows that most of this is imaginary. That your own life is more of a drama to yourself than it ever is to anyone else, and that if she had simply said, aloud, "Paul's mom basically bought us this house, of course" or "Are you afraid of what's going to happen to Jane?" or something like that, she might have become, at once, the sort of person who earned the answer, earned the house.

But these had seemed impossible statements, for reasons that, much later, she will begin to piece together.

Because then there is something else that happens next. What happens is that Amy goes temporarily crazy. Looking back this is how she puts it to herself, though it is not at all the same kind of crazy she went in college, in fact the two experiences will hardly seem to deserve the same name, especially as she continues to appear very sane—to others, anyway—and even to herself she will seem basically rational and responsible.

It begins when she decides to see a therapist because she is having terrible nightmares. In these nightmares she is trapped in a basement—it is the basement of her elementary school, not a proper basement but the indoor play area, where you were sent when it was raining at recess. The basement has painted lines on the cement floor for foursquare and a brightness coming from the high windows, which are covered with metal cagework. There are pillars here, and also men, many of them, not exactly hiding among the pillars, not taking too much trouble to conceal themselves, but rather lurking, drifting in disorganized packs. She knows these men want to kill her. First they will rape her, then they will begin stabbing her with a knife. Or shoot her with a gun. They are sometimes black men, but not always. The fear that comes to her in these dreams is indescribable—it is dream fear, a plain message from whatever lizard-center it is in the brain that sends out these signals.

It gets to the point that she can't ignore it anymore, and she tells Paul. She is shaking when she does. She is embarrassed, angry, that she cannot control the tremble in her voice, so when she speaks to Paul he believes, at first, that she is angry at him.

She asks, when she is done describing the dreams, what he would think if she would decide to go see someone.

"You mean therapy?" he asks.

She can only nod.

This is, for her, the worst moment of the marriage. It seems to her everything she has worked so resolutely to silence has returned, redoubled. He would be justified in leaving her now, in taking Peg. But he just says, "Sure. Why not?"

"Because I should be able to do this myself!"

"But you can't," he points out. "So you should get some help."

He is calm, rational, unjudgmental, though he is judgmental about everything else, everyone else. It did not occur to her that he would be this way, that he would not recoil in disgust. She failed to imagine that he might use her troubles to demonstrate something about himself.

Her therapist's name is Rebecca Stein. She is Jewish, Orthodox, of some strain of Judaism that is among the most extreme—she wears long denim skirts and long-sleeved blouses. Her office windows are tinted to admit only a portion of the afternoon light. The office has a studiously neutral quality: the chairs beige and nubbly, the carpet light gray, the pictures on the walls pink flowers, pastels—placeholders for other things, platonic in their near non-existence.

"What seems to be the trouble?" asks Dr. Stein, after they have completed the preliminaries.

"I'm having nightmares," she says.

"For how long?"

"A few months."

"How often?" Dr. Stein's attention is already caught. People simply do not expect Amy to be troubled, she just does not look troubled, she is so pretty, so composed. And it is probable, too, Amy supposes, that more often people come having exaggerated their problems, not minimized them.

"Two or three times a night."

Dr. Stein takes a breath. "Oh dear, that's terrible. You must not be getting *any* sleep."

No, she hasn't been.

"How do you do it?" Dr. Stein asks. "You must be absolutely exhausted!"

She can only nod.

"You poor thing."

This is too much—she begins to cry. Just a little, at first. Then, she can't help it, she is sobbing. *Racked*—to be stretched horribly—but the sobs compress her, she can hardly breathe. She is blind with tears. It is shameful, not to be witnessed, even by herself. Dr. Stein rises, takes a place beside her on the sofa. Dr. Stein embraces her. She is crying helplessly, speechless. This is all they do that first week, and the next. It is a guilty, terrible pleasure—to dissolve so completely like this. It is very hard to leave the sofa, to make herself presentable again leaning over the sink in the little washroom, to go down in the slow, anonymous elevator to the blazing street. Surely everyone can see what she has been up to—her eyes red, her lips swollen, her hair a wiry frizz.

She does not tell Paul all this. Sometimes she wants to. He notices nothing wrong.

She's just so *mothering.*

She's just—she just puts her arms around me—

(Oh, it is awful, but she can hardly think it without crying.)

And she can't tell him, anyway. Because it is humiliating to find herself so far out in the world, and to be so naked in this way. She had grown a shell, had she not, and now, somehow, she has lost it.

But it does not help. The nightmares grow worse. She wakes sometimes convinced that behind the bookshelves, which line the long hallway, there is nothing—actually nothing, just empty space, a horrible emptiness, that will draw her somehow *in* and *through.* She has to lie there, sometimes for more than an hour, until she can bring herself to go to the bathroom. The darkness has an attractive power, it looms there. It gapes, a great invisible hole in the house.

She is a terrible mother.

Or they are at the zoo, climbing one of the gentle hills the zoo is built over. Paul is carrying Peg on his back and she is chattering into his ear—but they are far enough ahead that Amy can't hear what she's saying.

Her daughter's hair is straightening, growing darker.

And she hears a helicopter, making its way somewhere nearby. Then it rises, slowly, with a strange purpose, a black hovering insect, bug-eyed, above the trees. It is nearer than she thought. Its black blades chop the air, *whomp whomp whomp,* and she can hear beneath the blades the storming churn of the engine. And then she hears, or almost hears, the sound begin to change. No—it is *standing on the verge of changing.* It is standing on the verge of becoming intelligible—becoming speech. The helicopter is trying to speak to her.

This is not true. And it is very frightening, because she is also quite sure of it—or quite sure, rather, that if she listens any longer to the helicopter she will begin to hear it say something. She cannot clap her hands over her ears—well, she just *might* be able to get away with this. But it will look peculiar. She hurries up the slope to catch up to her husband. She does not want to hear what the helicopter has to say.

Peg is craning now to watch her mother come up behind her.

"Do you know what you used to call helicopters?" Paul is asking their daughter.

Peg knows the answer: "Al Gore!" she exclaims.

The helicopter drifts away again behind the trees, as insinuatingly as it has appeared. It was not looking for her, Amy tells herself. She scolds herself for being so dramatic. Stop it right *now,* she instructs herself.

There follow more incidents of this kind. She is standing in line at the grocery store when she sees three white cars pass the plate-glass windows. She feels a flood of dangerous portent suddenly, a sense that the forces of malice are making arrangements and that if she does not leave at once they will have completed their plan, that she will be caught up in their net and never get home, seeing in her mind's eye the way in which they will be able to guess which way she's going, cutting her off, driving her farther from home. She is alone. Peg is with Paul. Her cart is full of strawberries, blueberries, cantaloupe, chicken breasts.

Or she is with Peg, at the playground, and the other mothers are grouped at the picnic table, and she hears one of them say, very distinctly, "That woman is completely ruined from the inside out," before they all at once, like a band of chimpanzees, look her way.

But it is the darkness behind the wall that haunts her. It does not leave. Deciding the therapy is making things only worse, she stops seeing Rebecca Stein.

It is as though a tremendous force has begun to move in her. She is powerless. In desperation, she begins telling Paul everything about her life—what she can remember, anyway. After Peg is asleep in her bedroom down the hall (the darkness in the hall) and their bedroom is dim, safe, quiet against the day, she tells him. This goes on for a few weeks as memories come bloating to the surface. The veterans' bar she would go to, at seventeen. The rape. And the other man who attacked her, held her down and cut off her bra from behind, only to leave her shaking on the gravel. When she told her mother, how her mother had blinked frantically, her jaw clamping shut, said nothing, nothing, said, "You make things up," before fleeing the room. Her father breaking her two front teeth off against the bathroom sink, in rage.

He hadn't known this.

"Here," she shows him. The faint line where the false teeth are affixed to the true stumps.

Finally a look of real distaste.

"It was mostly an accident," she supplies. "He was just hitting me, not trying to break my teeth off."

He asks her to open her mouth again. He examines the work, the discoloration. He would never have noticed.

"Is there anything else you want to tell me?" he asks.

She makes a vague, hopeless gesture, half-spinning. "I don't know what you want to hear. How much detail. I don't—"

She sees that he understands, that she doesn't want to assign it more importance than it really deserves. It is years ago, after all. Why bring it up after all this time?

But it was she who brought it up.

"Did you have an abortion?" he asks, abruptly.

"No." She shakes her head violently. "Never."

The relief in his face is stark. He watches her intently for a moment. Then he sinks back, his expression relaxing. He blinks. "Those were just—things that happened to you. It's like being in a plane crash. It has nothing to do with you." He settles further, until he can settle no more. "Just—accidents of circumstance."

It is insufficient.

"Really," he says.

She gets no release. The dreams continue. When she wakes in the middle of the night she must lie still for hours, silent under the quilt, assuring herself that the walls are solid, hiding no blackness, that no one has broken out the basement window, no one is creeping across the Herez carpet, up the narrow stairs, knife in hand—

She listens for sounds under the normal sounds: the creaking of the window fan, the push of traffic up the hill, the trains from all the way downtown.

It is all safe.

Lying there, too, she thinks of his relief. That this should be something—the one thing, evidently—he would have strong feelings about. And then it begins to seem as though this, too, is a lie: that in fact she *has* had an abortion, and suddenly she remembers it very clearly: that it was Sam's child, that he took her to the clinic on a weekday morning, rainy and chill, in the fall, October, she remembers the waiting area, the procedure—

She remembers it all too clearly. But she cannot remember if it is true, or if she has invented it.

For the months in which she lives like this, her life becomes almost intolerable to her.

But to look at her, you would never know.

And then, eventually, for no reason she can identify, the period of her life that these events describe comes to an end. She masters these feelings, or they peter out on their own. The nightmares recede. She regains a sense of herself. Her daughter is older. She herself is sleeping more.

She has pushed it all back down again, for now. She will consider it all again, later, when her daughter is still older, when she is older too. Later. She will. When it matters even less.

Her husband is at the end of the hall, the space heater blowing on his ankles, and she is in the bedroom, folding laundry, and the big house creaks and breathes around them. Their daughter enters first grade in the fall. Their son is three, and looks like Paul.

It can be said that they have gone their way.

They would be memorable, it occurs to her, in time. The two childless adults, not yet acting their age. The house, much too big. The way Paul had adhered, out of boyish loyalty, to his mother, to the wilds of his own family's past, plainly still in some hard thrall to his own history. Their obvious discomfort with their own lives.

So, we're happy.

They had cut, anyway, an interesting figure. So much so, in fact, that Amy is sure they exist in that version still, in the Pellikens' minds at least. They would be an object of curiosity, of retrospective inquiry: whether they had been happy, enviable, what has become of them. If the Pellikens could see them now, they would see contentment, or something like it. They would not see the lost months of that nighttime terror—none of that would be visible.

Every marriage is a mystery.

Still, now—in a minute she will stir herself from bed to get up and go down to check the doors, though she knows in her heart they are locked. She will look out at the empty street, to see if anyone is there. She will stand on tiptoes to peer through the front door's glass, to check the porch. She will do this resolutely, in the reasonable manner of adulthood. But really, she is still afraid, afraid of so much, although it is also true that she is beginning not to notice it anymore. Or rather, not to feel it as much. She is so accustomed to this. By now, already, there are certain things about herself that she seems to be forgetting. It is as though there are certain things she can no longer see, because they are so familiar. Things not gone, but forgotten.

PREPUCE

Thomas Lynch

IT WAS THE FIRST OF JANUARY THAT I QUIT SMOKING. THAT first winter after Sally died, late in October, the year before. Can twenty-five years be gone since then? We don't feel the time going. Dylan Thomas would be a hundred. The blink of an eye, the moment and twinkling—as if it were yesterday, and there I am, in the film always flickering out in slow motion, the matinee version of my life and times, sometimes in living color, sometimes black and white, and there I am, stretched out in the old tub on New Year's morning, soaking in the bubbles, trying to work up some excitement and contemplating the Feast of the Circumcision.

Sr. Rose DeLourdes had always kept us alerted to the everyday feasts in our daily missals, and taught us to pray to the saint of the day for guidance and good counsel and something she called *continence*. By which, we gathered, she did not mean pissing the bed or shitting ourselves. Though it had to do with our "nether regions." I'll hand it to Sr. Rose DeLourdes, she sensed what bedeviled the sixth-grade boys. And what would bedevil the old farts they would grow into, obsessed with their bladders and bowels, their eructations, ejaculations, emissions, and erections.

For most of the years of our marriage Sally would give me one of those word-a-day calendars to keep on my desk. The idea was to use the daily word three or four times before lunch in the normal course of your morning rounds. I'd say "imbroglio" or "codswallop," and friends would roll their eyes a little, thinking to themselves, "He must've got another of those vocabulary calendars for Christmas," but sure enough, I'd find myself talking way over my pay grade, and Sally liked that. And she liked the way it disappeared, one page with the day's date and the good word and its meaning, and on the back, a more fulsome explication of its etymology. How's that for a handful of calendar words? "One day at a time," she would say. "No need to get ahead of ourselves."

"*Continence*," I still say to myself. "Where is Sr. Rose DeLourdes when we need her?" Dead as a mackerel, myself replies. They're all dead—Sally, Major, the lot of them. And Sr. Rose, always telling the girls they were not to dress in such a way as to lead the boys into the "occasion of sin," which is, of course, all we ever thought of—such occasions, getting our hands on the fine new breasts of our classmates taking shape under their uniform blouses, safely ensconced in their brand-new brassieres. I said "tits" back then but learned that girls didn't like being called girls and preferred that their mammaries be called breasts. But how that nun could make it sound like St. Catherine of Siena, the anorexic mystic who lived for years on the communion wafer she had every day, could relieve us of our newfound urgency, is hard to know.

St. Catherine's feast day was at the end of April and even in Michigan the winter was sufficiently banished by then that the whole sexy, muddy miracle of mighty nature was pushing itself up through the soil, budding and busting loose—had we forsythia then?—and chirping and shoving itself into being, and even the fourteenth-century Dominican looked fetching in our *Lives of the Saints*, in which her mauve-toned likeness occupied the page next to a little biography. There was St. Catherine in her halo and chaste habit, bearing the stigmata and a crown of thorns and holding a crucifix and sprig of lily while gazing on the nearly naked, crucified body of Christ with a look on her face of such longing and piety.

Well, I don't have to tell you that among her several patronages—firefighters, people ridiculed for piety, nurses, and sick people—the one who said that her intercession would save us from "sexual temptation" turned out to be wrong, Sr. Rose DeLourdes's rosaries and novenas notwithstanding. We were all mad anxious to cop a feel and, according to what Sally told me years later, one night well into our marriage when she'd had too much champagne punch at the KofC dance, the girls really wanted to be felt up too. She'd never have spoken so brazenly without the drink. And she was a cheap drunk. A glass of champagne, a whiskey sour, a rum and coke. She'd get giggly and chatty and fondling.

Of course, I wouldn't have been lounging in the tub, smoking the last of my cigarettes and playing with myself to visions of my late wife in her girlish, preteen beauty if, by the grace of God, she were still alive. Still, a man has to conjure what he can. I let the ashes off the end of my smoke fall into the suds of bubble bath, then doused the hot tip, put it in the ashtray, and lit another. My limp member fell into the suds.

For years I'd been a closet smoker, ever since Sally quit. She used a rubber band around her wrist and every time she felt like smoking she would snap it. The little pain produced an "operant conditioning"—her words—against the impulse to light up another Pall Mall. I felt it only fair to keep my continued smoking hidden from her. I went out to the garage, where I kept packs of Kent 100s hidden among the bicycles and garbage cans. I'd smoke in a hurry and try to wave the smoke away into the air and keep the smell of it off my clothing. I never smoked in the house or car or on the job. I was always outside, in a hurry and huddle. I'd say I was taking old Major out to do his business—our golden retriever—and once I got down the block a little I'd light up. So to lay there in the soapy water without a worry over who might catch me at it was oddly luxuriant, just one of the mixed blessings of bereavement. I was alone.

St. Catherine hadn't much of a chance. Late April in northwest Detroit, in the hub of southeast Michigan, the light of the vernal equinox lengthening into the rest of the day, bright on the sides of the brick bungalows we all lived in —Sally on Eileen Street and me on Monte Vista—under a canopy of elms and sugar maples, littering the air with their pre-leafiness, up and down the street. I can see that light now, and Sally in it, if I close my eyes, angling its way through the tall windows of the classroom at St. Francis DeSalles, and the smell of chalk and Murphy's oil soap, as the afternoon edged toward our liberation and all of the girls in their blue uniforms and white blouses and anklets and saddle shoes and the whiter-still outlines of their satiny bras and the certain air of detachment they all suddenly adopted because there was some form of knowledge they had recently acquired, coincident with their new breasts, that none of us guys would ever have and it made them, however chaste, however determined they were not to be provocative in their manners and dress, all the more objects of desire, each and every one of them, and the look on sweet St. Catherine's face as she contemplates the broken body of Christ nailed to the cross for the sake of our sins did nothing but fan the flames of that desire—thus, no doubt, her patronage of firefighters.

But April is a long way off on the first of January and the snow everywhere and the bitter cold and the Feast of the Circumcision is one that Sr. Rose DeLourdes never mentioned in school. Of course, we'd still be on our Christmas break, not going back until the Epiphany—the little Christmas and the three kings that Sr. Rose DeLourdes celebrated more than the big one. But really, what's to celebrate about circumcision? How to make any sense of it at all? I have to say it always made me wonder.

When I asked Fr. Clement about it—this was later, when I was in high school, and we all got a kick out of how uncomfortable it seemed to make him to talk about penises and other body parts—he said it was probably best not to bring it up with the nuns but that the reason we celebrated "the octave of the birth of Christ," which meant eight days on from Christmas Eve, was that it was the first time Jesus's blood was spilled and therefore "the first episode in the story of our redemption." He was blushing when he told me this. Somewhere I'd seen a holy card with a painting of the incident replicated. The rabbi with his little knife, the infant with himself exposed, the helpful parents trying to hold him. And to say the look on our savior's face was, well, not exactly foursquare in favor of the proceedings would be the truth of it. My mother was a convert to "the one true faith," which she took instructions in before she could marry my father, and she had books at home that listed the rubrics and liturgical calendars and the various devotions and novenas and all the details of the magisterium.

I had interrupted our religion class to ask Fr. Clement about circumcision and the holy prepuce and how many churches claimed to have the relic when he told me to see him privately after class. I could call in at the rectory.

"As you, yourself, know, Doyle, we are redeemed by the sacred body and blood of Christ, who loved us so much he died for our sins and rose from the dead and saved us from eternal damnation and left us the gift of the Blessed Sacrament."

"Yes, yes, Father, but why circumcision? What was so special about the end of a penis?"

"Of course, you have to understand, my boy . . ."—he was turning bright red—"you have to understand, it was the Law of Moses. It's all there in the letter of Paul to the Galatians . . . the Jews . . . the Gentiles . . . it's all there in Paul's epistles, a longish disquisition on the power of the law."

When I think back now, I reckon that priest got "disquisition," whatever it meant, from a calendar. No telling which of the nuns might have given it to him. He'd learned all the churchy words at seminary—cardinal, venial, transubstantiation—but he took special joy in deploying words like *factotum* or *indefatigable* in the normal talk of the day. He'd pepper them throughout his Sunday sermons and stress the importance of *etymology, exegesis,* and *hermeneutics*, which were words we could look up in our own good times.

"Yes, Father, of course, but why, I mean, who exactly—who's idea was it in the first place?"

"He writes elsewhere to the Corinthians or Ephesians, I cannot be certain, except that he broaches the topic with them of 'spiritual' circumcision. It's in the Bible."

"But whose idea was it at the start?"

"Idea, Doyle?"

"Yes. To slice the skin off the end of little boys' penises in the first place?"

"Yes, of course, Mr. Shields, now I see . . ." He was beginning to sweat a little now and he brought a white handkerchief from the sleeve of his cassock and wiped his forehead and removed his eyeglasses—the fragile, wire jobs with octagonal lenses—and gave them a quick wipe with the cloth, then returned them to their place on his face, wiped his pursed lips with the kerchief, returned it to the sleeve of his cassock, and proceeded.

"Of course, that would go back to the very beginning to Abram, or Abraham, as he was later called, as we call him now. God was always changing names like Simon to Peter, for example, the Rock of the Church. Saul to Paul. So, it was with Abraham in the book of Genesis. It is all in there, Doyle: how he had a dream and God spoke to him about how his wife Sarah was going to have a child, though she was herself a very old woman at the time, going for a hundred if I'm not mistaken, well past the age you'd expect such things, but Abram—that is, Abraham—was told he'd be the father of the nation and his heirs would be as many as the stars in the firmament, or shall we say the sky."

I reckoned that "firmament" was one of his calendar words until I went and read it all myself in Genesis, all the begat and begetting and the deal they made—God and Abraham when he was ninety-nine, that his ancient wife Sarah, whose name got changed from Sarai, would bear him a son Isaac, and God would keep his testament with him so long as all of the kinsmen would be circumcised. I wondered momentarily if Abraham had to look that up—circumcision—or if he knew exactly what God had in mind.

And there was the part that always had flummoxed me, how the scribes in charge of the book of Genesis fell upon penis snipping as the sign of the deal between this little itinerant tribe in the desert and the Creator of the Universe. Why not a tattoo or cleft palate or pierced ear or eyebrow? Maybe a secret handshake like the freemasons were said to have. Wouldn't that be sufficient for the Jews? How is it they went right for the penis?

Such was the nature of my contemplations that starlit, predawn morning, twenty-some years ago now, the first of the year, the January after Sally died, lonesome and lazy and outstretched in the bathtub, smoking with impunity, considering the uncircumcised end of my miserable dick, which I was trying to get stiff in my sudsy right hand, if only to say that it might be a sign that I was still alive, if not the father of nations, at sixty-five, widowed and heartsore, sleepless with grief, that here at the opening of another year, another decade, the last of the twentieth century, the new year of the new life I'd been living without her, that I was nonetheless someone to be reckoned with—a man who, despite age and hard miles, type-two diabetes, and a broken heart, had a member in good working order, sufficient to the few if any tasks it might have to perform.

When that didn't work out the way that I wanted it to, I contented myself that cleanliness was still next to godliness. I got out of the tub, dried my parts, dressed myself, and made my way in the darkness downtown to the Main Street Deli where old farts like myself had talked the proprietor into opening up on New Year's morning to keep the routine of our daily offices of coffee and talk. We promised her a big tip and no mess if she'd open on the holiday.

That's where I heard that Ron Gillies and Joe Baker, the last of the smokers beside myself, had taken it into their minds to resolve to quit smoking from this day forth. Maybe, I told myself, this was meant as a sign, which is something I'd been telling myself a lot since Sally died, not incidentally of lung cancer—a slow eighteen-month subtraction of herself, first her fitness, then her comfort, then her voice, then herself, after the cancer moved itself into her brain so that she died within a few days of Halloween the autumn before after a horrible night of seizures and visions. It was just after daybreak and she was gone. We had the funeral luncheon at a club even though the ladies at the church had offered to do it—I wanted it to be first-class, like Sally—and so after the graveside at Holy Sepulchre and after the club with its condolences and cocktails, I came home to the house, which had never seemed so empty, and I hadn't been here long enough to make coffee when the first little trick-or-treaters, ghosts and goblins, came shouting for candy at the door. And my daughter, who thinks of everything, had thought of that, because on the straight-backed wooden chair by the side of the door where I always threw my coat was a clear plastic bowl full of miniature Baby Ruth bars, Sally's favorite, to give to the beggars on All Hallows Eve.

Surely, I told myself, it was a sign.

And so I said I'd quit with Ron and Joe. We'd make a clean sweep of it. All the other old farts were smoke-free. We were the last to carry on. But I'd take the pledge with them that day. No more smoking from that day forward.

"What the hell, God loves a chancer," is what I said and we put the ashtray that used to occupy our end of the row of tables back up on the counter and began being nonsmokers.

"We'll see," said Bert, doubting our resolve and launching into a story that no one was listening to about how he'd quit smoking years before. Bert had a memory like a steel trap, never forgot a name or a detail, and he could make a story that ought to be told in thirty seconds last for twenty minutes. He had the Irish gift for talking all day and never saying a thing. Still, as old farts go, he wasn't the worst. He sat at the end of the table with guys like himself who listened to talk radio in their shops all day working on some project they dreamed up for themselves, maybe cleaning a gun or carving a block of walnut into a model truck or whittling a walking stick out of some windfall.

Bert had been a machinist's mate in the navy and had a deft touch with little engines and other oddments. George did upholstery and had turned the business over to his daughter but still worked whenever she asked him to. He was hard of hearing so that Bert's retelling of the same story never bothered George that much. He'd just nod and smile and ignore what got past the low volume settings of his hearing aids. He had his own routines: orange marmalade on rye toast most days, eggs over easy on Thursdays, oats on Mondays and Saturdays.

It was the first of January, 1990. George Bush the first was halfway through his only term as president and the Dow Jones was holding above twenty-eight hundred. Gas was a buck thirty-five a gallon. As good a day as any to quit; I hadn't planned it but there it was. I'd said it in front of all those people, albeit the old farts, nevertheless resolved. So I left the deli and drove up the street, north of town to Dr. Rozella's office, the osteopath, and asked him to write me a script for the patch. I'd heard—was it that idiot Bert who told me?—the nicotine patch made it so if you smoked you'd get nauseated. I hated puking. The helplessness. The cold sweat. The toilet bowl.

Puking was, for me, sufficient deterrent. I was still praying for continence: to get more piss in the toilet than on the floor and not to dribble it out in my shorts after zipping my fly and not to be caught short needing to take a shit as sometimes happened. I'd get out of the car, feel my bowels move, and have to race to the toilet. I couldn't count on my sphincters the way I could in my youth. I'd get loose shits from good grease and some dairy products. If I had, just for old sake's sake, a greasy burger and chocolate shake for lunch with the alchies, I'd have to plan my departure and make my way home before I'd get what I'd call the sharts—half fart, half shit—and mess my trousers. Hell to get old.

I didn't smoke that day and put the patch on at night and couldn't believe the vivid, cinematic dreams I had—like going to a double feature back in the old days—and I woke wishing I was still back in the dream, which involved my beloved in ways that are none of anyone's business but mine. Suffice it to say I did, in fact, quit smoking, and I'm glad I did. My wind got better and my appetite improved, and the dreams remained so sumptuous and memorable. I quit the cigarettes but never the patch. I still keep a box of them in the drawer and still see Rozella if I run out. He renews the script out of habit, though it's been twenty-some years now and more. "Don't quit quitting, Mr. Shields," is what he yells from inside his office while his gal brings out the prescription to me. "Right, Doc," I shout back. "One of these days, the cure will take." Whenever the dreams disappear, I break out the patches and am back in the middle of things and feel alive.

Of course you've got to take the good with the bad. Some nights it gets a little too intense and seems more a nightmare than an apparition. Probably it was the same for Abraham, the father of nations, the man who dreamed up that first deal with God—his tribe's foreskins for the ancient covenant, the promised land, the chosen people part. I've tried to imagine the following morning. His tribesmen gather like we old farts do, for no apparent reason, just to chew the fat, and Abraham announces that God has spoken to him. There's some good news and some other news. He's determined to tell them.

"I'm going to be the father of nations," he tells them. "My descendants will be like the stars in the night sky, so numerous you'll never be able to count them all."

Of course his tribesmen know there's some trouble with this. His tribesmen know he's been trying for years to get old Sarai impregnated to no avail. They know—because like this place, it's a small town and people talk—they know that eventually he got the servant girl, Hagar, knocked up and she has given him Ishmael as a kind of consolation prize, a son and heir and someone to teach the religion to. But the wife of his heart, old Sarai, remains as barren as the desert. Until this dream about which he's telling them now, the good news of it. He and Sarai will have a son.

"And the other news?" one of his pals now asks. "You said there was something more to it."

"Yes, yes, I was only just now coming to that. God wants all of us to have the skin cut from the top of our penises. In exchange for which we are to be his chosen people."

"His chosen people?" They are looking at each other now, kicking the dirt with their bare feet or sandals. "Cut our penises?" Their eyes are widening and rolling now.

"Yes, as a sign of our agreement with God, our covenant, our testament."

It is at this point I am always trying to picture what happens next and I don't think Fr. Clement could tell me and there is no mention of it in the book of Genesis in the Bible. How many of Abraham's tribesmen do we see running into the desert as fast as they can to get away from this crazy old son of a bitch who wants to slice their penises? They want to get away and start another religion, another covenant with a god that doesn't think like that. This is before even those who would become the chosen people had come to understand that life is about learning to take the good with the bad. And that for every night old Abraham dreamed about Hagar and Ishmael, banished with blessings into the Jordanian hinterlands, he probably had some nightmares about killing Isaac, how close he'd come to it. Or the pharaoh fucking his wife, Sarai, who Abraham had claimed was only his sister—chicken shit that he was, frightened of the Egyptians.

In much the same way as for every night I dreamed of dancing under the stars, the firmament, at the Walled Lake pavilion to Glenn Miller or Tommy Dorsey tunes with Sally in my arms and her pressing herself into my tightening embrace that summer after our high-school graduations, between the day of infamy and my signing up and taking off the day after Thanksgiving in '42—that perfect summer of our brand-new lives when after the music and the moonlight and the rest of the gang, we'd drive my father's '36 Chevrolet out to Middle Straits Lake, down the bumpy dirt road to the clearing in the woods by the lakeshore, where we'd lie on a blanket and look up at the stars and try to imagine the life we could have if only there wasn't a war and I wasn't going to be fodder for it. That's when Sally would take my hand and place the palm of it on her breast and pull me down to kiss her on her mouth. We would do that for most of an hour or more before we'd head back home on Grand River Avenue. For every dream I had of reaching under her blouse and getting under her bra and holding the soft globe of her breast in my hand, my finger tracing circles around it, and the catch in her breath and then the heaviness of her sighing and the increasing difficulty with which she would plead, "Please, Doyle, not yet, not yet . . ." and I could tell over time how her resolve had been shaken by the pleasure of it, our touching, our kissing, our chaste embracing. "Don't go driving that bumpy road with anyone else but me," we would sing to the tune of "Don't Sit under the Apple Tree," which is all we were hearing that summer from the Andrews Sisters and Glenn Miller. That clearing in the woods by the shore of Middle Straits Lake is always turning up in my dreams and Sally is always willing but not quite ready. And I'm trying to tell her that we mayn't have time, what with the war and its contingencies, we mayn't have time to take our time and wait for a wedding in the easy future, that sooner than later I'll be having to go and do my part.

For every dream like that there are darker, violent dreams in which I'm utterly terrified, afraid for my life and certain I'm going to die horribly and alone. But the dreams of Sally keep me coming back for more and even though I have some in which she cannot be found, or when I find her, she's dying of cancer and her oncologist is saying there's nothing more he can do and there's really no reason to take her to the hospital, just keep her comfortable as long as we can at home and hope for an easy end to her struggle and she's only sixty-five and I can't imagine a moment without her ever since coming home from the war, like magi following their star all those Januaries back.

Now that I'm looking up the barrel of ninety, it has gotten well nigh impossible to separate dreams from memories. So whether we ever got naked out there at the lake, both of us eighteen and eager and earnestly in love, and went for a swim and lay on the blanket afterward drying, and whether I ever actually held her naked body with my naked body before I went off to the US Marines is not a thing I can actually say for certain now. But I have dreamed it and I know the tune I'm humming in the dream as she lets me trace her formerly secret places with the fingers of my right hand as I lie next to her propped on my left elbow and the moonlight shines on the lake and our bodies and we have the rest of our lives before us. Whether I dreamed it because it happened or whether it only happened in a dream, I cannot tell you. Still, it is real to me, and part of my settled memory of her. Whether it happened because she wanted me to have something to live for when I was thousands of miles away or it happened because on the Feast of the Circumcision the year after she died I quit smoking cigarettes with the help of a patch that gave me the most vivid dreams of my life is quite impossible to say.

Possibly it's like those matinees we'd go to on weekend afternoons. My father would take me into the bars on Fenkell Avenue. Bumming, he called it, when after Sunday dinner we'd walk up Monte Vista to St. Francis DeSalles, cross to the far side of Fenkell Avenue, turn left, and stop in the first of the three bars he'd always visit—the Italian, the Irish, and the Polish one. He knew the barkeeps and the patrons who all called out his name, "Hey, Frank! Whadaya havin?" or "Who's that good lookin fella with ya?" He'd introduce me all around: "My son, Doyle," he'd tell them, and buy me a soda and give me a quarter and tell me to come back when the movie was through.

"If I'm not in Carmello's, I'll be at Mike's," he'd promise, and Mike's was most often the one I'd find him in, glad for the excuse I gave him to tell his buddies he'd have to get me home. He liked to have a couple beers and maybe a shot off the top shelf, but times were hard and he couldn't afford to settle in for the long haul and the certain headache of routine excess.

I'd settle into the plush green velvet seat of the theater with my two Slo Poke suckers and a bottle of Vernors and wait for the cartoons to begin. After the theater darkened and the projector cast its first light toward the stage from the little square windows up behind us, the first images would hit the velvet curtain, which slowly began to open so that the light and the colors rippled with its movement. Then the images hit the white linen curtain underneath, almost sheer, so that we could see the big screen behind it, but still the images were undulant with the wave of motion in the opening curtains. It was like the word "apocalypse," the etymology of which Fr. Clement once told us had to do with the removal of veils, as in a dance when the face of the dancer is eventually uncovered, revealed—thus the book of Revelations at the end of the Bible and, he supposed, at the end of life, when everything finally becomes clear to us. Such is the nature of my memory and dreams now—it is impossible to know where one ends and the other begins, and the older I get, the worse I'm getting, and the better the dreams are, like going to the theater on Sunday afternoons while my dad killed a couple hours in the bar, then walked me home in the fading light naming the constellations he knew: "Orion, the dominant winter constellation," or "There are the seven sisters, the Pleiades," or talking about the Tigers and their chances this year, his hand on my shoulder, the world in order—the curtains and the veils shimmering with light and glimpses of images, promising that in the fullness of time, everything would become clear and known and certain.

Still, all I know for certain now is that I quit smoking on the first of January, 1990, twenty-four years ago—we don't feel the time going—and I've been dreaming ever since.

It was Saturday, the first of January, 1944, when we came ashore on the beach on Cape Gloucester, New Britain, in New Guinea. We were the last of the division. They'd already secured the airstrips at the north point of the cape, the west end of the island. We followed the battalions that'd been landing all week. We bivouacked just north of Borgen Bay. Yellow Beach on the operations maps. There'd been talk about scouts from the Seventh Marine Regiment, three of them, who'd been ambushed a couple days before and never got back to their outfit. They'd come upon an injured Jap and chased him up the trail to have a look-see when a platoon of screaming Nips rose out of the green with bayonets and rifle butts. Apparently they didn't want gunfire to alert the company from the Seventh a couple hundred yards away. Only one made it back to tell the story, so our battalion, the Third/Fifth, hardly slept all night there on the beach, knowing the enemy was out there, before moving out on the morning of the second, to the southwest, to join up with the Seventh Regiment.

It's crazy how it all gets smaller and smaller as you make your way to the actual business of battle. When I left Detroit on the Grand Truck Western out of Michigan Station for Chicago everything seemed to be opening up—the future, the world, the possibilities. Even the war was a big-picture event, a wide canvas of good and evil ever since the Japs surprise attacked us at Pearl Harbor the year before. After passing the back ends of Michigan's small towns—Ann Arbor and Tecumseh, Niles and St. Joe's—to see the skyline of Chicago finally, so much bigger than Detroit's, then out across the great space of the nation, prairies and canyons, the damn purple mountain majesty and fruited plain of it all before arriving at long last in California and the ocean, which I'd never seen before, and the distant mountains, and the southern turn from LA to San Diego for boot camp. It was a month before they gave me my M1 and it only took a week to make me a sharpshooter. The bayonet drills, truth told, were harder. Then to Camp Elliot where I qualified as a general clerk, then to Camp Pendleton for serious drills, jungle warfare, scouts and snipers eyes, hand-to-hand combat, machine-gun school. I got scraped up on the amphibious landing drill and spent a few days in the base hospital while the rest of my platoon, Lou Rogers among them, shipped out with the Second Marine Division. I'd met Louie on the train and gave him Sally's sister's address because she wasn't going with anyone and Louie seemed nice and needed someone to write to back home. I got assigned to K Company of the Third Battalion, Fifth Marine Regiment of the First Marine Division and shipped out on Friday, 25 June 1943, from San Diego on the *SS Lurline*, a luxury steamship turned transport, en route for the Pacific Theater, which they told us meant catching up with the Old Breed in Melbourne where they'd been regrouping and retraining since Guadalcanal. It's a big war on your way to it: crossing continents and oceans; meeting guys from every state of the nation—Billy Swinford Smith from Paris, Kentucky, and Donald Crescent Coe from Galesburg, Illinois; learning to stab and shoot and survive the elements; learning to keep from puking on a ship; watching out the portholes for signs in the firmament, the night sky, and the shape of clouds, as to what the future might hold for you; the V-mail and postcards back to the old neighborhood, to Sally and my parents and younger sister, the distance ever widening between us, so that when Madeline from Melbourne made it known to me that no man should risk dying before he had sex with a willing woman, I was happy to hear it and dove right in. That was something that made the war smaller—her lovely body moving beneath me with its tidal, undulant pleasuring. I'd just turned nineteen not four months before and here I was, a little buzzed from the Aussie beer, glad for the heroes they all took us to be, and grateful for Madeline's manifest eagerness to relieve me of my virginity. Suddenly the great adventure seemed a poor substitute for this actual pleasure, her dark-brown hair and darker eyes, her pale, white body, its actual chrisms and benedictions. After that baptism I knew two things immediately: that the nuns and priests were wrong about sex and that old men bereft of it were the ones who wage wars even if young men were required to fight them because no human wrapped in such an embrace could work up the intention to go out and kill or conquer. I suppose it was from Madeline I learned such things. By the time I'd left Melbourne it was clear there'd be no turning back, that those two months of relative ease and easy pleasure were compensations for what was coming next, the two months of intensive training on Goodenough

Island and the horrors of the jungle war on New Britain. When we left Milne Bay on St. Stephen's Day, with only three hundred miles of the Solomon Sea between there and Borgen Bay, I was thinking how tiny the sea seemed now with our fleet setting forth and our days numbered right down to the moment we came across that maggoty corpse of that poor gyrene scout from the First/Seventh who'd gone out a couple of nights before looking for Japs and a way through the jungle.

And we were really in it right away. Jap patrols we could only imagine in the thick green rain forest, and because it was always raining, we couldn't hear them, the noise of the rain made double by the leafy fronds of overgrowth. It was like fighting ghosts because you couldn't see a thing for sure, only some movement in the canopy of green, whether the low ground growth or vines at eye level or trees rising at various heights toward the sky and snipers in the higher trees rising above a patch of kunai grass. I saw one dropped like a box of rocks after Romero, who qualified sharpshooter with me in San Diego, dropped to one knee and squeezed off five rounds just as the Jap was taking aim at someone in the first squad up ahead of us. It was not long up the path we came upon one of the scouts from the Seventh who'd never made it back two nights before.

It was horrible what they'd done to him. He'd been tied to a tree where they'd clubbed his head to smithereens and apparently used him for bayonet practice, the thick lacerations in his thighs and thorax making him look like St. Sebastian in the *Lives of the Saints*, who'd been shot full of arrows by Diocletian's archers. This was in the third century, somewhere near Rome. Of course Sebastian had been found by a Christian widow and taken down from the tree and back to her house where he was nursed back to health. This seeming reprieve was soon reversed when Sebastian continued to insult the emperor, who then had him beaten to death and thrown into a privy. He was known as the saint who was martyred twice and it looked much the same for this poor gyrene limply hanging from the tree they bound him to. No one could say if he was dead from the clubbing before they started bayonetting him, whether the beating or the bleeding finally finished him. Nor could it be determined at what point in the proceedings the Japs dropped his dungarees, castrated him, and jammed his genitals into his mouth, which is how we found him, wide-eyed and full of maggots swarming his wounds and orifices.

That's when the war got proper small for me, down to a dose I could fairly manage. The Japs hated us, lay in wait for us, were watching through the rain for the chance to kill us, and from that moment onward, from finding that poor defiled corpse of a man in the jungle, never mind he was my countryman, I wanted to kill some Japs in return for what they had done to him, beyond the necessary bit of killing him. It wasn't about Pearl Harbor anymore. That was long ago and far away. I had no truck with the Japanese people or the Japanese nation or the Japanese version of current history. But I hated the Japs who had done this thing and were doing things like it every chance they got and I wanted to rid first this jungle, then this island, then this hemisphere, then this globe of them. And I feared such an end for myself. Worse than death, to be dismembered and defiled and left out to rot. The fear was like a dry prickling heat at the back of my throat. It was fear turning itself to hate. I quit watching for Japs to save myself and started watching for Japs to kill. I hadn't, as it turned out, very long to wait.

McMahon, our platoon leader, asked for volunteers to square away the dead guy and hump him back to the CP for graves registration.

"We're not gonna leave the poor devil here like that," the lieutenant said. He knew they'd already reconnoitered some high flat ground near the airstrips for a cemetery. A couple runners from the mortar section said they'd get him back the mile, maybe less, we'd advanced if someone else would get him "squared away." I said I'd do it.

The smell was awful, and the maggots, but I got some kerosene from the corpsmen and soaked some cotton in it and stuffed it in his nostrils and the gaping wounds from the bayonetting. And I laid some cotton over the pelvic incision by which they'd removed his genitals and poured more kerosene on it. The maggots that didn't drop off the open wounds or orifices quit wriggling and died. I was glad of that. It wasn't exactly a medicinal smell, the kerosene—more like a gas station—but it was better than the rotting. The corpsmen brought me two extra ponchos and I laid them out, wired the eyelets together to make one huge winding sheet, cut him away from the tree he'd been tied to, and laid him flat out on the ponchos and folded his arms across his chest. The poncho would make a serviceable shroud and I got three belts—one for the neck, one around the hips, one for the ankles. It would make the handling easier. That's when the corpsman offered me the needle and the thread. He actually threaded the needle and set it on the thigh of the corpse. Not the kind you'd sew a button on with, but thicker, like butcher-shop twine, and a needle curved like a long S shape. He said nothing. I knew immediately what he had in mind. I carefully pried the dead man's jaw open, yanked his genitals out of his mouth, and jerry-rigged them back where they belonged with four or five quick, looping stitches to hold them more or less in place. I was weeping now. And it was raining. It never stopped raining. Even so, I could see he'd never been circumcised.

I swabbed the maggots out of his mouth best I could, stuffed it with cotton and kerosene, repacked his nostrils with the same, then hauled up his dungarees with a grunt. I buckled him up, retied his boondockers, wrapped him up tight, and sent him on his way, feetfirst, covered by a flag. A man of parts, in part repaired—still, dead as anyone had ever been.

CEMETERY

Loren D. Estleman

ROY GRANGER—HE WASN'T "UNCLE ROY" THEN—SOLD HIS house in the territorial capital in 1871 and spent most of the proceeds outfitting himself as a prospector. The proprietor asked him what he was hoping to find.

"My fortune."

"You're past the age for fortunes, old-timer. Anyway, all the gold and silver that ain't been dug up belongs to big outfits from back East. Where you fixing to look?"

"The San Pablos."

"Hell, that's injun land. Even if you manage to outrun 'em, all you'll dig up's a nest of rattlers. The only pay dirt you hit will be a cemetery."

"I'll remember the advice."

And he did, nearly a year later, when he struck the richest vein of copper west of anywhere. Six months along, his little shack sat dead center in the middle of a canvas-and-clapboard metropolis, teeming with hard-rock miners, Chinese laundries, saloons, and whores. When it came time to petition Washington for a post office, he received a questionnaire asking for population figures and such. That first blank was easy: "8,000, give or take 100."

The second, asking the name of the town, gave him pause while he scratched a thinning temple with the cottonwood twig he used for a pen. Then he grinned and wrote:

"Cemetery."

Which in the early years was more than just a private joke. Claim jumpers, tinhorn gamblers, and all the rest of the vermin that flocked to money like ants to sugar swelled the local graveyard population and filled the telegraph columns as far east as Philadelphia with entertaining stories of gun feuds and stagecoach robberies; but a Committee of Public Vigilance was formed, bad hats strung up like dried chili peppers, and a hard-as-nails marshal appointed to sweep up the leavings all legal-like. A church and a schoolhouse went up and promptly burned to the ground, but that was nothing unusual in a dry place. A volunteer fire department organized, and by order of the new city council the ruined buildings were replaced with brick structures.

The opera house attracted musical acts and Shakespearean companies, then tourists, who marveled at the bright-red metal fixtures in the Copper King Hotel and visited the local saloons-palaces now, with crystal chandeliers, well-dressed bouncers seated in chairs on raised platforms with shotguns across their laps to keep the peace, and even side entrances where ladies could sip cordials in a separate room without fear of molestation. Some of the original prospectors grumbled about all that downright civilization, but they were in the minority now. The storekeeps, dress-shop proprietresses, and customers of the ice-cream shop didn't complain: for them, lurid stories of mirror-busting brawls and daylight back shootings were something you read about in *Captain Jack's Tales of the Border* and other sensational periodicals wrapped in bright colors and available in C. J. McGonigle's General Emporium for a dime apiece. By then, even the *St. Louis Gazette,* which has built its circulation on grisly accounts of daily life in Cemetery, was referring to it as "the Renaissance Capital of the Frontier."

It wasn't that, of course; but neither was it "Granger's Hell" any longer.

By this time, he was well established in the community as "Uncle Roy." For many years, adults who'd spent their childhood in Cemetery told fond stories of gathering around Fenner's Confectionery waiting for the old man to come out, his pockets stuffed with jawbreakers, peppermint sticks, and rock candy, and stand, laughing and squirming, while the little barbarians stripped him of all his sweet wealth.

He was a beloved character, not just because of the prosperity he'd brought or even his own good nature, but also because no one could tell by looking at him he was the richest man in town. His only concession to dressing up was an old necktie and a clean pair of overalls for church, and while others who'd hit pay dirt had lost no time building big houses, all gabled and gewgawed, on every hill tall enough to overlook the city, he retired each evening to a horsehair-stuffed mattress in the same cottonwood shack where he'd slept in his pick-and-shovel days.

"Uncle Roy," everyone said. "There's quality for you; and I don't believe he ever finished third grade."

It was no surprise, then, in the tenth year of the city's founding, when a special meeting was called in the community hall to discuss how best to honor the old gent while he was still upright and breathing.

Granger himself wasn't invited; pains had been taken to ensure he was ignorant of the gathering. Everyone knew he was a modest man, who would object to being singled out for public praise. Best to make all the arrangements before someone broke the news; then it would be too late for him to back out. He was too sensitive of his friends' and neighbors' feelings to disappoint them after they'd gone to all the trouble.

Jan Vandergriff, owner of the New Holland Mill, spoke for everyone when he said, "By thunder, we'll give that old man our gratitude if we have to shove it down his throat!"

Mildred Flood, the librarian, suggested a big picnic, to be an annual event named for Granger. That was vetoed: Winter was coming, and Gold alone knew whether Uncle Roy would still be around for favorable weather.

Postmaster Orville Feeny thought a gold watch would be appropriate. Vandergriff shut that down before it could be discussed.

"Appropriate, hell! That's what you give a banker when you boot him out for a younger man. Anyway, it's cruel. Why remind a man of time when he's past his threescore and ten?"

Someone envisioned inviting the governor to hang a medal around Uncle Roy's neck, with flags and bunting and the fire-department brass band playing "For He's a Jolly Good Fellow." Someone else—the town's only Democrat—said that if that august official ever set foot in Cemetery, he'd personally reconvene the Committee of Public Vigilance to hang him by his red sash.

Everyone had an idea, and everyone else had a good reason to call it bad. Then a Christmas festival brought the room to thoughtful silence: There would be a Snow Queen selected from among the members of the Young Ladies' Cultural Society, an "Ode to Uncle Roy" penned and read by Schoolmaster Henty, who considered himself a poet, fireworks, and a shooting contest.

"Why a shooting contest?" Mildred Flood wanted to know.

"Because Christmas Day and the Fourth of July are the only times a man can legally fire a pistol inside the city," Vandergriff replied. "Uncle Roy can take part and award the winner. I don't imagine at his age he can hit the obvious side of a buffalo, but he was a fair marksman in his day. Back then you didn't carve a ton of copper out of this country without winging an injun or a highwayman or two."

Mildred set her jaw. "It's bad enough men fire off weapons on the holiest of days without throwing a heathen circus."

This led to shouting, but Feeny came up with a compromise. "Let's make it Christmas Eve."

The librarian considered that, then nodded. "We need a central event. Roy can shoot a gun if he wants come Christmas, but surely we can come up with something more substantial than a homemade poem and a pretty girl prancing about."

The miller said, "I'd hate to think I'd get to his age without being able to appreciate a pretty girl."

There followed another lively exchange of opinions. When the noise died down:

"Why not an unveiling?"

All eyes turned to Richard Briggs, the telegraph operator. He was a young man who'd run away from his father's bicycle manufactory in Chicago to find adventure. Those who knew him thought he'd settled for his sedentary occupation out of bitter disappointment, leading to sullenness, the source of his reluctance toward conversation. When a quiet man speaks, others listen.

Reddening from the sudden attention, he touched his gold-rimmed spectacles and cleared his throat. "A statue of Roy Granger, Cemetery's founder, to be unveiled Christmas Eve before the community hall. I'm sure the stonemasons at Wilson's Quarry would know where to find a sculptor."

A vote was called for, and the motion was passed unanimously.

The sculptor was a Russian immigrant named Anton Grigori, who asked when his subject would be available to sit. Informed that the statue was intended to be a surprise, he demanded photographs.

"If he can't pose for you, how can we get him to have his picture taken?" Briggs asked.

"That is for you to decide. Shall I follow him about, making sketches and taking measurements?"

The telegraph operator was a man of ingenuity. When Granger came out of his shack to ask what Briggs was up to with a tripod camera, he told Granger the Cemetery Historical Society had asked him to prepare a photographic record of the city for future generations to appreciate, and the founder's modest home was a logical place to start.

"What do you want with my old pile of kindling? It should be the first thing the town tears down after I go to Glory."

"All the more reason to have it in the record."

"Go ahead on, then, and don't forget to come in for coffee after."

When he turned to go back inside, Briggs called out to him. "Would you stand next to it? I need something people can compare it to, to show its size."

"Can't you get somebody else? I never got my pitcher took and I'm not used to the idea."

"Who do you suggest? I have to get back to the telegraph office or I'll lose my job."

Granger looked up and down the deserted street. "Tarnation. Can't everybody be down with the ague."

It was indeed an unusual circumstance, involving mass cooperation.

"All right, then. Just don't show it to me after. I got certain opinions as to my looks and I don't like disappointment."

As an amateur photographer, Briggs, it turned out, was a perfectionist. He had his subject pose ten times, from ten different angles.

"Turn my back? Who in perdition has his pitcher took from behind?"

"I could give you technical details, but—"

"Yeah, you'll lose your job. Just squeeze the bulb." He turned around.

"Thank you, Mr. Granger."

"Call me Uncle Roy. And don't forget to come around later for that cup of coffee."

Working in his studio in the territorial capital, Grigori completed the statue in six weeks, carving Granger out of Carrara marble in a modest pose with his hands in the pockets of his overalls. It was too risky for all the people who voted for it to leave town to inspect it, so Briggs brought his camera. The picture circulated, and everyone agreed it was an excellent likeness. Arrangements were made to carry it by rail to the Lucky Duck Mine outside town until December 23. Then it was loaded into Mordred and Sons' hearse and taken to its right spot in front of the community hall under cover of darkness. Uncle Roy always turned in at sundown, but as an extra precaution the horses' hooves were bound in muslin and the hearse chosen for its rubber tires so as not to rouse the old man with the noise.

The conspirators stood at the foot of the canvas-covered sculpture, conversing in whispers.

"How do we get him here?" asked Mildred Flood.

Vandergriff said that was easy. "He loves to shoot off that old pistol of his. He lives for Independence Day and Christmas. We'll tell him we got his targets all set up, waiting for his approval."

All agreed with this, and the party broke up to retire. It would be an early day for everyone, as Roy Granger hadn't missed a sunrise in his life, and his morning walk always took him right past the community hall.

■ ■ ■

"Shucks, I ain't choosy. Hang a lard can on a fence post, I'm happy as a pig in a pile of compost." Uncle Roy stood on his doorstep in his everyday overalls, his Christmas pair awaiting pickup at Hip Sung's Laundry.

C. J. McGonigle said, "You'll like these better. I just took delivery on a ream of paper bull's-eye targets at the emporium."

"What do I owe you?"

"Not a cent, Roy. It's my gift this year to the sharpshooters."

"Well, it's your money. I don't need to take a look. I'm sure you got 'em set up where no stray rounds'll hit nobody important."

"You'd better inspect them," Mildred said. "You're the only one here with true field experience. If we're going to profane the holy day with gunfire, we should at least make sure it's safe."

"Heck's neck, Miss Flood. I only shot one man in all my born days, a Sioux kid fixing to run off with my mule. I caught him in the left ham by pure luck and lost a week's prospecting patching him up and spoon-feeding him broth from a buffalo liver. But I'll go along with you, since you're so fired up."

"You're a gentleman, Mr. Granger."

"No, I ain't. I never wore no tall hat nor swung no monkey stick. And I'd be obliged if you'd call me Uncle Roy."

The whole town seemed to have turned out to escort him to the town square in his bearskin coat. He stopped and turned. The crowd pulsed back as if he'd drawn down on it.

"This here's a business day. Ain't you folks got nothing better to do than follow an old man around?"

Briggs said, "We just want to make sure you're satisfied."

"Well, try and hang back a little. I don't much care for attention I didn't ask for."

He couldn't understand why they found this amusing. Then he saw something in front of the community hall that hadn't been there yesterday. It looked like a six-foot-tall sack of grain.

Henty mounted the steps of the hall, turned to face the crowd, cleared his throat, and drew a fold of paper from inside his coat. He opened it and read:

Ode to a Pioneer

There isn't a one in town, woman or girl, man or boy,
who doesn't love our Uncle Roy.
He made himself rich in his sixtieth year,
but the town he built is wealthier.
So let's all have a 'hear, hear, hear,'
and hope each day he's healthier.

Applause thundered. Vandergriff shook his head. "And here I thought the teacher was just bragging on himself."

The schoolmaster put away the paper and took hold of a cord attached to the canvas sheet. "It's my great honor to have been asked to reveal this small token of Cemetery's appreciation for the man who made all our lives possible."

A twitch, and the marble monument shone in the rising sun.

More applause, louder than the first round.

Granger, who was choking on his morning chaw, found himself pushed and pummeled by dozens of pairs of hands to the top of the steps.

Silence while he swallowed the plug. Mildred Flood, who also edited the *Headstone*, the town's weekly newspaper, got her lead right away. "On Christmas Eve, no one could but notice a tear in Uncle Roy's eye when . . ."

The old man blew his nose into a bandanna handkerchief. A swallow of tobacco would make a rattler's eyes water.

"Speech! Speech! Speech!"

"All I come out here for was a comfortable old age," he said. "I don't deserve this."

He stumbled down the steps and made his way through a hurricane of back slaps and outthrust hands back to his shack. No one saw any more of him that day.

"Well, that was short and sweet." Feeny's tone was dry.

Vandergriff said, "He's never been what you call a gabby coot."

"Overcome with emotion." Mildred touched her eyes with a lace handkerchief.

"He didn't look happy," Briggs said. "Maybe this wasn't such a good idea after all."

"Poppycock." Henty was still aglow with authorly triumph. "He's like all those gallant old men who braved the wilderness. Too proud to show their sentimental side."

"I hope you're right."

"Sure he's right!" Vandergriff whacked the telegrapher on the shoulder, nearly knocking him off his feet. "That pile of rock's the greatest idea anyone around here ever had since Uncle Roy sold his house in the capital."

Nearing midnight, Granger rolled off his cot, pulled his overalls on over his nightshirt, stuck yellow-nailed feet into his brogans, and went out into the deserted town square, lit bright as a day by the moon reflecting off a powder of fresh snow. He stared up at his marble image.

"It weren't no dream."

Christmas Day dawned shiny as polished copper, with a snap in the air and not a cloud in sight. Penelope McGonigle, C. J.'s seventeen-year-old granddaughter, rode down the street in the livery's best brougham, shivering a little in her white Snow Queen dress but with a smile that put her tiara to shame and a wave for all. Fresh-baked pies steamed on a trestle table covered with a checked oilcloth, ready for judging, the volunteer fire department played a medley of hymns (most frequently "Praise God from Whom All Blessings Flow," because it didn't make as much use of the broken key on Floyd Ott's clarinet), and McGonigle set up a row of pickets with bull's-eye targets tacked to them; he hadn't lied about those. At noon, all the town's self-professed Wild Bill Hickoks turned out with their pistols and carbines and lined up to take their chances at a twenty-pound turkey donated by Ernest Schriftseller, who'd raised it himself from a chick on his 160 acres.

"Not so fast." Vandergriff, the event's self-appointed chairman, stepped forward just as the first shooter was approaching his mark. "It's only fair Cemetery's leading citizen take the first shot."

Richard Briggs, still looking troubled, asked if anyone had seen Uncle Roy.

"Not since the unveiling," Mildred Flood said. "Someone ought to check on him."

"I don't need no checking on when there's shooting to be done," said Granger, stepping through an aisle that had opened up for him between bodies. He had on his best overalls, a clean shirt, and miner's stovepipe boots, old and cracked but blacked to a high shine. His old ball-and-percussion Colt sagged in a worn leather holster strapped around his waist. "Stop that," he snapped, when the clapping started. "I got a hankering for turkey meat."

When the spectators started to step away from the targets, he raised his voice. "Better clear the square! I ain't just sure but that the whole cylinder might go off all at once, like it did in '72 when I shot at a prairie dog and slaughtered all its neighbors. Also, I'm old and half-blind. I wouldn't want to mistake young Briggs for a paper target."

The throng obeyed, withdrawing into the mouths of the streets converging on the square.

"Go ahead, Uncle Roy!" said Vandergriff. "Show these tenderfeet there's still plenty of powder in the old barrel."

"Shut up, Jan. I got to concentrate." He drew the hotleg and aimed.

In the silence that ensued, a restless shoe squeaked in the snow, loud as thunder.

But not as a loud as the blast when Uncle Roy Granger turned parallel to the bull's-eye, squeezed the trigger, and touched off the bundle of dynamite he'd buried in the earth at the foot of his statue.

WALK-ON

Gloria Whelan

LAURA CASTOR, IN HER JUNIOR YEAR AT THE UNIVERSITY, was going to change the world. She was taking Russian because of the brave Soviet Union. Germany had invaded the Soviet Union and Laura wanted to show her sympathy. She wasn't exactly a Communist, but when a delegation of Russian generals came to nearby Detroit, she was there cheering for them in spite of their being her father's age and having pudgy faces and awful haircuts.

Ann Arbor during the war was a costume drama. The dormitories were crowded with reserve officers, medical and dental students conscripted into the service who wore their uniforms to class. In the law quad middle-aged, overweight JAG officers played dogged games of handball. It wasn't all war. On Saturday nights there were dances at the student union, a mingling of uniforms with formal gowns in velvet and taffeta. A student band played "In the Mood" and "Moonlight Serenade."

Laura lived in a sorority house with a new wing named for her mother, who, first as a student and then as head of the chapter's alumnae association, had been a member and then a patron of the sorority. Laura's father gave the money for the addition as a memorial following her mother's tragic death. Laura lived at the sorority out of her loyalty to her mother, but she had better things to do than go to dances.

Laura had red hair, which she wore in a pageboy, and blue eyes that were almost extraterrestrial in their translucence. She was tall at a time when height was considered a disadvantage for young women. Her shoulders were hunched, her body folded in on itself as she tried to make herself smaller. An only child, she was uncomfortable in a group, which always appeared to her as a phalanx. During rushing she hardly said a word. If it weren't for her mother's connection with the sorority, she would never have been pledged. Laura's sorority sisters teased Laura about her Russian. "Say 'thank you' in Russian." "Say 'I love you.'" She would say the words and everyone at the table would laugh.

Within the sorority Laura was a member of a clique considered unsociable, even a little weird. There were four of them. One was the only girl in the school of architecture, another was premed, the third was in the English honors program, and there was Laura. The four girls didn't date much, and a recent Saturday night was spent on the roof where the housemother, Mrs. Alexander, couldn't see them drinking Chianti and reading T. S. Eliot's *Four Quartets,* which had just come out. They boycotted the weekly chapter meeting with its ritual and its inane songs, but to avoid the housemother's wrath they followed rules about wearing silk stockings and high heels to dinner. Dinners were served to them in a formal dining room with student waiters in white shirts and black pants. Mrs. Alexander, with a lace handkerchief tucked into the pocket of her blue suit, presided at the head of the table. When she walked into the room to take her place, all the girls stood up.

Laura couldn't imagine what Mrs. Alexander would think if she could see Laura with Evan on this autumn Saturday morning going door-to-door with the CIO's Political Action Committee to lobby for Roosevelt's re-election. Laura was in love with Evan for his intelligence. She considered intelligence in a man incredibly sexy. Evan was the first Communist Laura had personally known. He mentioned in an offhand way stories about the International Brigade in Spain and the fall of Bilbao to the Nationalists, describing it as if he had been there, but that was six years ago when Laura figured he must have been in high school. He always had a book with him. Lately it had been Camus's *L'Étranger,* which was about a horrible man who seemed to hate his mother, smoking and eating in front of her coffin. It made Laura think about her own mother and how awful she had been to her and now her mother was gone and she could never make up for the things she had said to her.

Evan lived in a dormitory conscripted by the army. He was one of a squadron of soldiers drafted by Military Intelligence for postgraduate work in the Japanese language. For so tall a man, Evan had delicate features—a narrow, sardonic mouth and a secretive smile. Although no horses were involved with his training, he wore boots and spurs with his uniform. Soldiers weren't allowed to be political, so today, ringing doorbells, Evan wore slacks and a jacket that was too short at the wrists and had a high-school logo. Laura liked him better in his uniform, especially the boots and spurs, which gave him the look of a character in a Tolstoy novel. To the people who opened their doors Laura was polite and deferential in her pitch for Roosevelt, while Evan shoved the literature reluctantly at the residents, as if it were too good for them. For the most part the residents were cordial, though every now and then someone would rant about how Roosevelt was a Communist and would ruin the country. Laura's father supported Dewey. Actually, he was for General MacArthur, but at the convention MacArthur had only three delegates.

When they were through soliciting, Laura and Evan wandered off to the university arboretum, a kind of chaste and orderly arcadia with its acres of carefully pruned and labeled trees. It was early October. All of Ann Arbor seemed to be burning leaves, leaving a veil of smoke, as if a coat of old varnish had been spread over the landscape.

Evan was angry. "It was a complete betrayal," he said. He was talking about Earl Browder, the head of the Communist Party in America, and how Browder had dissolved the party, changing it into a political action committee. After being attacked by Germany, the Soviet Union had joined the war on the American side and now everyone was supposed to be friends. There was a hectoring, tutorial quality to Evan's talk. "Browder thinks we can work with Norman Thomas and the Socialist Party, which is crap. You can't collaborate and keep your ideals. Thomas is a bastard. He'll weaken the party." Laura felt guilty. Last spring when Thomas was in Ann Arbor, she had gone to a picnic for the Socialist candidate for president. She had thought him rather grandfatherly and sweet.

Evan flung himself down on a patch of grass. Laura hesitated, half hoping Evan would spread his jacket for her. She had on one of her best pleated skirts and she didn't want to get it grass stained. When he made no move she dropped down next to him and asked, "So there isn't any Communist Party to join now?" She felt she had missed out.

"There's a rumor that a small cadre is still meeting and planning the next move." He ran his hand casually over her breasts, as if he were petting a cat. She pulled back, afraid someone would see them.

"God, you're so repressed. Don't tell me you're a virgin."

She was, but she wasn't going to admit it, for he had once told her, "I don't have time for virgins."

"Of course not. I had a steady my senior year." Even that wasn't true. She had gone to the senior prom with a friend who took her because he had a crush on a girl who was going to the prom with someone else and he wanted to torture himself by watching them together all evening.

Evan pulled her down and rolled over onto her, his weight frightening. She felt his arousal. It was as close to sex as she had ever been. She wanted to put her arms around him but she heard voices and pushed him off, springing up as if she were a plant suddenly released after being crushed by a boulder.

"I'm not going to play games, Laura." He got up and brushed himself off. "I might as well go back and get some lunch. See you next week."

He strode off and she followed like an afterthought, struggling with her longing to tell him she wanted to give in and would have if only it had been the right place and he had been more romantic about it. She felt her chastity was valuable and a prize worth fighting over, like knights with their ladies, and not a hindrance to be dismissed as not worth the trouble. Why couldn't he instruct her in sex as he was instructing her in Communist theory?

The next Saturday Evan brought a girl with him for the door to door. Her name was Ann. She wore a dress that came to her ankles and earrings that reached her shoulders. Her hair was in a long black braid that snaked down her back. She didn't take a list for herself but went along with Evan.

When they were through they handed in their reports, and because the late October day was warm and welcoming, the three of them settled down on a bench in a nearby park. A swarm of children were playing tag. The brightly colored jackets they had shed were scattered like flower beds over the ground.

"I hate to go inside," Laura said. "Another week or two and we'll have snow. Why don't we get some food and go to the arboretum for a picnic?" Even though she was jealous of Ann, she included her.

Ann said, "I have to get back and prepare for tonight's discussion, and so do you, Evan."

"We're in the same study group," Evan explained.

Laura felt a child's exclusion. "What are you studying?

"Probably nothing you would be interested in," Ann said. "Evan told me you live in a sorority."

Evan said, "We're reading Freidrich Engles's *The Origin of the Family,*" and there was that secretive smile that Laura saw as a closed door.

"I'm taking Russian," Laura announced, wanting to show she was as dedicated as they were.

Evan said, "She's preparing for the revolution."

"It's an intensive course and it meets five days a week. I'm reading *War and Peace* in Russian on my own." That was an exaggeration. She had read two paragraphs and those with the help of a dictionary.

"Good for you." Ann headed off, expecting Evan to follow.

Laura watched them until they turned a corner, then she headed for the quad and the library where she looked Engles up in the *Britannica* and discovered his real name was Simon Buttermilch. With a name like that, how could you take him seriously? What's more, he went foxhunting, which was cruel. If she saw Ann again she would taunt her with that.

Laura had planned to study, but Jean, the premed student from the sorority, said she was cross-eyed from memorizing the little bones of the hand and was going canoeing on the river and Laura went with her. The bright-blue thread of river spun out, reflecting the October sky. A kingfisher followed them, alert to the insect hatch their paddles stirred into its path. Laura's father was a fly fisherman and she had heard him name the hatches: caddis, stonefly, and mayfly. Since her mother was killed he fished all the time as if the answer to the question he was asking lay just around the bend of the stream he was wading. She thought of him alone, grieving. She ought to go home more often, but memories of her last argument with her mother there kept her away.

It was nearly dark when they got back and Laura stayed up late doing her Russian homework and thought again about Evan and Ann, shaken by how much she hated Ann when she hardly knew her. Laura's Russian course was divided between Professor Natler and Madame Petrovna. Natler was responsible for the basic fundamentals of grammar. He was an enthusiastic supporter of the Soviet Union and taught the class Red Army songs and songs from the Spanish Civil War, "Los Cuatro Generales" and "Hans Beimler." He talked to the class about the Siege of Leningrad and how the starving people there were boiling books to get at the flour paste holding the bindings together. He was humorless and a hard marker, and Laura felt he hated them for their privileges.

Madame Petrovna taught the conversation class. There must have been a shortage of Russian instructors, for she seemed to have no qualifications other than a passion for the language. She was in her sixties, a stout woman who trod rather than walked. Her neck was lassoed with strings of beads, and like a rustic peasant she draped her square body in a shawl. She smelled of the insides of old suitcases. Tears slid down her rouged cheeks as she read them Lermontov's love poems. Madame referred to Leningrad as Saint Petersburg and the Soviet Union as Russia. Her favorite students were invited to her apartment for her "afternoons." Laura was always included.

On those afternoons Madame Petrovna answered her apartment door in a silk kimono embroidered with dragons. Her dyed hair, tightly controlled in the classroom, fell over her shoulders in springy curls. There was a faint odor of incense in the small living room. A samovar was lit with a copper spirit lamp, and set out on a tarnished and dented silver plate were sticky cakes that tasted of perfume. Red velvet drapes were partially drawn across the single window, leaving the room in half-light. One wall was ennobled with icons, the gilded saints staring relentlessly down at them with wide-open eyes. On the opposing wall, garnished by a dried rose, was a faded picture of Czar Nicholas and Alexandra with their four handsome daughters and their invalid hemophiliac son. Through a partially open door you could glimpse Madame's bedroom with its tatty silk spread and more icons. "Moscow Nights" played on an ancient windup Victrola.

Laura attended the afternoons with Janet and Donald. Donald was a senior who planned to go to Russia after the war, start an export business, and make a lot of money. Janet was president of the university's Postwar Council and thought Russian would be useful when everything was divided up. Madame Petrovna and her apartment dazzled Laura. She had never seen anything like it. Her spacious suburban home was without surprises. She decided that when she left college, she would live in New York's Greenwich Village and have a room just like Madame Petrovna's—though not the cockroaches that skittered along the baseboards and not the dusty red velvet drapes, and of course her own religion didn't call for icons.

A photograph in an ornate frame stood on a small brass table. It showed a man in a Cossack uniform. Madame Petrovna would take it up and clasp it to her copious breast. "My son Grisha, slaughtered by the Bolshevik beasts." Laura had heard this many times, but it always moved her. She imagined the man to be like Vronsky in *Anna Karenina*. Madame went on, "Think what those murderers did to the children of our beloved czar—slaughtered them like animals. They couldn't kill dear Anastasia. She sewed the Romanov jewels, diamonds and rubies, onto her corset and it deflected the bullets. She escaped and is in hiding and waiting. When this nightmare of Communism is over, she will become our empress." Madame would wipe away her tears and nod to Laura to serve the tea.

"I was on the last train." Madame lowered her voice as if the enemy were nearby. "Bolsheviks were pulling people off the train and taking them to Stalin's Lubyanka. It was a miracle I survived."

It did not bother Laura that Madame's feelings toward the Soviet Union were the opposite of her own worshipful attitude. It was as if the country were two books, and one could read and enjoy both.

Madame told about her escape to Paris, where she was employed as a seamstress in the workroom of the great designer Schiaparelli. She showed them the gown Elsa Schiaparelli herself had given to her before Madame made her way to America. The workmanship was exquisite with stitches so tiny Laura could barely see them.

Laura never tired of hearing Madame Petrovna's stories and thought in comparison how dull her own life was. Maybe after the war she would skip New York and go right to Paris. Every birthday her father gave her a five hundred dollar bond and then made her put it right in the bank. She would have plenty to live on, although it might be that near starvation was part of the experience.

One day Madame invited Laura to dinner. "You are so *simpatico,* Laura." A small table was set in the living room. They ate by candlelight. The napkins were trimmed with ragged lace and the thin porcelain dishes were chipped. There was balalaika music on the record player. They ate blini stuffed with cheese. The blini were slippery, and Laura didn't like the cheese, but it was the best dinner she'd ever had. Madame told her stories of sleigh rides through the Russian winter nights with a full moon and, silhouetted against the sky, the black skeletons of trees like an ominous script that foretold the tragedy to come. Laura had tried to write some poems about Madame's life, but you couldn't write a good poem about a secondhand experience.

For dessert there were cakes soaked in rum, and after dinner Madame served several thimble-sized glasses of Slivovitz, toasting the czar after each one. Laura got a little drunk and told Madame about her mother's fatal automobile accident.

Laura had been a senior in high school. Her grades were excellent, but she didn't have a lot of friends. She was the editor of the high-school paper and wrote editorials about how in their suburb, Jews, Negroes, Asians, and Catholics with Italian or Polish names were awarded points. If you had a certain number of points, a Realtor wouldn't sell you a house. After the Realtors association complained to the school about Laura's editorial, the principal had called Laura in, telling her she was too young to understand such things, and to stick to school subjects.

Laura was sarcastic at family dinners, asking her father, who headed an investment firm, how many millions he had made that day.

"Enough to keep you in the expensive clothes you wear," he said, "and to pay for those incendiary books written by men who would like to have me taken out and shot."

His tone was amused, but Laura's mother spoke seriously to her. "Laura, you're fouling your own nest, damaging the reputation of your community. I heard one of the Detroit newspapers has been asking questions about the so-called point system you describe. They're going to write it up. Of course any discrimination is all nonsense. We simply want a congenial neighborhood. Those people are happiest with their own kind."

Laura exploded. "Why don't we just build a wall around us? I can't wait to get to college and meet *real* people."

Her father had looked at her over his coffee cup, "Shut up, Laura. You don't know what you're talking about." His voice was patient as if he were talking with a young child.

The week before she started at the university she received an invitation to a rush party from her mother's sorority. Laura told her mother, "I'm not going to pledge." They were in the kitchen. Laura had come in hungry and was cutting the crusts from a peanut-butter-and-banana sandwich. Her mother was handwashing the Spode luncheon dishes she had used that afternoon for her bridge foursome. She turned around from the sink, her soapy hands dripping water. "Laura, if you're saying that just to get a rise out of me, I'm not going to bite. Of course you are."

"I don't want all that togetherness and those silly songs I've heard you sing. I want time to study and go to lectures. Anyhow, they probably wouldn't have me."

"Have you? Why wouldn't they? You've been a straight A student all though school."

"You said they don't want grinds, they want well rounded."

"You write little poems. I've seen them on your desk, though I certainly haven't read them. I know how you feel about me touching your things."

"I don't think that's what they mean by well rounded."

"You have nothing to worry about, Laura, and when you're initiated you can wear the pin I was given the year I was president. It has a real diamond."

"If they don't pledge me, will you take back the pin?"

"Sarcasm is the language of the devil, Laura, and you're too fond of it." Her mother didn't say another word, but Laura saw her wipe her eyes with soapy fingers and then have to rinse away the soap's smart. The accident happened a week later.

The university was a two-hour drive from their suburb. It had been a rainy evening on a dark stretch of highway. Her mother was returning home from a sorority alumnae meeting. She tried to pass a twelve-wheeler and the water from the truck's wheels blinded her. Her car went off the road and into a tree. She was killed instantly and everyone said that was a mercy, but Laura would have given anything for even a second in which she could have made amends to her mother. She pledged and, when initiated, wore her mother's pin with the diamond.

As she told the story to Madame Petrovna, Laura cried. "I was horrible to her."

"Ah, Laura, we always see ourselves at the center of a great tragic play when we are only, how do you say it? An actor with a small role."

Laura was embarrassed to have made herself the center of her mother's tragedy, when, as Madame said, she had only a small role. "A walk-on," she said.

"Yes, that is very good, walk-on. It is in our nature to exaggerate our part in the world; how else would we keep up our interest in living? Forgive yourself." She poured Laura a little more Slivovitz.

The next Saturday Evan came without Ann. It was to be their last day of soliciting. Tuesday was the election. The little park was empty of children and in the nearby yards the last leaves were burning in a haze of endings. Streets were crowded with cars surging toward the stadium and the football game. After they finished, she settled down on a bench and Evan sat down beside her. She huddled next to him for warmth and he put his arm around her and she had never been so happy. She dated but she regarded her dates as boys whose lives were no more interesting than her own. Although he wasn't much older than she was, she thought of Evan as a man, as someone who had moved into the larger world she longed to enter.

"I should head off," he said.

To keep him Laura told Evan about her evening with Madame Petrovna, exaggerating Madame's Russian accent and leaving out the part about her mother's accident, not wanting him to see how vulnerable she was.

Evan was dismissive. "How can you believe a word that woman says? She's the sort of person the revolution was meant to get rid of. Ask her sometime about Bloody Sunday when the troops of her beloved czar opened fire on unarmed demonstrators and killed a thousand innocent people. Children included. And what about the millions Nicholas slaughtered in the First World War he got Russia into? That Cossack son of hers probably rode through shtetls raping and shooting Jews. It's a crime to be poisoning the minds of impressionable students with lies when millions of Soviet soldiers are dying under Nazi guns. I'd like to write a letter to the university and get her canned. They'd be interested to hear she plied you with alcohol."

"Plied!" Laura laughed, but she worried that she had betrayed Madame Petrovna. "You wouldn't really write to the university?"

But Evan had moved on. "Laura, I want to see you again, but I'm not going to tramp around the arboretum in snowshoes."

Laura thought of the dances at the union, but Evan would never go to one of those, and anyhow you couldn't wear spurs to a formal dance. She knew what he wanted and she wanted it too. "I can get you into the house." All week she had been thinking of how she might have him to herself and what would happen. She believed she would do anything not to lose him. She needed his secrets.

He gave her an amused look. "Stroll into your sorority and ask the way to your room?"

"We have a rec room in the basement," she told him. "It's where we have our chapter meetings, and there's a Ping-Pong table and sofas. I could wait until midnight when everyone's asleep and then I could unlatch one of the windows and let you in. No one would bother us." He saw what she was offering and for an answer he moved closer to her and, brushing her hair away, kissed her cheek and then her mouth. At first she tensed in his arms, then she opened her mouth for his kiss.

He left saying he had to get back to the dorm and study, but she saw him later through the window of the Pretzel Bell where the army's Japanese language school hung out. He was back in his uniform. There were girls at the table. Ann was sitting next to him and he had his arm around her in a possessive way. They were all laughing. Laura was hurt and angry at not being in on the joke and wondered if they were laughing about her. She didn't see how Evan could be with Ann, after the plans they had made. She hated them for making her see herself as they might, a foolish rich girl playing at being a revolutionary.

She tried to put him out of her mind, but she couldn't and waited eagerly for midnight. She put on her best nightgown and the robe her grandmother had given her for her birthday. She put on lipstick and a sprit of Shalimar she borrowed from one of the girls in the house. At a little before midnight, she crept down into the basement. She hoped he would wear his uniform and worried that he would arrive in slacks and his high-school jacket. The room was furnished with several comfortable leather sofas and a podium. Folded chairs were stacked against the wall.

The overhead lights were garish and unflattering, but she had brought her own shaded lamp. She had a thin volume of Lermontov's poetry in Russian to read to Evan, either before or after. She didn't know how long the lovemaking would take or whether he would stay or just climb back out the window and leave her. His staying in the house, and his leaving, were both worrying. Laura couldn't forget the picture of Evan with Ann. Would he tell his friends about sneaking into the sorority house and having sex with her? Would they all laugh? There was just one girl in the sorority who admitted to losing her virginity, and while the other girls were excited by her adventure, they were a little sorry for the girl. They said she was lucky not to have become pregnant, which they regarded as the ultimate punishment for her sin. Laura believed Evan was experienced and would know all about what to do.

When the time came, watched over by the podium where her mother once stood as president of the sorority, she couldn't do it. He tapped at the window. She didn't respond and he tapped again. Through the curtains he could see the light from the lamp and must have guessed she was there. When she didn't open the window after a third rapping, this one very loud, he threw a brick that broke the window and landed at her feet. The noise brought the housemother hurrying down the stairway, her gray hair nestled in a net, her satin robe an unexpected garish red.

"I was just doing my Russian homework," Laura said, indicating the book. "I didn't want to keep my roommate awake."

Mrs. Alexander, excited at having this melodrama in her own house, as if the war had spilled over from the trenches to Ann Arbor, called the police, but no one could discover who had thrown the brick or why. In the end they thought it might be the dishwasher who had been fired for being drunk on the job, but he had moved without leaving a forwarding address, and so nothing came of it. Laura did not see Evan again and never learned if he threw the brick in impatience or anger. Years later when everyone thought nothing of having sex, Laura wondered if unlocking the window would have changed her life. She tried to find Evan on the Internet, but he wasn't there, either dead or not important.

Next day Madame was absent from her conversation class. Instead a Mr. Grisky, a graduate student, came and read Pushkin to them. He appeared to have no politics but dwelt extensively on the use of Gallicisms in Pushkin, which was the focus of his PhD dissertation.

The minute class ended, Laura hurried to Madame Petrovna's apartment. The samovar and Victrola had been packed. On the walls were ghost-like blanks where icons had watched. Madame's hands shook as she crushed the dresses she was packing with a layer of books. "I said to the dean, a stupid man, 'Why should I not talk of Russia? How can my students understand a language if they do not know the country? Who better to instruct them than someone who loves it?' That Professor Natler teaches lies to his students. I am sure he is the traitor who turned me in. Who else could have done it? He hates me because I speak from the heart and tell the truth. *Nechevo*, what does it matter? I am used to being thrown out. I won't starve. I know of someone who has a connection with the alterations department at Saks in Chicago. They will be delighted to have me. I can show them what I learned from the great house of Schiaparelli. Let them see my dress and know what exquisite work is still possible.

"Give me your address, Laura, and I will write to you when I am settled. You, my dear, are *simpatico*. We have much in common." But Madame never wrote.

WEEP NO MORE OVER THIS EVENT

Ander Monson

I CAME UPON HIM AS HE WAS RUSTLING THROUGH THE DVDs downstairs, throwing them into a sack in what appeared to be a self-congratulatory way, as if laughing to himself, probably at the selection, which was my wife's, and I was doubly enraged. I don't know why I thought of this when action was required, but I wondered where people *get* sacks like this, as in can you buy them at the supermarket, or are these specialized burglary tools endorsed by criminals? I was standing on the steps coming down from the spacious landing to the main floor of my house, and I wondered also how he got through the alarm system I had installed after my wife saw too many of those threatening commercials on television and I felt the pressure of my husbandness coming down on me, and I called and got jacked by the small print but had it installed nevertheless, a gesture that did not stop my wife from leaving.

I found out later you can set the system, which is admittedly pretty glorious, to keep someone from *leaving* the house, too, though I did not read the entire instruction manual at the time and it would only seem important to me later, like most realizations I have had in my life.

So I was watching and he must have heard me coming down or something because he turned to me, and it must have been hard to see me in the dark because he began to walk toward me. That's why I shot him. He *advanced* on me. He was an *imminent threat*. This is what the police told me later as I sobbed, more for the loss of my marriage than any kind of ruined innocence.

■ ■ ■

The fat policeman explained it like this: *To shoot him where he stands is allowed now by law in this state, and is more than allowed—is, in fact, requisite of the situation—which is to say that you did the right thing and should weep no more over this event.*

I liked that he said *weep no more*, like this was all a tragedy or a musical or a spiritual. He asked if anything was missing and if this had occurred before, seeing the new alarm system on the wall and its array of lights blinking into a new configuration. I told him no, nothing was missing as far as I could tell without inventorying the entire house, and no, it hadn't ever happened before. Then I told him about the commercials.

Mm-hm, he said, *I've seen those too. It's good you had it, because it shows a lack of premeditation on your part, not that it matters since he was in your house, dude.* He might have said *sir* instead of *dude*, but it's hard to remember the exactitude of language in moments like these.

I said I found the pattern of the lights to be beautiful. He stared at me and did not blink until I spoke again.

I explained about my wife. How she had left a month ago and I think he divined the implied emptiness because he had a ring still on his finger. He looked at me like he was thinking of his own wife in this moment, like this is what anyone would do. He took down my information, brought me to the station to give my statement, said it would only take an hour and then I could come back to my domicile and lie down, watch some news, or whatever I needed to do to get it off my mind.

■ ■ ■

The event weighed on me, though not in the way I expected. I was out in the middle of the department-store floor contemplating a couple blow-up Christmas decorations to add to my menagerie, when I had what I guess you could call a flashback, except this one was like fiction. In it my wife and I were in bed, and we had been crying separately for an hour, and had just drifted off to sleep, when I heard someone downstairs and so I got the gun and went downstairs and there he was, and I was on the stairs with my wife's presence behind me, like I was guarding her from him, and when I shot him all I could see was light, and then she was gone, and it's true, she is gone, she had gone, gone a while ago, and all I had left was light, and the house, her DVDs, and the system, and my menagerie.

Men of a certain age begin accumulating collections. Some are private, like my father's collection of over six thousand toy rocket ships. He had two whole rooms devoted to them. This was when I was a teenager, before I left that house, after Mom had died, after it had seemed so empty for a couple years, and he had started to fill it up with this stuff. I was a teenager then and wanted to blow them up, but didn't because I feared his anger. I still fear his anger, really. When I called him to tell him I shot a man and should weep no more about it, since he was in my house, since he was advancing on me, Dad told me it was OK. He had shot a man in wartime but never talked about it. We waited on the phone, neither of us saying much of anything, which was how most of our conversations went. I had expected him to have some wisdom for me, but he never was much for wisdom. He said, you sound lonely, son. You should get a cat. I told him I would think about it. He said to go shoot for a while at the target range. Sometimes others will come to a house once it's been broken into, even when you shot the guy. You should be careful. You have all that Christmas shit to protect. He was joking, but it was true.

My collection is on my lawn, all over the exterior of my house. I tell myself it's for the kids, the families in the neighborhood. My neighbor, Rutan, has a competing collection, maybe because of his name. His display is spectacular. He has twice the inflatable Christmas decorations, even makes stuff by hand. There are lights and moving parts. I got the idea from him. When Katie and I would come back at night and go by that house with all those inflatable things alive, the air compressor humming, with them moving back and forth in the night, it impressed me. You could see it from our bedroom window. I could see it as we fucked. I could see it after. It was like I was fucking Santa, the reindeer, a series of penguins, Dora the Explorer. It glowed all night. Sometimes it was all I'd look at. Rutan was a single guy. I think for him it was a little desperate—he was into Christmas, sure, but he didn't have any kids, no wife. I think he was trying to attract them, and still is, by accumulating the trappings of Christmas cheer. Now I have a collection of my own. He and I are making our own society here. They wrote an article about us in the paper, and people came from across the whole city after they read it. Rutan spent most evenings outside, adjusting the compressors and the angles, talking to the gawkers, suggesting photos, giving hugs. It is not impossible that his method will work.

■ ■ ■

Here's the problem: my domicile immediately began to appeal to me less—it felt like a mausoleum, or, if not that, a crime scene, then. A place where I couldn't forget the past. If someone could be shot there, if I could be home invaded and, potentially, if she were still here, Katie could have been carried off and raped, or traumatized because of this, then it was a problem—my problem, this city's problem, America's problem—but I was the only one able to take action. I had already taken action. What I needed was I needed more action.

I couldn't stop thinking about it, like the way I thought about my mother at unexpected times and couldn't get her out of my head, like when Katie and I were having sex one of the many times we called our first for effect, and she was high, but I wasn't, and she was talking about the thousand needles all around us, by which I take it she meant the stars. I did not tell her about my mother's face hovering above me because women don't want that kind of honesty, no matter what they say.

Some nights I would sit up at my own darkened window and watch the lights wink off in the neighbors' windows, or what I could see of them through the trees. You'd see silhouettes, a setting sun of motion in a window. I felt increasingly sure that eyes were looking back at me. So I installed a more robust system with encrypted codes and a super-spectrum something or other that transmits signals to itself and its backup systems via infrared. This may have been about sexual jealousy, but I don't like to think about very much.

■ ■ ■

Of course at first I tried some spells that I found on the Internet, but they had no effect at all. I don't know what I expected but it was worth a shot and I thought back to days playing D&D with friends in high school and how magic was one option, and Katie had gone and we had said some things, and it had been weeks by this point, and I wasn't sure where she was—she'd said just don't fucking call her for a while, that she had things to work out, probably in Cancun. So I had the alarm system—a kind of spell of protection—updated and I lit some candles for the incantation, too many as it turned out, since it set off the fire alarm, which triggered a manned response by the security team—this is why I signed up for them, the personal responses, the sense that we, that I, have a security team ready for response at the slightest electronic dip or tuck or wavering—and I had to call them off and tell them the code word and all that.

They do a good job with all of this. Like in the commercials, they make the effort to make it realistic for you. I was charmed. I felt completed. And happy that I purchased the second gun they recommended after the invasion: a .357 pistol, big and loud and hard, an exclamation point in my hands. My forearm holds the memory of firing at the range, shot after shot, meaning something probably in Morse code, followed by muscle soreness, which wasn't much different than firing at the guy on the carpet in the main room, the intruder, the interloper in my domicile, attempting to make off with my—with Katie's—probably ridiculous shit.

■ ■ ■

I don't know what exactly I'm trying to tell you here, why this is emerging the way it is, what secret I have to offer up that you might be amazed by. I look down and see a spider slowly skittering up to me. I hold my ground. I will live in peace with it, even if I am terrified of them. It will spin its threads and capture interlopers and slowly consume them: nature's defense. It disappears. See. I can coexist with something. This is already helping.

The more I contemplated possible entrances into the house—the twin skylights upstairs, chimneys, the forty windows—the more I became convinced that I would have to try out each of them. The security system wasn't wired to the skylights yet, you see, because I hadn't asked and I hadn't thought it realistic to deal with that. I purchased some burglar's tools on the Internet, including the cool suction-cup thing that you attach to glass and cut out a circle and it doesn't fall in, waking whomever's inside. I tried it on the window. It took longer than I thought it would but it worked eventually—with practice

I could take out a pane of glass in a minute, I thought. I added this to the list of additional skills that I could deploy to impress Katie or possible employers. She'd be excited when I demonstrated some of these.

You could see Rutan's lights just past my lights outside. I thought it important to appeal to passersby. The lights, I realize now, may have been a defense mechanism of another sort. They warmed the exterior of the house. They warmed my heart. They warmed a thousand visitors' hearts inside their bodies as they drove by with their families' bodies and their eyes adjusting to our sudden light explosions.

■ ■ ■

I didn't take off the guy's mask. When the cops showed up they shooed me out of the house so I didn't have to see his face. Maybe they thought that would make a difference in terms of my psychological recovery time. The fat and sensitive cop gave me a couple cards for psychologists to talk to after an event like this. They said to be careful upon waking—and to unload the gun for a couple weeks. People sometimes went a little nuts after.

I admit I couldn't sleep. Not before, even, really, but certainly not now. Part of that was Katie's fault: she'd want to sleep *on* me, like it gave her peace to be warmed from underneath, which was fine as far as it went, but I got hot too fast and would have to eject her for a while, and then she would get cold, and we would repeat. Sometimes it led to sex, which was better than the other times.

I began to think of myself less as a person and more as a force. I was becoming a force of vengeance, of redemption, a force of comeuppance for those who broke into homes and tried to make off with loot, who made off with our neighbors' daughters, who left no trace at all behind.

■ ■ ■

A month later, I broke into my first house. It's hard to explain why. I don't even think I know. I made sure he was gone, casing it for a couple days. Chose a neighbor, Danny, whose wife had died two years ago. His daughter had also disappeared. I'd gone to his wife's funeral and not known what to say. And in any of our subsequent interactions, I still didn't know. I considered this a failure as we had briefly bonded over discussions of the World Cup soccer matches just before his wife has passed, and what we had—which wasn't much surely, but it was something—has collapsed.

But being in his house (he had no security system) in his absence was exhilarating. I did not bring my gun. I didn't plan on taking anything. I just wanted to be out of my space for a while, in somebody else's. It had been a while since I had last been inside his house—a Super Bowl party a year ago that Katie and I had attended which was a sea of awkwardness because I knew how much she hated football, and I had said we really should go, and she wouldn't be the only woman there, which turned out not to be true, and she had left a quarter and four beers in and had not returned in spite of Danny's hospitality, which was impressive, considering he had to learn to do a lot of things for himself after his wife died, and so every occasion was an occasion for him to commit a major social error; I knew he thought about it because he talked about it after he had a couple drinks oftentimes, him knowing that I was interested in systems and constantly trying to figure out what to do or say in any situation. I had felt torn between these two obligations: a sort of approximation of maleness, what he and I were supposed to be able to do together, and my love for Katie who had no love for football or Danny, and no pity either for his predicament—this particular brand of loneliness, the still-empty room he had kept that way, just as it was, for his daughter if she ever came back, if anyone ever found her, or if at least what happened to her became apparent, like if the body was found. I felt we could cut him a little bit of slack considering. Katie had said before that he was a clueless dick, and losing his wife didn't make him any less of that, though I argued that it gave him complexity, and she said well then he is a complex clueless dick, which even I had to admit was true, though the complexity itself was an achievement, I said, something to aspire to. This was our problem, she said later, after I stayed for the rest of the game: my inability to commit to her needs at the expense of society's. And she said it like that, that my connection with Danny was just a social obligation. I said well what is our connection then, and that didn't go well at all. Marriage is a social institution as is a neighborhood, and both come with obligations: the lawn, the trash, the lights, the packages we give each other because of grief a couple times a year or because of fear of loss or change, keeping up the appearance of the exterior of the house, attending events you have no interest in—my list went on for a while, ever increasing the more I thought about it. The point I was trying to make was that we were both part of something besides ourselves. She may have agreed, but she wanted finally to be ranked higher in one of the many lists I made of my priorities in order to keep myself on task, make sure I met all the obligations I had committed to.

Sure, yeah, I trawled through his stuff. I looked at the insides of whatever I could find. I had held myself back for so long it felt like freedom. I went into his daughter's room and sat on the bed, tried to envision her, to imagine the last time she was in there. It wasn't untouched—it was clean but still recognizable as the room of a fourteen-year-old. I don't know how to describe it except to say you could feel the past there.

Shortly after the shooting I added *assess self for post-traumatic stress disorder* to the list. The literature said this was often an aftereffect of a shooting, that the experience would persist in a halo of related symptoms. I wondered if burglary could be a direct result of that, if crime could perpetuate itself in this way and continue spreading out into a matrix in the world, and if so, maybe that was the reason why the guy was ransacking Katie's DVD collection and I was in the middle of Danny's living room, all the furniture curved inward like a fortress, with several televisions at the center. Danny'd acquired something like a dozen cats since his wife's death, which probably meant something in terms of his psychology, and they moved around my feet as I padded softly around the carpet, inspecting his DVD collection, which included what appeared to be a complete set of *Emmanuelle* films. Interesting. They might have been his wife's, or perhaps he bought them as a tribute to his wife, who looked, before the chemo, more than a little like Sylvia Kristel, the star of the majority of them.

I slid one in and turned it on. I looked at the photos of the two of them and their daughter on the wall. I looked at the screen. It was a little like watching a ghost. A sexy ghost.

Obviously I didn't get through more than a half hour of the film without resorting to masturbation. I admit it. It was not my house, not my DVDs, not echoes of my dead wife. It was barely even my body by the time I finished and hit eject, ashamed, though I wasn't yet sure why, then powered off. Then the house was dark and his little girl was still vanished, his wife was still dead. The cats were everywhere.

Headlights started to pass the house and soon it was regular, a metronome. Where does this sudden traffic come from? Could it be police? Could I be surrounded? What I feared is what cannot happen, that Danny might come home unexpectedly, that Danny would see me here among his everything that is no longer either *his* or everything, since I am here and his wife is not, and he would shoot me down, an imminent threat, as I stood to go toward him, to shake his hand or offer explanation, as society would deem appropriate. I would make it easier for him, I think, even now. Another pair of headlights passed through the window shades but did not approach. I could tell him he really should get one of the security systems filled with lights. For the memory of Marie, his wife—I thought of her name just now in this equilibrium we can call a developing situation in my mind if not in the real room here in front of me. I could go, I realized, or I could stay and wait for him. But what would really happen is something unexpected. Maybe the cat-sitter shows up and dies of fright, or a plane drops from the sky through this roof and takes me down in flames. Or he could never return: maybe he left for good, abandoned it, what remained of his life, or maybe he was on that plane. Maybe he was dead in one of the rooms of the house and his life had eroded to the point that he would lie undiscovered here for four days, no one here to check on him, flesh torn off in tiny bits by cats, only to be found by his masturbating, home-invading neighbor, himself the victim of a home invasion, and the beginning of a wave of them, every home invasion leading to another.

But nothing happened. Everything collided in my mind and there were cats swirling through the darkness. Katie would disapprove. She hadn't even called to harass me, which means she cared even less than I would have thought. It was unfortunate. I was singularly unfortunate. But I had power. I have power. I have a gun. I shot that man down and continue to do so every night. I came all over the DVD case of *Emmanuelle in Space* while thinking about a dead woman and had to clean it up. This is a personal low for me, I thought at the time, though I don't think that anymore. I've since surpassed it.

I cleaned up, got up, and left his space. I did a couple dishes, which seemed appropriate. I felt ashamed a little after, but mostly I felt new. Maybe this was post-traumatic stress disorder, where you go a little crazy later and start masturbating in your neighbors' houses? I reasoned my behavior could easily be explained in terms of biological irregularity in the brain.

■ ■ ■

The worst part for Danny was when his daughter had been gone for a week—her name was Marie, too, but she wanted to be called Mary in the way that kids want to differentiate themselves from everything they dislike about the world—and speculation in the neighborhood began to turn on Danny and Marie. We didn't want to speculate about the rest of us. None of us could be responsible. We couldn't even start to think it. We were all responsible adults with cars and cats and curs yowling through the nights, proclaiming their alarm at our perversities. The police weren't releasing any new news. No leads. The parents were naturally persons of interest in the investigation, but nothing was disclosed to connect them to her vanishing. Statistics we saw on TV said that in 75 percent of missing persons cases, the one responsible is a family member or someone who knows the girl well. But the woman on the television said that Danny and Marie were surely beyond reproach. And you could see it in the shot of them on camera as Marie delivered her tearful plea. It was moving, it really was. It could have been any of our daughters if we had daughters, that lovely trouble. Their faces were drawn like their window shades. The two of them had taken to living in near darkness and left the house as undisturbed as was possible while still living in it just in case there was some kind of useful evidence not yet identified by the authorities.

This was five years ago. As soon as Mary had disappeared my wife had started her conjecture, throwing out theories, identifying creepy people we had encountered, even wondering privately about the perverts in this neighborhood who she claimed would follow girls around, to stores, and with cameras in their shopping bags, trying to take photos up their skirts and post them on the Internet. She'd seen it happen a couple times and had heard about it even more. She had this theory that the more leisure time our neighbors had—and let's face it, we lived in a neighborhood that bespoke nothing if not leisure—the more fucked-up they became. She would constantly be asking me if I thought Gary's wife was a lesbian, or if any of our friends were gay. Fuck, I loved her, but it drove me crazy, this constant speculation, like all of us were mysteries that we could crack open by the action of our brains. My feeling was that as friends, as family, as members of a neighborhood association, we owed it to the others to take them at their word, their closed blinds, their brusque greetings on the streets. It felt gossipy, particularly with Danny and Marie, because they had been our friends. Our neighbors were all interviewed by the police—this was before my wife had left, you understand—and so whatever speculations they had were encouraged. I know because we were all encouraged to speculate, to attribute meaning to any tiny transgression or strangeness or outlying car or lurid comment or open window late at night or whatever we had possibly noticed, and in some cases had actually logged or blogged or journaled about already. These things were wheedled out of us, even if we appeared that we didn't want to say. Anything could matter, they told us. This was important, they told us. Tell us the story. Don't leave anything out.

■ ■ ■

Here's what I didn't say to them, nor to Katie. I had seen Danny looking at Mary in what I assessed as unfatherly ways more than once. She was fourteen. She was going to be a beauty. She was a beauty already. Which made her a sort of myth. The women were allowed to say it, but the men were not. I don't blame him or think it means any more than it did. And now she was gone. And had any of us entertained our thoughts about what might have transpired? Yes. I'm sure the answer's yes. But, fuck, Danny was already getting the treatment from the police. Everyone assumes the guy's responsible in the absence of another story, another angle to consider the disappearance from and keep it breaking news; of course it would be best if she was found alive, but in the absence of information people are going to talk and fill things in, and it was awful when my wife started doing it. We got into a confrontation over it.

Had I thought about murdering my own wife before? If I'm being honest I'm saying yes. Not to say I would do it, but I had considered it, entertained the thought, let it through the logic gate in my mind and back out into the submerged whatever of it. Had I thought about making out with, off with, Mary? That answer is yes also. We can hold a lot of ideas. We can hold a lot of grief. We can wonder if our lives might contain that other thing, just for a moment. Thought is the wrong word. Thought implies intention, which it should not. You are aware of the temptation, what is within you, what you are capable of in spite of all the social interactions and the neighborhood associations, and you might erupt at any moment—you could tear down anything in your sight. And then you back away from that precipice. You don't have to verbalize it, make it part of a conversation, make it part of the theories on the whiteboard in the police station. You can keep it to yourself, fortress yourself in on weekends, maybe watch a couple *Emmanuelle* DVDs and think of the dead.

Adjust the sensors on your security system and reconfigure the programmable thermostat. There is a lot to keep you—me, any of us—busy with the world so we don't have to open up our silences.

■ ■ ■

When Marie died, then, almost two years later to the day, the vans reappeared along the curbs with their transmitting equipment. This time it wasn't the real reporters but the interns or the fact finders or something who were going, again, door-to-door, trying not to appear intrusive, but looking for material. They are always looking for material. Katie asked, well, could you blame them? They want to know. We all want to know. Do we want to know, I said. Yes, we want to know, she said. And pretty soon after that she was gone.

I didn't change much in Katie's office, leaving the things she left as she had last arranged them. In a way it was just like what Danny did for his daughter. They could both come back. They could both reintegrate themselves into our lives. At least he had a garage sale after Marie's death, after his family had come in to help him clear out some things and get some distance from it. The whole neighborhood was there, at the sale, too, and lots of random people, maybe looking for items that had some connection to Mary. I bought two alarm clocks, overpaying for them, frankly, at ten dollars a shot, but it felt like doing something. Both were nearly identical, still in the package, different colors. His and hers, it read, in a faux-elegant script. I keep them on my nightstand now at home. Most of the stuff he sold was pretty crappy and nondescript. If I were him I'd sell everything I could so that the spaces in the house didn't remind me of my dead wife. Some of us bought to remind ourselves of Marie, and some of us of Mary.

■ ■ ■

Later, I received a note in the mail informing me that I could go down to the station to receive my copy of the police report featuring my shooting and my no more weeping. I had taken to waiting for the mail with suspicion, as if the mailman knew things he wasn't telling about me, about Katie, about Danny and Marie and Mary, about the final destinations of all of us and our newly separated lives or what remained of them. He had seen the forwarding information, surely, and noticed the decreasing supply of women's magazines to the house. I could see it in his posture as he slid the mail truck up to the driveway, killed the engine, and slumped out toward the door, avoiding eye contact. They must teach you that, I thought, in the training, not to personalize, to avoid confrontation, to carry pepper spray or mace or a Taser in case of dog or other attack. He had to deliver the note from the police in person since it was sent certified mail. He looked at me as I signed it. I said hey, thanks, I appreciate your service. He asked me how I was doing. I said good, good. The weather was looking up again. I asked him if the police ever talked to him about that girl's disappearance, if he had seen anything, if he'd care to add a story to the world. This was a successful social interaction, I decided, and so I said never mind and thanks again and have a good one, and he was gone, with whatever darkness was in his eyes too as he started up the truck again and pulled away.

My copy of the police report listed the facts as I had described them, which was reassuring. It described the intruder as *the decedent,* the incident as self-defense, me as *shooken up*, which I'm fairly sure is not a word. It listed *the decedent*'s name as Lewis Klatt. There were several sections redacted for some reason, blacked out with rough strokes of marker, and the whole thing had been photocopied a couple times and so had that deteriorating look. It didn't list much information about the decedent. It had his age listed as seventeen. It did not list his address or surviving relatives. You couldn't tell much about it.

It took a couple days before I found his address on the Internet. I found his social-network page, which had a bunch of sad comments left after his death from those who were his friends. There was no note indicating that the page would be deleted, but it listed the last log-in as being the day after I shot him. His mother, probably, learning things she didn't know about her son only after he had gone on and through this world. I found the address where he lived with his mother, apparently, his father not being listed or mentioned anywhere. A couple days later I drove by his place in the evening. It was a foursquare, maybe fifteen hundred square feet, in what Realtors would describe as an emerging neighborhood. A good investment, surely. No lights were on. I wasn't sure what I was doing there as I sat in the heated car. The air was clear. Little was happening on this block. There were no streetlights. The whole place reeked of sadness.

There aren't any streetlights in this city because it is a darkened city with regulations against streetlights on most blocks and the use of halogen headlights, and even powerful flashlights are discouraged. This is all so as not to interfere with the important work being done at the observatory just past the valley. The trade-off is that we pay more for our police department in the neighborhood where I live, because the lack of light demands more frequent patrols. I parked outside the house. I sat and watched. Nothing happened by virtue of my being here. I wrote a couple memos to myself and went back home. I could feel something building inside me.

■ ■ ■

I did not think I wanted forgiveness for shooting the intruder. The report spelled out the justifiability of the situation. I knew I had acted in self-defense, even if I might have been, in retrospect, projecting some of my substantial reservoir of rage about Katie onto the kid and when I shot him he was shot, and Katie was not, and the world waiting outside of teenage girls' windows was not shot or even deterred from whatever they might continue to go on doing, and that was the end of it. And I didn't want any kind of retribution. Or even an encounter with his family. I wanted to riffle through his things. I wanted to break in and achieve the kind of intimacy a person can only gain by breaking into a house. When I broke in, I wanted to find his life laid out for me. What fucked-up things he masturbated to. What things he did beyond his life as described on the social-networking page, and we all know you can't trust those facades anyhow.

So I found myself outside the house wearing dark green-and-black sweatpants. I moved from window to window, sliding out of the security light in front toward the back where nothing was activated by motion. I pressed my hands to each window. There were no pets. In the house there was only silence.

In the back window you could see the flickering LED on what appeared to be an answering machine. It flashed a number, twenty-eight, and had several blinking lights. I tried the latch on the window. It was open. These people, who were these people, who thought nothing of the possibility that someone could come in and take their lives apart?

I entered through the window. I waited for something to happen.

I felt like all my life I was waiting for something to happen.

And things did happen to those around me. Katie left or was forced to leave, depending whom you talked to about it. Danny's life fell apart, his wife, his daughter gone.

And now I was in the decedent's house, leaving a card on the kitchen table for the home-security company that I used. Let this be a lesson to you, I thought. Let me make my point this way.

I heard a string of firecrackers going off, maybe a block away. It started up my heart. I thought it was a gun, an uzi maybe, that was how uncomfortable I was in the neighborhood. But that thought receded with the sound into the silence.

I went upstairs. Each stair creaked distinctively. Though I knew no one was home, you never really knew anything about anyone, I thought to myself. What if Danny did it, I thought to myself.

The door read *Lewis*. I checked out the other rooms first. Then I opened his door.

All of his possessions made up a pile on the floor of his room. It looked like it had been searched. The blinds were open and I looked out into the street. Cars passed. I held my breath, then let it out. I sat down on the decedent's bed.

The question I had was whether I'd done something unforgivable, or if Katie had, or if anyone had. When I went to college and applied for the requisite set of credit cards, I found out that my parents had been applying for credit in my name for a couple years, having exhausted their own creditworthiness, and my whole score was shot. I was angry. This was years before I met Katie, but the credit traces shadow you for a decade, so I had to explain it to her. She believed me at the time, but later, after she left, she told me she had come to doubt me. I had not forgiven my parents for this, nor for their many other transgressions, and I had told them this, and when they died it didn't change a thing.

Later, when having breakfast with my sister on one of her rare returns to this town, this country, we were talking about this, and she told me she had forgiven me for that time when I had hit her in the head repeatedly with a set of igneous rocks that I had stolen from the church when they had their rock-and-gem show for kids. She was a little drunk on the mimosas when she told me this. I had not remembered what I was thinking. She said she knew that, that she wondered what I had meant by it. She dabbed off the makeup to show me the scars across the side of her face. I told her I didn't remember that at all. Did I do that? I touched her face. It smelled like lamb. She said there were many things that I had done. Was it possible that she had made up this story for her advantage in future family gatherings? Or were they actual wounds inflicted by my hands? She was twelve, she said. Don't you remember when we had to go to church and when we spent most of our time breaking into the world of Boy Scout paraphernalia hidden away in one of the storage rooms? she said. You know, when you had touched my face and we would listen to muffled hymns being sung a room or two away? I had only vague impressions. I guess it didn't mean that much to me, I said.

The question was whether I had done something unforgivable to Katie, to break her heart and send her away from me, to her many adulteries. Were they a punishment for something I had done? I asked. She said that was stupid, that her affairs were stupid and didn't mean anything, and she was sorry. What did she mean she was sorry? I remember asking. What could anybody mean by that? She had done things. She had done a lot of things. She was not asking for forgiveness, she said. She just felt bad about it and wanted me to know it. I was very angry as I sat on Lewis's cream-colored sheets contemplating his mass of stuff piled on the floor. What a useless set of possessions. It looked like mostly underwear, a couple dozen books, some video-game paraphernalia, and, most impressively, a collection of sixty-four model rockets organized in boxes at the base of the heap, all the disposable engines removed and lined up on the floor. Were they even his, I wondered, or had he stolen them? Did that make them his? Was that it, I wondered? Was that all he had amounted to?

I had said some things to Katie. I had told her stories about what I might have said or done to Mary in her last moments. Tell that to your gossip columnists, I said. Tell that to the CNN reporters. Are you happy, having wrung that out of me? She was white. All my blood had drained too as this story came out of me. For the first time I can remember she looked utterly surprised. We had crossed a line. I had carried her over the threshold and into another house, her in another wedding dress and me already naked. And we were held aloft in that moment, suspended somewhere above our marriage and the neighborhood and the rules that the world had set out for us, that we had agreed to. And that lasted for about a minute. And then her expression turned, and she had turned, and she had gone, and that was it, and was it possible that that was really it at last? I had been drunk just as I was drunk with my sister, receiving her drunken forgiveness as she sobbed. They both were sobbing. I was not sobbing. I didn't sob when I shot the intruder down. I did not believe in this catharsis. I would finger all my wounds and allow that pain to penetrate. I would bathe in it, fortify myself with it.

I paused. I kept waiting for something to happen.

If this scene turned out as I hoped, I would hear the shrieks of the stairs, the clicks of weapons being armed. The door would open suddenly and the room would fill with the sound of angry voices. I would feel nothing as I lay back on the decedent's bed, pants around my ankles, headphones on, as I pleased myself furiously, thinking of all of you, your naked bodies, your open mouths. I would barely be aware of any force as gunshots bloomed across my chest like wildflowers in a spring field on fast-forward. Time would slow and somebody would understand something, and I would at last be carried away by consequence.

CARD NIGHT

Mardi Jo Link

THEY'D INSISTED SHE ATTEND, STATING THE OBVIOUS: three-handed euchre was just no good. Josephine was gone and according to the charter, daughters were required to take up their mother's chair. At least that was supposedly what the document said, though Charity couldn't know for sure because she'd never seen it. Hadn't even known it existed until after her mother passed.

The women had hinted she'd be allowed to read it and the curiosity must have gotten to her. Otherwise, why stand on Sylvia's stoop, alone, without her mother, in the cold, in the dark, in spite of her antisocial self, in spite of her grief.

The porch light was on, and she could hear strains of dated jazz from behind the heavy door. Charity removed a mitten, then rapped hard with bare knuckles and the door opened as if on a trip wire.

"You're just in time for cocktails," Sylvia said, reaching a boney hand for her coat. After she'd shrugged out of it Sylvia opened the foyer's antique highboy to reveal a full bar. Charity rarely drank, but in the face of Sylvia, and her ice tongs shaped like talons, refusing didn't seem like a possibility. She took a polite sip of gin and tonic, shuddered. The fumes alone could thin her blood.

"This way," Sylvia instructed, grasping Charity's free hand, an odd gesture coming from someone who'd always treated her with such reserve. Charity felt strange inside. The alcohol, the physical contact, and her own pent-up anxiety combined into a sudden vertigo. She didn't like socializing, wasn't comfortable with small talk or her mother's friends.

"Right bower, left bower, ace-king-queen," Charity mumbled to herself. She'd never been able to keep the rules of euchre straight in her mind, no matter how many times her mother had tried to explain them. Aces were high in every other card game she could think of. In euchre, it was the jacks, but they weren't called jacks, they were called bowers, and only two of them mattered. How you figured out which always caught her off-balance.

The hallway between the foyer and the study was long and dark. In her high heels Sylvia marched the two of them at a forward lean, as if fighting a headwind. She halted at a set of French doors, let go of Charity's now-sweaty hand, placed her palms on the wood, and pushed.

"Here she is, girls," Sylvia announced. "Our new member."

Every December, Charity had accompanied her mother to this room. Once a year the women brought their daughters for a special card night. She'd never wanted to go—had dreaded it, even. When she was little, her mother had simply put a hand on her back and guided her into the car. As she'd gotten older, it was the pleading that forced her. Only one night a year, she told herself, and for her mother she'd endure it. But their personal questions had made her uncomfortable. Where had her green eyes and her curly hair come from? Did she have a boyfriend?

The mood was different tonight somehow, and the room looked grander than she'd remembered. Walls of full, well-ordered bookcases. Red leather club chairs arranged around a square card table. The jazz she'd heard from the front door crackled from an actual record player, and overhead, sharp light shone from an elaborate chandelier. Her mother downplayed their family's wealth, but Sylvia put hers on display. She wasn't afraid of being ostentatious in a small, conservative town. She wasn't afraid of anything.

The two remaining members were there too, and already seated. They smiled at her, and their chalky faces offered a surprisingly genuine welcome. And the moment inspired a longing for her mother so powerful it would have knocked her down if she hadn't reached out a hand to Sylvia to steady herself.

"I miss her, too," Frances said. "It can't be easy, so soon after losing your dad." Frances was Sylvia's younger sister, and there was a shaky tenderness in her voice.

"Thank you," Charity managed.

"You're alone then, at the house?" It was the other woman, Helen Bartlett, asking. She was retired now but Charity had once dissected a fetal pig in her honors biology class. The memory brought with it a whiff of formaldehyde.

"I have the dog," Charity said, pleased by how satisfying it felt to correct her old teacher.

"Sit down," Sylvia told her then, pointing. "Right there, across from Frances—that was your mother's place."

The card table itself was polished maple with herringbone inlay. In each corner were built-in drink holders and a divot with a removable tin ashtray shaped like each of the four suits. A diamond for Sylvia, a heart for Frances, a spade for Helen, and a club where Charity's mother, Josephine, had sat every Monday night for decades.

A box of playing cards sat untouched in the center of the table, and noticing them caused the chant to hijack her thoughts again. "Right bower, left bower, ace-king-queen," she mouthed. And again. "Right bower, left bower, ace-king-queen."

Sylvia shifted in her chair and arranged her shawl, flapping each side like wings, a bird of prey about to dine.

"You won't need all that," Sylvia snapped at Charity, waving her hand in dismissal. "We're not here to play a game. *Life* isn't about playing a game and neither are we."

With Sylvia's eyes upon her, the dread that had been tempered by Frances's kindness returned. Yes, she'd wondered about the so-called charter, but she still hadn't wanted to come. Tonight, or any of those other years, either. Felt no kinship with these women, didn't like cards, didn't like small talk, was awkward at the kind of socializing most women came by naturally.

Card night was her mother's weekly escape from the strictures of Charity's straight-laced father, no more, no less. Why did four old fossils need some secret piece of paper to tell them what to do?

"Then what—"

"Don't interrupt," Sylvia snapped, both fingers pressed to her temples and looking as if she were about to start drilling. "This is important. You need to know what we do here. Your mother did her part and now that she's gone, you'll take over her week."

Sylvia reached under the table and there was the sound of a thin drawer sliding open. She retrieved a yellowed sheet of paper and slid it across the herringbone to Charity.

"Read," Sylvia ordered.

At the top of the page were typed the words "Card Night," boldly underlined, followed by three sentences:

> *A weekly game of chance.*
>
> *Help only women and their children.*
>
> *Daughters, carry on for your mothers.*

Charity read it twice, then looked around the table at the other women. All these years she and her father had seen her mother come home from card night with alcohol on her breath, had listened to her effervescent tales of tricks taken, of loner hands so good there wasn't any need to play them out. Her mother had just fanned them down on the table for the win. That had all been a lie?

Someone's hearing aid whistled as Sylvia reached for the deck. She passed the box to Frances, saying, "Your week."

Frances nodded, opened the box, took the cards out, and shuffled. Euchre was not played with all fifty-two; only the face cards and the nines and tens so the bundle was small and awkward. Even with her tremor, Frances completed the task easily. When she placed them facedown on the table and turned over the top one, there was handwriting scribbled over the face card. Frances read what it said out loud: a woman's name, but not one Charity recognized.

Sylvia had already pulled a computer tablet out of the hidden drawer, and she swiped her finger across the screen.

"She needs her rent paid, three hundred seventy-five dollars," Sylvia said flatly, as if reciting a to-do list. "And a girl's winter coat, color choice lavender, size four."

Frances exhaled. Relief? "Done," she said.

Sylvia retrieved the paper charter, put it and the tablet back into the drawer, slid it closed. She leaned back in her chair then, looked at Charity, and steepled her fingers.

"This is what we do here," she explained. "We don't play cards, not in the usual sense. We arrange for charitable contributions, like rent and clothing. Though some weeks, our work can be a bit more . . . *involved*."

Charity tried to imagine her mother shuffling the cards, her mother turning one over, her mother helping some anonymous woman who couldn't pay her rent or clothe her child. Logic dictated there had to be women that desperate around town, but she could not imagine her mother knowing anything about them.

"And my mother—"

"Your mother was an enthusiastic participant," Sylvia said. "The week after Frances's was hers. That week now belongs to you."

■ ■ ■

Driving home, Charity kept trying to picture her mother being involved in what Sylvia described as "charity work." Was *that* where her name had come from? The story went that when Charity was born her parents had thought they'd been past childbearing—certainly too late to add a Faith or a Hope. She'd asked them about her name, several times, yet had never received a satisfying answer. "It suited you," was all her mother would say.

She could neither remember nor imagine her mother being interested in or knowing of any women in trouble. A mother who couldn't even afford a child's coat? She pictured some miscreant high on drugs. Not at all the kind of person her mother would offer compassion or counsel to.

"Suck it up, buttercup," had been Josephine's solution to any difficulty, whether Charity had suffered a skinned knee, lost a favorite book, or endured a taunt from the popular girls at school. Her mother had been a matter-of-fact kind of parent, a woman who did encourage effort, though never with physical affection. Charity had overheard stories of her mother's youth, and in all of them she'd been the one running wild.

Charity's father was as straight as a row of feeder corn, which was why Charity had assumed card night was her mother's euphemism for getting a load on with her friends. What else had her mother kept from her? The grass on her grave wasn't even grown over yet and thanks to those women, Charity now felt like she hadn't even known the person buried underneath it.

Anger rose from her gut into her neck and pressed on her jaw like mercury through hell's thermometer. If they thought she was going to join up with them, they were the ones who should suck it up. She was driving her father's car—it had been a comfort to sit in his plush seat, navigate the outside world—and she thumped the steering wheel with the heel of her mittened hand. A light from the dashboard blinked on: Fuel Level Low.

"Not now!" she blurted into the quiet of velour and leather.

And there it was. Charity wasn't sure when it had happened, but it had. Her life wasn't important, exciting, or, now that her parents were dead, even useful. It was boring and sad. And sometimes, like now, not even that. To the world at large she was nothing but an irritant, a middle-aged woman who mattered about as much as a dashboard warning light.

She pulled into Mapleton's only gas station, slid a credit card through the slot, pressed the button on the pump marked "Premium," and leaned against the car while the tank filled. She felt like an idiot. It wasn't just her mother—she'd known the three other women her entire life, too. At some point, anyone with half a brain would have realized they weren't playing cards—they were playing God. Well, screw their weird traditions. Screw their cashmere and their crystal and their pathetic need to control other people's lives.

At least the solitude of her parents' empty house awaited her, barely a dozen miles down the road. She was considering the best way to extricate herself from card night when a corroded station wagon lurched to a stop on the other side of the pump. A woman in a dirty fur jacket slid out, jammed her hand in the pocket of her jeans, and extracted a small wad of bills. She smoothed them against her leg one at a time and Charity watched as the wind blew the woman's long hair into her mouth and held it there.

From somewhere a rap song started to play, but it didn't sound like it was from a radio. There was a cell phone in the long-haired woman's hand now—that was the source—and Charity noticed three unfledged faces, one craning its neck from a baby seat, in the station wagon's backseat.

"So what if he ain't," the woman yelled into the phone, "the girls are yours!"

The long-haired woman was an impressive whirl of activity. She carried on a telephone argument, stopped the pump, returned the nozzle, screwed the gas cap closed, rapped her knuckles on the back window, pointed aggressively at the faces, recounted her cash, and walked toward the gas station. Her movements were so efficient, they seemed choreographed. Charity could never have managed them. She had a hard time not getting her feet tangled up between the car door and the hose on the gas pump. As the long-haired woman walked past her to the gas station, Charity studied her face. The woman stared back, flashed her a middle finger, and also seemed to score a point in her cell-phone battle.

"Seeing them and paying for them don't have nothing to do with each other," Charity heard her snarl, before the store's glass doors swung closed.

Then the gas tank clicked full and Charity returned the nozzle to its perch, leaving the hose in an awkward twist. She waited for the receipt to print, felt the faces from the backseat of the station wagon, looking, and willed herself not to return their gaze. She made a habit of not engaging with random people, children included. Children especially, and she slid back into the quiet of her father's Cadillac and shut the door.

She had the keys in her hand, was about to put them into the ignition and drive home, escape to the solitude of an empty house, escape the card women, escape the grit and grease of the gas station, escape from small children with dirty faces and angry mothers, when the back door of the station wagon creaked open. When a tiny booted foot poked out Charity looked toward the store.

The long-haired woman must have finished paying for her gas because she was outside again, pacing by the trash bin, her mouth alternating between yelling into the cell phone and sucking on a cigarette.

Charity didn't know much about male/female relationships, having never experienced one (something the card-night women were so fond of reminding her of), but she knew what feeling preoccupied felt like and that's what the long-haired woman was. She hadn't seen the back door of the station wagon open, didn't seem to know one of her children was walking through the busy parking lot. And without a coat, too.

The girl walked to the long-haired woman, coming close enough to take hold of her hand or hug her leg the way Charity had seen some small children do, but this one didn't. She sat down on the curb a few feet away instead, pulled a tiny doll and a tiny doll hairbrush out of a pocket on her dress, and started brushing. The wind pressed the thin material tight against her tiny legs.

It was snowing—only lightly, but still, what the hell was that woman's major malfunction? The girl had to be cold. The woman either didn't care or was too stupid to notice. *Drive away*, every instinct in Charity's brain chanted, but she found her hands leaving the steering wheel instead. Found the car door opening, and her hand grasping the squeegee from the gas pump bucket. Charity busied herself with the Cadillac's windshield, but in the reflection watched the girl go inside the store.

She briefly considered following but would have had to pass the long-haired woman, so she returned the squeegee and got back into her father's car. Sparrows pecked the pavement near the trash bin. The long-haired woman yelled into her phone and flicked her cigarette butt at them. People going in and out of the gas station were staring but she either didn't notice or didn't care. She jerked the phone away from her ear and held it, straight-armed, down at her side.

Her head was turned away and she held the phone like that for a long minute, then threw it into her purse, walked back to her car, got in, and slammed the door. Then the station wagon squealed a horseshoe turn out of the parking lot before speeding away into traffic.

Charity watched, transfixed, as the car drove toward a busy intersection, picked up speed, ran a red light, and disappeared over a hill.

Had that just happened? Charity grabbed her knees with both hands and squeezed just to make sure she was really in her father's car, at the gas station, in the dark, watching a child be abandoned.

That couldn't be right. The long-haired woman would notice the missing girl and come back. She was probably turning around right now. Hopefully safely, but probably not, and Charity unrolled her window and listened for the crash. Nothing but the Michigan wind on asphalt and far-off traffic.

The woman had seemed the type who'd yell at her kids in public. Maybe she'd even hit the girl for getting out of the car. Were you supposed to intervene when that happened? Charity thought about calling the police, but by the time they arrived the woman would surely have returned and then she'd feel like a meddler. For all Charity knew, the girl knew someone who worked at the gas station and dropping her off there had been the long-haired woman's plan all along.

Except that if she *didn't* know anyone, it couldn't be safe in there alone. People coming and going. Anything could happen.

Charity opened the heavy door again, hardly felt the cold rushing in, swung out a leg, and sat. A car drove up to the pump but it wasn't the station wagon. She got out of the car, locked the door, and leaned against it but thought that probably looked odd, so she lowered her chin against the weather and went inside.

There were a few people in line at the cash register and a guy in some kind of uniform was grabbing an energy drink out of the cooler, but no girl. The gas station was the kind that had a convenience store attached and Charity walked up and down the aisles, pretending to shop. She found the girl at the back of the store. She was sitting cross-legged on the scuffed floor, a cereal box on her lap.

"That stuff any good?" Charity asked.

The girl shrugged but didn't look up.

"I'm forty-one. How old are you?"

The words sounded false, even to her nonmaternal ears, but the girl looked up. And Charity took her in. Her dirty face, her chapped lips, the threads of bangs that hung into her eyes.

"Are you Mommy's friend?"

Charity shook her head.

A tiny silence seemed to fill the whole store while the girl considered her.

"You get your check?" she finally asked.

Then it was Charity's turn to have nothing to say. Did she get what check? A beat later, the meaning registered. Welfare, public assistance, child support, or something of that nature, surely.

"No," Charity said, reaching into her purse. She pulled out a fifty-dollar bill, held it out so the girl could see. The brown eyes, already huge-seeming in such a small face, widened.

"You're *rich*," she whispered.

"Indeed," Charity admitted.

Charity had never acknowledged that out loud to anyone. Growing up, she'd sometimes felt embarrassed by it, though she could not have said why. In the month before they died, her parents had sold off most of the farm to developers, so she was probably even richer, now.

"If you could buy anything in this whole store," Charity asked the girl, "what would it be?"

The girl cocked her head, considering. Licked her lips. She looked back down at the cereal box. "This," she said, holding it aloft. There was defiance, not glee, in her answer. The girl would accept aid, but she wouldn't grovel for it.

"Pop-Tarts." The girl added, "The kind with sprinkles. Some ChapStick. And chocolate milk."

Charity walked to the front of the store, hooked a shopping basket under her arm, and looked out the window. No station wagon. When the long-haired woman returned for the girl and took her wherever people like that take their children so late on a weekday evening, at least they'd have a bag of food. She returned to where the girl was sitting, smiled, and extended a hand. The girl frowned and crossed her stick arms over her chest.

"Where's Mommy?"

Charity let her proffered hand drop to her side and took a breath. When the answer was bad, were you supposed to lie to kids? Her own mother had apparently lied to her at least once a week her entire life.

"She drove away," Charity said, trying to keep her voice neutral. "I saw her drive away."

If she expected the news to land badly, she was wrong. The girl didn't even change her expression.

"Will she come back this time?" she asked.

"I don't know," Charity said.

The girl handed Charity the cereal box, stood up, then reached into her pocket and pulled out the doll. It was so small the girl's hand covered everything but the head and the feet.

"I'm cold," she said.

Charity eyed the thin jumper, the tights with a hole in one knee. "Yes," she said, "I expect you are."

In ten minutes the basket was filled with the kind of food Charity never bought. Artificial colors, artificial everything. Were these manufactured things even food? But she wasn't her daughter.

They got in line to pay and Charity looked through the big windows and scanned the parking lot again. The cashier took her money and they pushed through the doors. The wind hit them square in the face and the girl sneezed. Charity reached into her purse, wiped the girl's nose and mouth, threw the soiled tissue away in the same trash bin the long-haired woman had just been standing next to. What had it been, twenty minutes? A half hour?

But Charity had heard it. The girl had said *this time*.

The two of them could wait in her father's car. It was probably still warm inside. Her father had a blanket in the backseat for emergencies. This, she thought, taking off her own coat and wrapping it around the girl, certainly qualified.

■ ■ ■

On the security tape, she looked like a monster. With only three clicks Sylvia had brought the news story up on her tablet, and there Charity was, hiding a defenseless child under her coat, scanning the horizon like a criminal, then hurrying the tiny bundle into a sinister-looking Cadillac.

Charity watched with horror as the sheriff department's emergency number flashed across the screen along with the words "Amber Alert!" The drums in her head started pounding with abandon then. *Right decision, wrong decision, arrest, court, prison.*

The on-screen Charity, hideous in the florescent lighting, closed the car door and drove away, beyond the range of the gas station's security camera.

"And to think," Sylvia quipped, when the footage turned into snow pixels, "it's only your first week."

"Is this some kind of *game* to you?" Charity hissed, gesturing toward the girl, asleep on Sylvia's daybed.

She was going to wake up. In an hour, or maybe two hours, or perhaps in only five minutes she was going to wake up and wonder where she was, what she was doing in some old woman's house, and where her mother was.

Her dirty face was calm but her eyes moved rapidly under the lavender skin of her eyelids. Charity couldn't know the girl's sleep patterns—didn't know anything about her at all, including her name. But she wanted to. She wanted to know the sleeping girl with the dirty face and the hair that needed trimming and the torn tights that needed mending—or just to be thrown away—more than she'd wanted anything in her life, ever.

"Oh, my dear. This is anything but a game," Sylvia said, her voice like ice.

As if to prove it, she stood and walked to the card table, picked up the deck still sitting there, and handed Charity a playing card and a black marker.

Charity looked at her, mystified. "What am I supposed to do with these?"

A smile started small and took its time spreading over Sylvia's timeworn face.

"Sign your name, put the card back in the box, and hope for the best."

THE WARRIOR

Desiree Cooper

INVALID, AS IN NOT VALID, WITHOUT FORCE OR FOUNDATION—indefensible, as in the blaze of a father's knuckles that sends a boy running into the arms of an uncle. Sam enlisted at sixteen with an ID that was fake, as in fabricated or without legal merit, just like the war Sam took up looking for anyone's ass to kick. Not three weeks in Sadr City and he realized his assumptions were invalid, as in deficient in substance or cogency; weak. The sand niggers were not his enemy; they were kerchiefed, weepy-eyed widows and toothless old men. They were villagers abraded by dust. They were young men rotting on fence posts as children walked past on the way to school. One day Sam made another invalid assumption. He bent to help a boy (or maybe it only seemed like a boy since he was small and his bones were thin), and before Sam could scamper far enough away, the IED exploded. That day, Sam became a member of the armed forces disabled during active service: an invalid. As in a person who sleeps only in snatches, between thunderstorms of hair and flesh, and who dreams of bare-knuckled fists. As in a person paralyzed by fear—who doesn't know who the enemy is or when to stop fighting. As in a person without legs who can't stop running—a person without eyes who can't stop seeing.

CHANCE

Peter Ho Davies

THERE WAS A CHANCE THE BABY WAS NORMAL. THERE WAS a chance the baby was not.

Fetus, he told himself.

There was a chance the fetus was normal. There was a chance that it was not.

She, he told himself. That was the result of one of the tests on the fetus.

There was a chance that she was normal. There was a chance that she was not.

Jesus.

■ ■ ■

No one could tell them the exact odds, but there was a small chance the baby was normal. A tiny chance. BB-sized. No bigger than a bean. And there was a large chance she was not. A full-grown, adult-sized chance. Big as a whale, big as a house.

"Stretch marks," his wife said, gazing at the pregnant women across the waiting room like distant mountains. "That's what I used to be afraid of."

■ ■ ■

The chances of what was wrong with the baby being wrong with the baby had been a million to one.

Before the test.

Except there was still that tiny chance it was wrong.

A million to one was a figure of speech, he knew. The condition was so rare there were no reliable statistics. It was so rare the genetic counselor hesitated to put a number on it. *But if you press me.* Fifty or sixty cases worldwide. Ever. So rare that even after a positive test the doctors couldn't be sure the baby had it. But they thought so.

■ ■ ■

He was a writer now, this father, but he had studied physics once—the science of the unimaginably vast and the unimaginably small, as one of his professors boasted—and still the numbers meant nothing to him. Unimaginable. He didn't like that word—as a writer, had a professional dislike of it. Sometimes, he wondered if the baby would grow up to be a scientist. If the baby might make sense of the numbers. What would the baby say in his place, what would the baby decide?

The list of things the baby might have was four pages long. Single-spaced. The list was not numbered. When he cried and stared at it, blurred, it looked like poetry, free verse. Short lines, long lines, run-on lines. He couldn't make any more sense of it than language poetry. He would start to read, and a page in, or less, his mind would drift. Perhaps the baby would be a poet. He felt proud of himself that he wanted the baby to be smarter than him, better than him.

■ ■ ■

There was a chance the baby would be a poet or a scientist. There was a chance it would die in the womb, live a few hours or days or months in pain. Unimaginable pain.

It was June. The due date was December 7. "A date which will live in infancy," they'd joked.

Then it was July.

■ ■ ■

"Chances are, it's not hereditary," the genetic counselor counseled them. She deftly drew the elongated chromosomes upside down on a pad between them. "More likely a spontaneous mutation. A random copying error during meiosis—cell division."

He nodded rapidly. He wanted to tell her he used to be a scientist.

"A freak," he agreed, and her face, radiant with concern, flickered.

"Just bad luck," she said with the infinite care of diagnosis. "Very bad luck."

■ ■ ■

There was a day-care center down the street. He jogged past it every day. The kids in the little playground. They'd thought it would be convenient, his wife and he. *Lucky*, they'd said.

They'd been used to thinking of themselves as lucky, until a couple of years earlier. They'd just bought their first house, taken a week to unpack, hung the last pictures, shelved the last books, gone away for the weekend. A pipe had burst, a $1.99 plastic tube running into the base of the toilet tank. When they came home, water was running from the light fixture onto the dining table, like a fountain. Water was running down the bulging walls, it was running *behind* the paint like veins. For days they watched dark-brown seams spread across the ceiling.

He'd felt like it was God's fault. He'd felt as if it had been hubris to buy a house. It was the worst thing that had ever happened to them in their life together. And yet months later, when they had a much nicer house, they'd kidded each other, *Thank God for insurance*.

They had wanted the house to start a family. They had worried about a child drawing on the bright new walls.

He didn't fault God for the baby. He didn't believe in Him. Couldn't imagine Him. The numbers were too big. They dwarfed God.

■ ■ ■

They couldn't know—no one could—so they decided, this mother and father. Someone had to and, in the absence of God, it was them. They waited as long as they could. They waited for more tests. They waited with hope, but not hope of good news. The later tests couldn't refute the old ones. The best the new tests could do was confirm the worst. So that is what they found themselves hoping for, as they held hands. The worst.

"Do you ever wish we hadn't done any tests?" he asked her and she squeezed his hand so tightly he felt the bones must fuse.

The tests were inconclusive.

So they had decided anyway.

And that was all months ago. The baby would have been born by now. They'd have taken the baby home from the hospital by now. The baby's grandparents would have visited by now. The baby would be smiling by now.

■ ■ ■

Months ago. They were licking their wounds. They were gardening for the first time in their lives, the sunlight heavy on their shoulders and necks. They were starting to tell people they might try again—trying out the idea of trying again, the words ashy on their tongues. They told their friends, the ones who, even though they knew the truth, said encouraging things like, "So-and-so had a miscarriage; they tried again."

Once, in bed, in the dark, his wife had whispered to him, "I *wish* we'd had a miscarriage."

It was just a thing people did, he knew. By the kind of chance he was growing numb to, the rhetorical figure was known as *meiosis*. Calling one thing something else, something safer. It made his wife furious, but to him it seemed only human, as if the events, the circumstances, so rare, so unheard of, shouldn't have a name. Perhaps in ten years, he thought, it's what we'll say. "We had a miscarriage." It seemed so easy to spare themselves explaining it again, over and over. Perhaps it was what they'd even say to another child, if they had another child. And then he knew it *was* what they'd say, because how could you say what really happened to a child, your own child. If you had another child.

■ ■ ■

Cars with pro-life bumper stickers were everywhere on the roads that election year. *93% of women regret their abortion. If Mary was pro-choice there'd be no Christmas. What part of "thou shalt not kill" don't you understand?* His wife tailed one to a convenience store, followed the driver, a woman, inside. "I wanted to tell her how she made me feel. I was going to, and then I saw her at the register. Know what she was buying? Lotto tickets." They laughed until they cried.

The next week he saw one that read, *The Number of the Beast? 50 Million Abortions,* and found himself, despite himself, coldly comforted. For once the numbers seemed with him.

"Will you write about it?" his wife asked. It was his way of making sense. "You can, if you want."

But he didn't know how to make a story of it. The odds were too long. The case too special. "People would only believe it if it was true."

"Nonfiction, then."

He shook his head so slightly it felt like a shiver. "It's too shameful," he whispered. "Not *that*," he called after her. "Too shameful to be this unlucky, I mean."

He stared at the white of the walls. Ashamed, and ashamed of his own shame.

If he ever did write the story, he thought, there was a chance that it would be true, a chance that it would be not. A story, at least, could be both.

■ ■ ■

He rejoined his poker game. Not a game of chance, he knew. But now when he lost a hand, the winner apologized: *Bad beat, man.* The next week, he started playing online. He had always been a good player—good with numbers from his physics days—but he played badly now. Drew to inside straights, chased cards. He figured he was due some luck. But when he told his wife, when she saw the bills, she said, "You think that'd make up for it? You think that'd make it better?" And he quit. But he could tell she thought they were due something too.

■ ■ ■

There was a chance the baby was normal, he told himself. There was a chance the baby was not.

Even now they didn't know for sure. But they could if they wanted. Somebody did, somebody somewhere in a white coat, in a lab. There had been more tests. Afterward. *Post-*. Finally, the definitive tests could be done. They had agreed to them. *If it helps science,* they said. *If it might help other parents some day. If some good could come out of this.* There were results to these tests and they were conclusive. And they were out there in some file, just waiting to be asked for. "Whenever you want to know, or never," the genetic counselor told them.

Were they those "other" parents now? Was it "some day"?

They talked about trying again, but they didn't. Trying again, she said, just didn't feel like anything they'd ever tried before. Instead, they talked about the results, whether they wanted them. They couldn't decide about the results. They could decide about the baby, but they couldn't decide about the results. It felt like a cruelty that the results existed. It felt like someone out there with a gun. They had agreed about everything, but now, sometimes, they disagreed.

She wanted the results, and he didn't, just as once and for a year or two, she'd wanted a child and he hadn't. Perhaps she thought he'd come around again.

"Someone knows," she said. "Some doctor, some technician. If they know I want to know." It was the same argument she'd used when talking about finding out the baby's sex. It had made sense to him then.

"I can't bear it," she said. "The not knowing. How can you bear it?"

■ ■ ■

He had been a scientist. Could have been one. It was the path not taken. At parties he used to joke that he was a "lapsed" physicist: *A bit like being a lapsed Catholic. They still feel guilt; I still feel gravity*. All he remembered of his physics now was the uncertainty principle, and the famous thought experiment about Schrödinger's cat. The cat in a box with a vial of poison. The poison to be released by a random radioactive decay. According to the physics the decay might or might not have happened until the physicist looked in the box. Only then, only when observed, would the cat be finally either dead or alive. He was thinking, of course, of the baby in the box. Wriggling. Squirming. Heart racing. The gray, grainy baby from the ultrasound that his wife still had somewhere in the house, not exactly hidden away, but put somewhere he wouldn't stumble upon, somewhere he'd have to ask her where it was, as if she were protecting it from him. When he imagined having sex with his wife again, he pictured the milky ghost of his penis, entering her swirling, snowy womb as if on the monitor at the doctor's office. It looked very cold in there.

He thought of the results. If they got them the baby would be normal, or the baby would not. Issue settled. But he couldn't do it, couldn't ask for the tests.

All he could think of was the old physics line:

How can you know the fate of Schrödinger's cat without looking in the box?

Throw it in the river. If it floats, the cat's a witch.

He wanted that box to stay shut.

"But why?" his wife implored.

He couldn't tell her.

Why, why, why, like steps, receding.

Not because if the baby was normal, it would make things worse (though it would).

But because, even if the baby wasn't, it wouldn't make things better. He didn't *want* to be relieved of this shame, when it was all he could feel, all he was allowed to. All he had left to remember her by.

That was why.

Because the baby was already dead.

There was a chance the baby was normal. There was a chance—tiny and miraculous—that they had killed their baby.

■ ■ ■

Here was a thing about numbers, he thought for years after. The chance of a flipped coin coming up heads a hundred times is a half times a half times a half one hundred times. Astronomical. But on one flip, the first or the hundredth, the chances of heads are still just fifty-fifty. The coin doesn't care how it's fallen ninety-nine times before. The coin doesn't give a fuck. That's what it is to be random. That's what chance is.

A HISTORY OF WATER

Natalie Bakopoulos

With what spirit, what heart, / what desire and passion /
we lived our life: a mistake! / So we changed our life.

—George Seferis, "Denial." Trans. Edmund Keeley and Philip Sherrard

THE HISTORY OF CASSIS IS A HISTORY OF WATER, AND THE jagged cliffs that flank this town prove the power of currents, of ancient river mouths. At night the waves crash over the lighthouse at the end of the pier, and my bedroom with its small terrace feels as though it's a boat, but with trains rumbling below all night long. I imagine awakening to a newly carved landscape, but when I throw open my shutters and see the same saturated blue sky, the golden potential of morning, I'm relieved. There is Cap Canaille, one of the highest sea cliffs in Europe; there is the green-tipped lighthouse. I have been here four months, since December, and the raw brightness of each new day still feels like a generous, unexpected gift.

Late Saturday morning Luc and I dress and go to the market, then undress, shedding our bags in the kitchen and our clothes on the floor. The sex is raw and quick but we're exhausted and sated afterward and I mention this because the moment I roll from atop him my phone begins to ring, like enthusiastic applause, a raucous request for an encore.

Without looking I know who it is, his impeccable sense of timing, even though it's been weeks. I burrow my head into my pillow. But Luc must see Aris's handsome face lighting up the screen, because he laughs. "Dignified of him to let us finish," he says. He kisses my stomach and disappears into the bathroom. Now his phone buzzes in his jacket, which is draped over my chair. After two tries, it stops, and then I hear the buzz to voice mail, which I didn't receive.

When I get out of the shower Luc is on the phone. *Re malaka,* he's saying, the only Greek he knows. *I'll pick you up at the train.* I stand at the nightstand, rubbing lotion into my shoulders. My phone shows two more missed calls and three text messages. Before I can read them Luc snatches off my towel and feigns shock at my nudity and motions for me to be quiet. I wrap the towel around my wet hair and crawl into bed next to him, pulling up the covers, waiting for him to finish the call. I can't hear what Aris is saying but I recognize the choppy cadence of his voice.

Eventually I knew we would face this.

I know Aris, now head of one of the Greek ministries, has been having some trouble in Athens, with the way the Greek political system is hovering precariously above the people, ready at any moment to be snatched away by the hands in the right place at the right time, by those who see the power lazily idling in those narrow, busted-up streets, or carelessly tossed into the backseat of a Mercedes, double-parked at a kiosk.

For the past two weeks, though I've been trying not to pay attention, friends in Athens have sent me newspaper articles and gossip magazine nonsense, which out of a sense of retrograde loyalty, I don't read. The accusations are often outrageous, and never in line with the Aris that exists in my mind: a bookish political scientist who left his academic career in the States years ago. That was really the beginning of the end—before my marriage, before his—and for years I tortured myself wondering what would have happened had he stayed in the States. Dangerous, pointless *what ifs*.

"Well he's obviously coming to see *you,*" Luc says. "He's already almost to Marseille, on the train. He had no idea if I was there or in Paris."

I nod. Luc's work often brought him to Marseille, where he keeps a small flat, and his parents, incidentally, live here in Cassis, up higher into the hills overlooking the port. In fact, I first came to Cassis with Aris, years ago, and we stayed at Luc's parents' house while they were away. It was our first trip together, after his daughter was born. I was in graduate school and fell in love with the place. Now I've returned, years later, for work. I admit I found comfort here, with its affiliation to Aris while still existing outside the place he calls home. It is impossible to compartmentalize anything.

I get dressed while Luc watches me.

"You haven't told him," he says. It's half declaration, half interrogation.

He knows I haven't.

"You can tell when two people are fucking," Luc says.

"Is that what we're doing?" I ask.

"He sounded a little desperate. And also like he had already planned to see you."

Anything I say will sound like a defense. Neither man has claims on me, yet somehow I am acting as if they both do.

Luc knots his scarf, puts on his waxed cotton jacket, and kisses me. "At least we're used to Aris and his drama by now, no?"

I feel sick and enraged, not because Aris is going to realize what's going on with Luc, though maybe it is a bit of that, but that Aris can still manipulate me this way, insert himself at any moment. That I allow it has always been the problem. It has been our history. Though this is the longest we've ever gone without contact, ours was a story of extremes, of sudden interjections and abrupt departures, of intense entanglement followed by radio silences as empty as the moon.

At the door Luc hesitates, turns back to me.

"You know we haven't spoken in weeks," I say. Aris's last visit three months ago was supposed to be the final visit. We have broken up, but we have broken up before, and when you're not really together to begin with, a breakup holds little relevance. This is how it was with us. A series of final good-byes followed by next times. Like quitting smoking: That first drag after weeks away from it was just as addicting. The quitting part was easy.

■ ■ ■

The morning is bright and cold. With the mistral wind comes clear, fresh weather, but earlier in the week when the gusts blew I could feel it in my teeth and eyes, a nervy ache that was beyond physical. I know there's a sort of clarity that comes with pain but I couldn't help imagining the warmer Greek *meltemi* winds that arrive in the summer and, though dangerous to sailors, bring respite from the parched heat.

When I open the door Aris tries to block the glare with his height, and all that bright sun behind his head makes him seem like an apparition. When he leans in to greet me with a kiss, I only graze his cheek but my fingers drift to the back of his head. Muscle memory knows nothing of reason. I quickly withdraw my hand.

"Sorry so last minute," he says.

We regard each other like startled animals. I turn back inside, not inviting him in. He follows me. I wonder if Luc is close behind.

"It's nice to see your face," he says, looking at my legs. His lip curls up, like he wants to say something else. "I'm sorry I haven't been in touch. Things have been difficult." I don't know why, but I feel sorry for him, knowing that the Aris that exists in my mind is one who does not exist at all.

"No apologies." I place his expensive leather duffel in the hallway closet outside the bedroom, where Luc's thick sweater is draped on my chair. At least I have made the bed, picked up the clothes from the floor. I turn on the stove for coffee. Aris stares out the long, narrow window at the sea. The sun is coming in and his hair looks almost reddish and I know I will remember him in this moment, standing in my kitchen.

"I was hoping I could stay here awhile," Aris says. "With you. Until things blow over. What do you think?"

And then Luc walks in, having just parked the car, and greets me as though we haven't seen each other in months.

"Nice to see you," I say.

"Always," Luc says. "You look good," he adds.

Aris's request hangs there, unanswered, and I'm grateful.

■ ■ ■

Sometimes I think my own divorce was harder on Aris than it was on both me and my ex-husband combined. In such an unconventional relationship (even after a decade of our involvement neither of us has ever uttered the word "affair") any change of status quo can be threatening: a vacation, a new job, a haircut. New variables can send you reeling; the contemporaneous marriage is a kind of solution. But if a decade into a marriage affords a comfort, a decade into an affair and it starts to spark and hiss and demand more attention, a plan, a road or escape hatch. A mercy killing.

When after my divorce the department of geology at Aix-Marseille offered me a visiting researcher position, I jumped at it. When I first arrived

Luc sometimes came to Cassis and took me to lunch, and I'd hear about the women who were giving him trouble or stories about Aris when he was younger, when they were both students at the London School of Economics. For some reason, he always made me feel better about things. Maybe simply because he knew, and his knowledge left a trace.

One day, shopping in the next town, we ran into Luc's parents, and his mother, Nathalie, a petite woman with sparkling green eyes and a slight limp, eyed me with great interest, like I was a new specimen of study, so unlike the cool, tall blonds Luc usually surrounded himself with.

"We're just friends," I told her.

"*Tant pis*," she said, and grabbed my hand.

Later that afternoon, Luc brought up my divorce, the first time he had ever mentioned it. I wasn't in the mood to talk about it, and I told him so.

"But it's enough for you now? I could understand before, when you were married."

Luc was infamous for falling for unavailable women but the last one had destroyed him, and now he seemed a little dampened. How to answer such a question? With Aris it would never be enough.

"If this is the scene in the movie where you, the smart-ass best friend, tell me he's not going to leave his wife, please. I never asked him to leave her."

Luc looked offended. "Well maybe you should have," he said.

I didn't see him again until weeks later. I walked into a meeting, and there he was, in a beautiful pinstripe suit and his arrogance. I was doing a project with the French Geological Survey, working to ban the American company that wanted to extract oil and natural gas through fracking, and he was part of an affiliated team of lawyers. After, Luc approached and said that my presentation of seismic surveys impressed him. He was very serious, as if he'd never seen me before. We had a strong case, he continued, and the other lawyer agreed. There was professional admiration, sure, but also something else, as though I were speaking some sexy, foreign language he'd never heard but liked.

After the meeting, we went for dinner in the Panier, where we ate pizza and calamari at a place called Chez Etienne, and our colleagues left but we stayed and had a drink, and another. Seeing each other at work, outside the realm of secrecy and the confining world of Aris's perpetual crises, created a new narrative, apart from him. Luc told me of his divorce, years before, and this time I felt less reticent to talk about the ways in which I existed outside the constrained, confined space of a love affair. It was the first time I acknowledged my other life, my *real* life, and finally I told him about my sweet ex-husband and his bright new marriage and the beautiful newborn twins. And then I stopped, not wanting to tell him anything else, that feeling coming back from the first time he'd asked. It was too much an acknowledgement of all that unaddressed betrayal and sadness. There was a moment of heavy silence as Luc finished rolling his cigarette, though I could feel him studying my face. It was thrilling, honestly, to be watched like that.

"We've known each other a long time," he said. "You know you just don't age?"

I laughed. "Take a closer look," I said.

I was used to his unthreatening flirtation, but something charged passed between us then, and when my phone buzzed on the table—Aris—Luc's expression turned dark. Protective? Proprietary? I didn't take the call. It was a strange relief.

On the way down the dark, almost eerie staircase that led back to the old town, Luc pushed me up against the wall. I thought he was going to kiss me but he just held me there, touched my hip, my throat, and waited for permission.

Luc had always been our alibi in case Aris's wife, Eva, called and wanted to know who he was with. I never questioned the cowardliness of this but now the whole thing seemed ridiculous, like when I was in high school and claimed I was sleeping at a friend's house so I could spend the night in the backseat of my boyfriend's giant Chevy, a ruse that worked twice until my parents called the friend's mother, something I hadn't expected. A child of immigrants often wrongly expects her parents to be oblivious.

We spent the night together and I awoke feeling elated until Aris called me, suspicious, and asked if I was alone. It was the first time I had lied to him about anything. I mouthed to Luc to be quiet, and he stared up at the ceiling.

Then Luc began to visit me on weekends, or sometimes he'd just drive in for the night. Other times I'd take the train to Paris.

Do you want to come Friday? he'd text.

Sure, I'd say. We never talked about it. Maybe we should have, but we didn't.

■ ■ ■

The three of us walk down to the town, and on this bright, sunny Saturday afternoon so many bodies crowd the port that I think it will submerge. If one more person, one more tiny dog, one more fur coat steps off a boat or appears from down a narrow passageway, poof! We'll sink into a subterranean world, with the secret river, the two streams I know flow under the sea: one saltwater moving inland and below it a freshwater one escaping, unable to be tapped.

I feel energized, humming with adrenaline. On a whim, I suggest we take a touristy boat ride out to Port-Miou, and from the side of the boat I show Luc and Aris the swirling waters that bubble and ripple and spread from beneath the sharp, steep cliff. I'm pointing and standing on my toes and Luc, not Aris, grabs me and kisses me, and I am stunned until I realize a young Russian couple is taking pictures, and if we are captured in the background it will look as though I am with Luc, not Aris. But of course I *am* with Luc. The dizzying complications.

I laugh and push Luc away, glancing to see how Aris reacts. He's more than usually irritated by Luc's playful advances. "What the fuck, Luc?" Aris asks.

"The weather is perfect," Luc says, and he walks away from us, striking up a conversation with two younger women.

"So, do you want to tell me what's going on?" I ask.

Aris's eyes, dark like kalamata olives, are usually so easy to read, but I'm distracted by Luc, the lilt of his flirtatious French, the laughing, golden-haired women.

"It's Eva," he says.

In Greece, Aris's wife is a minor celebrity, with her own talk show on which she spends half the time in quasi–political discussion and the other half cooing in a baby voice. It is confusing. But a lot of people love her—she is charming and feminine and nonthreatening—and I recently heard she was going to run for a seat in Parliament, a rumor just bizarre enough to be true.

"What about her." I think of the recent newspaper article a friend sent me, an article speculating on the naturalness of Eva's suddenly larger breasts and the ethics of such extravagance while the rest of the country financially derailed. Yet her frozen expression in the accompanying photo told such a sad story, of insecurity and a husband who strays, that I could offer no derision but instead my secret atonement. After all, wasn't I the villain?

Aris hesitates, as though he's talking about a simple domestic fight, but of course I know better. He wouldn't come to me for comfort, especially not now. In all these years we rarely spoke her name.

"It's not what you think."

"No?" I ask.

"I'll ask Luc to give us some time this afternoon. So we can talk."

"And what if Eva calls then? And your chaperone isn't there?"

"Don't be sarcastic."

"Talk about what?" I ask. But that feeling returns again, pity, something I never used to feel for Aris. He cannot seem to realize that most of the things that go wrong in his life have been all his doing. There is something so sad about this.

I glance back at Luc and the women and am relieved to see him walking back toward us, looking down at his feet.

Aris looks back at the land, the rugged terrain, the houses up high. "So beautiful. It just looks so much like Greece," he says. "Don't you think?"

"It *is* the Mediterranean," I say. But I know what he means. I love this town because it feels like Greece without the accompanying heartache of its tongue, because I can speak in a language I know but whose rhythms don't send me careening into the pit of the night sea. I always thought that someday I'd end up back in Athens, where I was born and lived until I was six, but the whole city has become too painful for me to see: the immigrants being beaten in the streets, the busted-out buildings, the junkies lying on the ground in the middle of the day, shooting up as casually as someone might roll a cigarette in an outdoor café. My mother hasn't gone back since my father's funeral five years ago and now probably never will. The demonstrations, the poverty—I hate the way the foreign media sensationalizes it all and yet somehow the reality is worse. A bleakness I couldn't have imagined.

The boat docks and we thank the handsome, grumpy captain and disembark.

■ ■ ■

Back at my apartment we begin to drink. I pour myself a whiskey and Luc and Aris share a bottle of bordeaux. When Aris disappears into the bedroom to continue a phone call, Luc kisses me on the head. "You impress me," he says. It's not sarcastic at all, but I don't know why he says it.

We keep drinking. We play music. Luc and Aris sometimes talk as if I'm not there. I put out some snacks that Luc and I picked up early that morning at the market: cheese and bread, some olives, and we devour it like a fleet of foxes. We are starving and it's not enough. I stand up to prepare some more but I feel unsteady and walk out to the balcony instead. The sea glitters, dazzling and near calm. The previous night it had been so loud that it seemed deceitful now, the grinning wolf who has swallowed a lamb, and though I've spent much time near water and waves, studied the effects of erosion, not until I moved to Cassis did I truly contemplate the sea's power: to lull to sleep and stir awake, to destroy and create, to kill and keep alive.

When I come back inside Aris and Luc are talking about the Germany-Greece soccer match, beginning any moment. "You don't have a television," Luc says, as if discovering this for the first time.

"I know the perfect place," I say. "We can eat there." And while we walk, I'm reminded of those early days, when we three ambled around London together, before silence and codependence became such an integral part of our shared histories. Those days when Aris made me feel like the only woman in the world, and Luc approved. Before my own short marriage, in fact, and of course before the divorce, when I couldn't imagine anyone else would be as important to me as Aris, when my choices didn't have the weight of being choices, when they felt wholly reversible. When there was beauty to my foolishness and potential in it too and I was just living my life. I don't want to think about what Aris mentioned earlier, about staying, and I wonder if Luc knows.

We pass the old carousel, the run-down hotels and the overdone new cafés, the boutiques selling overpriced clothing and the traditional brasseries. Just up the hill is my favorite place, a small restaurant owned by a man named Khaled. It's cozy and dark, with long booths and photos of Arabic and North African and French film stars and musicians on the walls. Inexplicably, a strobe light hangs from the ceiling, hence the appointed name of Disco Pizza. I don't know what the place's real name is; there is no sign, and I realize now I have never asked.

Khaled's wife Anouk sits at the bar, reading an alternative French weekly. Anouk and I quickly became friends; she teaches history at the university. Fifteen years earlier she had wandered in, just visiting the town from Paris, and Khaled charmed her with his long eyelashes and handsome, gentle face. At first I was shy to tell her about Aris, but one night after Khaled had gone home we finished a bottle of wine and opened another and I told her everything. And then much later I told her about Luc. Anouk was wise and nonjudgmental and made me feel comfortable, but I didn't want Khaled to know the sad details of my love life. He is older, traditional, and I am afraid of his judgment. My own judgment is bad enough.

I introduce Anouk to the two men and they sit. Anouk doesn't flinch as she says hello, though I know she registers my company as significant. She eyes me, wondering how my mood can be so light. The place is filling up because it's one of the few places in town that shows sports on television, or any television at all.

In fact, this is how I discovered the place, and Anouk; I am nonplussed by most sports but love watching soccer, and I had wandered in late one afternoon to watch a game. The place was full of men, and when I sat alone and ordered a beer, Khaled called Anouk at home and she arrived to keep me company. I am always amazed by the absence of women in certain settings here. Back in the States, women would be wearing cropped shirts emblazoned with their team logos, cheering and downing beers.

The crowd is divided in its allegiances, with half the men, including Khaled, rooting for underdog Greece—Prime Minister Angela Merkel was even at the match, looking smug—and the other half finding allegiance with Germany, not wanting to condone what it saw as Greece's thirty-year party.

Germany scores. Luc claps.

"What are you doing?" Aris asks.

Luc takes a long drink of his beer and exchanges good words with some of the fans of Germany.

"Whose side are you on?" Aris asks. He's seething.

I am surprised, too. Luc always roots for Greece, a country he fell in love with through Aris. Luc ignores him and orders another beer, returning to his conversation with one of the young German fans. He's already drunk, sloppily so. I have seen him pleasantly buzzed before but not like this. Luc is always perfectly dressed, perfectly in control: pressed, well-made shirts, beautiful cashmere sweaters.

When his new beer arrives he turns back to Aris. "You want Greece to just have everything it wants," he says. "With no repercussions. If they win they'll act like they defeated the big, bad guy. Then they'll tear down their own city."

I am stunned.

"If they lose, they'll do what they do best. Little blameless victims," Luc continues. "You're like narcissistic children. Honestly. Grow up already."

I wait for Aris to quip back but instead he lurches, knocking some of the silverware off the table and charging Luc like a crazy bull, shoving him against the wall. Two pictures thud to the ground, a glass frame breaks, and some of the men howl. Luc tries to move from his grasp, but his face is calm.

But Aris doesn't back down, and Luc grips Aris's arms to calm him. Aris is in decent shape, but Luc has the upper body of a rower, and they're both just strong enough and drunk enough to do a frightening amount of damage. Khaled rushes over, yelling in French.

Two young guys wearing soccer jerseys, as if they've just come from games of their own, laugh, and for a moment I think the way the crowd is handling it, watching, though not horrified, will defuse the tension. Then one of the young guys says something about Greek savages, and this is it.

Aris is infuriated. His hair is wild, in all directions, and he lunges at Khaled, maybe thinking he made the rude comment.

They're going to kill each other. I scream Aris's name and fling myself onto him, as if putting out a fire, and I do it to try to prevent the fight but I am shocked at the force with which I throw myself. Years of resentment and frustration. Aris loses his balance and flies into an empty table, taking me down with him, knocking over the already-set water glasses. The crowd gasps, two men run toward us, and Luc shouts my name. My weight is all off-balance and I'm hanging on to the corner of Aris's shirt so I don't crash into the table behind me, into all that glass. My cheek stings; I'm sure it's bleeding. I need Aris to get me back up, and he does, and then we're both standing, facing each other. The look in his eyes isn't anger or even concern but fear. Aris has trusted me with everything, for years, and all those times I looked the other way, all those times I pretended not to understand his dealings or those quick meetings where more than words were exchanged. I never knew what was shady and what was legit and I also never asked. He never asked me to get involved but he never quite hid anything from me completely. My complicity, if I was complicit, was unspoken but my discretion understood. I have always thought our relationship was structurally imbalanced, and I was always at his whim, his openness, his availability, emotional and otherwise. Now, looking at his ripped shirt and his messy hair I see how much power I have always had. I could destroy him and his marriage and his political career too. All of it. I feel sick to my stomach.

I pull my hair back out of my face and wait for Khaled or Anouk to tell us to leave but Khaled laughs it off, telling the crowd inside that these two *mecs* were friends and fighting not over soccer but over the beautiful girl, pointing at me. I am seething, but when Luc dabs my cheek with a wet cloth I relent. I'm fighting back tears.

Soon everyone goes back to the match. Khaled's son sweeps up the broken glass and I try to help him but he waves me away. By then Greece is losing and I know they will continue to lose. I ask Luc for a cigarette. He asks me if I'm OK, and I say yes. My face is throbbing.

"I'm going to stay, finish watching the game," Luc says. I know it's best that I get Aris out of there. Ashamed, I quickly bid good night, and Aris follows me. Khaled and Anouk watch us walk out, and Khaled calls my name but I hear Anouk stop him. "Let them go," she says. I give a defeated wave. Luc, who's made friends with the boys in the jerseys, turns back to the television.

Aris and I walk home in silence. My cheek is bleeding and I hold the towel to my face. Aris smokes most of my cigarette and then stops to ask two teenage girls for another, and they give us two, and I am assaulted by the suppleness and sophistication of their youth. One of them glances at my face with curiosity, but the other one seems wrapped up in her own affairs. To them we are old and irrelevant. Wasn't I just so young, beaming up at Aris as though he were some movie star, like all those handsome, dark-eyed stars that line the walls of Khaled's restaurant? Since meeting Aris I have been in a constant state of displacement, outside both the emblematic and physical borders of the things I desire, which wouldn't be so demoralizing had I not been involved with Aris most of my adult life. Because I have so much of my life in Greece, time *zones* have always entered my consciousness with great force, and no matter where I am, each glance at the hour bringing an instant, natural corollary: the time in Athens. But not time. Not a real passing of time.

Back at my apartment, I examine my face in the bathroom. Aris watches as I clean it off, place a Band-Aid over the cut. I hope I don't need stitches. I pour us another whiskey. I haven't drunk like this in years but I can't seem to stop. "What happened in there?" I finally ask.

"You tell me," he says. We walk outside and sit on a large chair on the terrace, a blanket around us. But it's too comfortable, too familiar, too dangerous, and I get up and lean on the stone half wall of the terrace. If I wanted, I could dive and hit the water. I climb up on another chair, as if the extra two feet might give me a new perspective, but the view is exactly the same: the twinkling carousel and ember red of the Hotel Liautaud, the proud lighthouse and luminescent Cap Canaille.

"Why did you come here?" I climb down and turn back to face him. "We're supposed to be done. We're not supposed to even be talking."

"I didn't know where else to go," he says.

I don't say anything. We rely on each other even though we shouldn't. At one point Aris and I were actually together, a real couple, one year before he returned to Athens. I was in graduate school, and after he went back to Athens I imagined it would work. It's laughable, now, but I truly believed it. Even then, I knew the way Aris made me feel was probably the way he made everyone feel. At first the thought tortured me, but the sun feels just as warm on your face and shoulders whether you're alone on a rocky cliff or surrounded by hordes at the beach.

Until a pregnancy, not mine, and a quick wedding, also not mine, and then my naïveté became embarrassing. Life kept happening for us both and now it was more than a decade later, I had married and divorced, and somehow sometimes I still managed to think our separateness was temporary, a small mix-up.

"It's all too much sometimes," he says. He touches my aching cheek.

For a moment I think we're going to sleep together, another last time. How quickly we could ease back into the patterns we've had for over a decade, those deeply carved grooves, unhealed wounds.

"I'm freezing," I say. "Let's go inside." But there is no suggestion in my voice.

■ ■ ■

Aris falls asleep atop my covers, and I sit in the armchair next to the bed, watching a movie on my laptop to distract myself. I text Luc and he asks to stay the night. Before I can respond he calls: he is drunk, he cannot drive back to Marseille, and he doesn't want to wake his parents. I am happy to hear his voice, though for some reason I treat him with cool indifference. I tell him I understand, which is the misnomer of the year. I throw on my sweater and meet him on the road, taking his hand and leading him back through the gate and down the stairs to my place. He pulls me in to him and I can smell the beer and cigarettes on his breath.

"Luc," I say. "Please. Not now."

He straightens up, brushes my too-long bangs out of my eyes, and now he seems far less drunk than I had thought.

"Your face," he says. We go inside.

"Who won?" I whisper.

"A stupid question, no?" Luc says, but gently. He knows it is not so stupid.

"A fan of Germany now," I say.

"No."

"Nice kiss today, on the boat." But I realize it wasn't to reveal a secret or to mark his territory. In fact, it had little to do with me. It was a move between Luc and Aris, a challenge. *Stop making me be your confidante. Whatever fucked-up shit you've done, I don't want to know.* In short: *My loyalties have shifted. You can't trust me anymore.* And this, even if Luc is abandoning Aris for me, makes me very sad. It *is* all too much sometimes.

We sit at the kitchen table, and I open the large window because I know he will want to smoke. Instead he gets back up and opens the fridge.

"There's gelato," I say.

From the freezer he removes two small containers. I hand him a bowl and a scoop, and he takes a small portion of each.

"Nothing happened," I say, and I feel again like I'm going to cry.

Luc shrugs and offers his spoon. "Did he tell you why he's here? About Eva? He was planning to leave her, then this."

Aris hadn't told me that. "She's pregnant again?" I ask. I'm joking, only because it seemed Eva's three pregnancies always came just when Aris resolutely claimed he was ready to leave her. But untruths radiate from his face like beautiful beams of light, and though I always knew he was lying, for some reason I still found warmth in the persistence of those rays.

"God, no," Luc says. "She's too old, isn't she?"

"You're such a pig."

But Luc turns serious. "It's complicated. I know he wants to talk to you about it."

I am quiet. I jump for the kettle before it sounds. "Well he hasn't."

"It's why he came," Luc continues. "You know what he told me, on the drive? That you're the only one who—" He stops a moment. "Who believes in him."

"And?" My stomach turns. I pour myself some hot water with lemon. "Look. Luc. I'm exhausted. I'm tired of Aris's moods and little games and his acting like everything is a major crisis. It's his only mode."

"Eva really fucked some shit up," Luc says. "For Aris. She was taking money she shouldn't have been. Bribes. Favors. Who knows. Aris claims he had no idea about any of it."

"He probably didn't," I say. "Eva acts like a little doll, but she's not stupid." Luc often makes the mistake of thinking that people who look ridiculous are unintelligent.

Luc removes his turtleneck sweater. Beneath it is the old Cornell T-shirt I love, a perfect fit. He was wearing it the first time we slept together. He smirks and motions for me to sit on his lap, which I do. "So you're *friends* now," he says. "OK, sure."

"You don't believe him," I say.

"When will you take him off that pedestal?"

"Believe me. That happened a long time ago. But come on. *Claims.* You said *claims.*"

Luc smooths out my hair and holds my head back, looking at my face. I stand back up to get ready for bed. I don't want to think about any of it.

When I leave the bathroom, I try not to dwell on Aris's foot dangling off the bed, his face lit up by the moonlight. He doesn't seem to age. Or maybe since we could never really proceed together, to him I was still twenty-three and not thirty-five, and he still thirty-five and not almost fifty. The last time I saw him he said I'd never lose my bloom, and I told him I despised the jackass who came up with the phrase. It's men who take the bloom away, rip it from us. In a world made only of women we would remain youthful until death, but what would we do without men to tell us we look good for our age?

I make up a bed in the den, my office, for Luc, but he insists on staying on the couch, though when I crawl into the bed he flops down beside me. I'm so grateful for his presence, the softness of that T-shirt, the protection from the loneliness I inevitably feel with Aris, that I forget Aris could walk in any second. When Luc retreats to the couch I slide my foot over to where he lay, that warmth. I try not to dwell on the strangeness. I fall asleep, to swirling, anxious dreams: breaking glass, shouting, carousel animals coming alive and running in packs.

When I wake in the morning, my cheek feels tight and my head aches. In the bathroom the assault of bright light hurts my eyes. I wash my face and carefully change the bandage. The cut looks horrible, and now my cheekbone is bruised a deep blue.

Luc and Aris are already on the balcony, drinking coffee. I can tell they've been arguing. Who were the lovers here, really?

I strain to hear what they're saying. Then I come out to the balcony, holding my mug up against my face.

Aris stands, but I can't hear what he's saying. There's a helicopter above, low and loud, and for a moment I think it's coming for Aris, swooping in to grab him and flying straight up into the sky.

"I'm going for a run," I tell them. I set my coffee cup down on the small table. When he's here Luc and I usually run together in the mornings. Luc says nothing and goes inside.

"You never said whether I could stay," Aris says. "Would you rather I stay with Luc?"

"Now you need me again," I say. I want him to admit it.

"Don't be like this," Aris says. "I'm stuck. I was planning to leave Eva. I was. I'm serious. This time it was for real. Then this happened." He waves his hand, as if whatever mess he's referring to is there, in front of him. "Now how will it look?"

"Right. Do you care about anything else? Only how things look?"

"I don't have a choice, Marina."

"Of course you do," I say. "You've always had a choice."

I pull on a sweatshirt and place my phone and keys in the front pocket and when I step out the door I shout to no one: "We all have a choice!"

I immediately begin to run. No warm-up, no stretching. Later, the Calanques will fill with hikers, casual walkers, tourists wearing the wrong footwear, panting and turning corners as if expecting an espresso stand. But now it's quiet, and at certain points I, though terrified of heights, veer recklessly from the paths to stand on precarious edges. Too many beers at Disco Pizza, and my throat is dry, my lips chapped. My calves ache, but I charge up those hills until my heart is pounding out of my chest, until I can taste the cigarettes I smoked last night, until I force that punishment.

On my way back I stop to sit on the smooth, white stones of the beach. An older woman I passed on the trail lies on the rocks not far from me, splayed out like a starfish. For a second I think, *Is she dead?* When I stand up to check, the woman stirs, looks up, yawns, and falls back asleep.

Then I hear the footfalls of another runner pounding down the rocky staircase and I expect it's Luc. But it's Anouk, and the white-hot shame of last night washes over me.

"*Çava*?" she asks. She's wearing bright yellow-and-black running clothes, her long hair piled high atop her head. Sunglasses.

I shrug, I moan, and we lie back and stare at the morning sky, welcoming the sun, not talking.

"I'm really sorry," I finally say. "I'm so embarrassed."

Anouk waves her hand. "It's nothing."

We're quiet awhile, and I can tell Anouk is waiting for me to talk. But I'm so confused I can barely form a sentence.

"So Aris knows, I take it," Anouk says.

"No," I say. "Not yet. He wants to stay here awhile. Who knows what that means: a few days, a week, a life. For all I know I will return and he'll be gone, as quickly as he came."

Anouk waits a while for me to say more, but I am quiet. "This place sometimes can be so oppressive," she says, finally. "This place, it will suck you in. You have to be careful." Anouk sits up and so do I.

She applies lip balm and then stands, walks forward, her hands on her hips, and looks out at the sea.

"You know how many soccer-match fights I've seen in there? Or political arguments? Not to mention romantic distress?"

"I imagine," I say.

The starfish woman glares at us for disturbing her morning nap. But then frustrated with waiting for the sun to fully rise, she gets up and leaves.

Anouk stretches her arms over her head and then toward Cap Canaille, pointing as if directing traffic. "It looks beautiful to you now, but you'll grow to hate it. It's always there: when you wake it blocks the rising sun, when you go to sleep it'll make you feel you're suffocating. I wish they'd knock it down. Just get rid of it."

Knock it down? Get rid of it? I don't want to laugh, but the notion is wonderfully absurd. *And who's they?* I think of the energy company, fighting to extract natural gas from these rocky cliffs, to inject hydraulic pressure to get what it needs. But that of course is not what she means. Yet I nod, suddenly and strangely empathetic. You can wish for something even if you know it is impossible. That's the point.

The knot in my throat returns and my eyes well up and I take my sunglasses from my head and put them back on my face. Anouk touches my arm and pulls me in for a hug. "Well," she says. "They both seem nice." And we laugh until I am crying, wiping my eyes on the sleeve of my sweatshirt.

■ ■ ■

When I get back to the apartment Luc is there but Aris is not. I check the balconies, and Luc laughs when I peer under the bed, in the closets. I wonder if he's gone—it is not unlike Aris to just disappear; sometimes he'd vanish in the time it took me to go out for coffee—but Luc tells me he went out for a walk, wanted to find Khaled and apologize. I am surprised.

"If he wants me now, again, it's because he's finally lost me. Don't believe otherwise."

Luc kisses me, and I don't know if I believe what I'm saying, but at this moment Luc's all I want—not his approval, not conversation, not even love, but just the way his warm skin and strong body are some kind of defense against despair, the way sex can resist the scarring of time.

Aris returns an hour later, and we drive up the steep hills and switchbacking roads to visit Luc's parents, who are having friends over for lunch. I am introduced, by Luc's parents, as "Luc's friend." They and their friends remember Aris from years ago. I wonder what Luc has told them, what his parents might think, if they know that when Aris, whom they love, stayed in their house years before I was sharing his bed.

They fuss over the bandage on my cheek, and I tell them I tripped, running in the Calanques, and landed on a sharp spike of limestone.

After lunch, I'm coming out of the bathroom and Aris pulls me into Luc's father's study, where it is quiet. We slept in this room years ago. I slump down into a large, leather desk chair and look out at the sea.

"You can't keep doing this, Aris. We can't."

Aris twirls an old, antique globe around, running his finger across countries I have never visited. He stops at Greece, so tiny, with its jagged coastline almost swallowing it up.

He sighs, heavy, but doesn't say anything. That's the thing with Aris. He still somehow believes his actions are without consequence, that he can live two separate, nonintersecting lives.

"When you look at a globe, what do you see?" I ask. "Land despite all the water, or water despite all the land?"

"I'm sorry?" He's expecting my petulance, my sarcasm, or maybe an answer to his earlier request. His voice is tired, as if the way he answers *my* question has strong bearing on everything. He stares at the globe.

"I don't know. I'm not sure what I mean."

Aris's phone rings again and I can tell it's Eva. Afraid she will sense my presence through the phone, I go back outside and stare out at the water, at the cape with its red rock and vineyards, the Aleppo pines and olive trees. When the Greeks took Marseille, did they overlook this place, with its Skopelos-like cliffs and urchins harvested fresh from the sea? There, there, right under their noses, there like so many loose-rocked islands? They could recognize the landscape as familiar, could introduce the growing of grapes and the making of wine, but a landscape so spectacular with its grand, towering limestone Calanques they could not quite acknowledge. To find a place so like their own outside their borders would be to acknowledge that the one within was not very special at all.

On the terrace outside two women burst into laughter, and I'm equally distracted by the party and the phone call. Luc goes inside, not into the den but into the living room. The music changes, grows louder.

When Gilbert Becaud's voice fills the terrace, Luc emerges with a fresh bottle of wine, dancing, twirling his mother around. He's played the song for her. Then his father cuts in, reclaims his wife, and the two of them move across the terrace, their glasses of wine behind each other's heads, exaggerating their movements. Some of the others—the jovial couple with the matching scarves, the handsome widower from next door, Luc's friendly aunt—join them, as if it were scripted. I am aware of this moment as a moment that is happening now and will never happen again, unfolding against the pink-and-purple light of the late afternoon, the patches of glassy turquoise water next to inky-dark depths.

Aris joins me outside. "Your father loved this song," he says, and for a moment I forget where we are. "Did you know that?" he asks. I didn't. When my father moved back to Athens, those years before his death after my parents had split, sometimes he and Aris had coffee. My father thought we were simply friends. The knot in my throat returns, my lower lip trembles, and I think I'm going to cry. There is so much I have already lost. Yet what is it I'll miss without Aris? The comfort of attachment, of shared histories?

Then Luc dances toward me, singing, saying my name instead of the one in the song, and it doesn't fit at all except suddenly I'm filled with a strange, light energy, a bit like I felt yesterday morning at the port.

Luc takes my hand and touches my hip, wanting to dance. He refills Aris's wine, and Aris tips his glass, and for a moment he's looking at me in that open, vulnerable way, that way he used to, when everything was simply potential.

"I'll join you in a moment." Aris motions for us to join the dancers. "I want to take some pictures from here. The gorgeous view."

We all look to the cape then, majestic in the glow of late afternoon. "Oh, that *thing,*" I say. "I wish they'd knock it down."

THE SHRINE

Michael Zadoorian

STEVEN DIDN'T HAVE A DARK SIDE. HE WISHED HE DID because everyone who was great and talented and yes, *cool,* had a dark side. For him, it just wasn't there, as much as he wished it were. Sure, he drank too much, smoked his share of weed, and was mildly depressive. He had his moods, as his wife would attest, but you couldn't really call him dark. You're either dark or you're not. If you're not dark, you're just gray. In most ways, he was fairly normal. Married for thirteen years, no children by choice, decent job as a senior copywriter at a good-sized ad agency in suburban Detroit. That's where he and Boyle met. The two of them found each other the way a lot of people found each other at agencies: through the walls. Not that they communicated with a wall between them like in some badass seventies prison flick—the walls in an agency communicated in a different way.

In the Creative Department, the walls revealed most everything you needed to know about someone. It was where people proudly displayed their interests and allegiances and obsessions—right out there where the world could see them, a way to make an unabashed statement:

"I love this totally unknown indie band that you've never heard of."

"I am an appreciator of the quirky films of Wes Anderson."

"I think manga are awesome!"

"Look at the painting I did in art school six years ago."

You could put most anything up in your cube in Creative (within the boundaries of what was deemed office appropriate by Human Resources, of course). It was one of the perquisites. And if someone had some obscure gig poster or piece of graphic design or image of an unknown ironic "celebrity" (say, Heino) on their wall and you recognized it—you were a member of the club, you "got it." Thus, you could approach.

Steven had passed Boyle's cubicle many times on his way to the coffee room and had noticed the twenty or so black-and-white postcards tacked up on the wall. Each time, he would recognize a different person on one of the postcards. Some took a while to identify. It wasn't long before he realized that the wall was a kind of shrine. They were all great musicians, writers, poets, artists, comedians—all incredibly talented, all undeniably fucked-up, and all dead: Kurt Cobain, Jack Kerouac, Lenny Bruce, Billie Holiday, Ernest Hemingway, Iceberg Slim, Hank Williams, Dorothy Parker, Charles Bukowski, Charlie Parker, F. Scott Fitzgerald, Jean Cocteau, John Belushi, Chet Baker, Tennessee Williams, Tupac Shakur, Rimbaud, and a few others.

I should talk to this guy, Steven often thought as he walked by. But Boyle usually worked with his back to the doorway and wearing earbuds connected to his laptop. Steven felt weird just going up to him, until one day when Boyle was just sitting there, no earbuds, casually paging through an issue of *MOJO*. He noticed that the man didn't fit the Creative Department profile—forty-ish, sandy hair, wire rims, an academic vibe. These days, Creative was filled with pierced, pink-haired, tattooed, bearded young'uns who spent a lot of money on artfully wrinkled clothes from Urban Outfitters designed to make the wearers look like they had just crawled out of bed. In a way, Boyle's look was merely a variation: the carefully cultivated, intentionally rumpled preppy look. Steven himself had his own variation, with his retro yet expensive versions of the thrift store clothes he used to wear. All of which made him wonder why everyone wanted to look like a worn and tattered version of himself.

"No live people allowed on your wall?" blurted Steven.

Boyle peered up from his magazine and pointed to a photograph of a grumpy-looking, jowlish older man. "He's still alive."

Steven didn't know who this folded-face curmudgeon was but didn't want to admit it. "Oh. Yeah," he said.

Boyle shot him an angled glance. "No, he's not. You know who he is?"

Steven tried not to stammer. "Uh. No."

Pause. "It's Gregory Corso."

"Oh."

Boyle exhaled through his nose, almost indiscernibly shook his head. "Probably shouldn't act like you know something when you don't. Bad idea."

So there it was: his first interaction with Boyle Petersen. Steven felt like he had just been shoved into an intellectual mud puddle.

"You're Steven, right? I've passed you in the hall about a thousand times without acknowledging you." He held out his hand. "Boyle."

"Good to meet you," Steven said, shaking it. "I like your wall. Besides, you tricked me."

Boyle smiled, obviously pleased with himself. "Yeah, I did."

"Still. Nice to see photos of writers and artists and such."

"You're the first person to say that."

"Really? You'd think in an ad agency, we'd have some readers floating around here."

Boyle emitted a skeptical *pffft*. "Are you kidding? Most of these fetuses haven't picked up a book since college. No one reads anymore."

"I guess you're not counting tweets?" said Steven, hoping it sounded wry.

"Easier to just proclaim *The Death of Print*, than to dare read something longer than a hundred and forty characters." Boyle then smiled at his own statement. "Jesus, listen to me." He affected a geezer voice: "Darn whippersnappers with their Twittering and their new-fangled Ataris." He shook his fist. "*You hipsters get off my lawn!*"

Steven laughed, feeling as though Boyle had just flung himself into the mud puddle with him. The two kept talking. Since it was almost noon, they went over to the Coney Island next door and talked more over Greek salads and chili fries. Was it surprising that they loved the same writers, the same music, the same films? Most of it made by the same junkies, alcoholics, and deviants up on Boyle's fabric-covered cubicle wall. It was also revealed that each of them harbored certain artistic aspirations, specifically writing fiction, though neither had enjoyed much success at it. Steven had a few stories published in some tiny online literary journals but that was it. Boyle stayed up late and wrote obsessively as only an insomniac can, reams and reams of it, to hear him talk, but he didn't send his stuff out. Not yet, at least. Steven didn't ask why, but for some reason, he assumed the work was amazing.

After lunch, back in his own cubicle, Steven felt the excitement he sometimes experienced after great conversation with someone of common interests—the jittery exhilaration of maybe finding a friend.

Soon they were going out for drinks a couple of nights a week, almost always after working late, which was happening more often since a recent round of layoffs at the agency. There were many drunken conversations. Steven had never known anyone who was so well read, well watched, so well listened as Boyle. They discussed the junk-soaked grind of the early nineties Seattle scene and how, though it was good, the Velvet Underground blew it the fuck out of the water; how people said that *Naked Lunch* was a classic, but what they really loved was the mythos of Burroughs, the drugs, the William Tell routine incident, the authenticity of his madness (Steven didn't say, but he preferred *Junky*, Burroughs's most disgustingly accessible book); how hilarious was *The Man with the Golden Arm* compared to *Trainspotting* or *Requiem for a Dream*.

It soon became apparent to Steven that Boyle was much deeper into the world where most of their heroes resided than he. Which made Steven even more fascinated with him. Boyle drank more than Steven (who drank a lot), enjoyed recreational prescription painkillers, and told stories of earlier days living in Detroit, off Jefferson Avenue, west of Alter, in an area where Steven wouldn't even think of venturing. Boyle casually mentioned ex-friends who were thieves or addicts.

"How did you get to know these guys?" said Steven.

"Just from around. I had friends who were dealing."

Steven tried not to seem too impressed, but couldn't help himself. "Wow. That must have been interesting. I mean, like good material. For stories and all."

Boyle gave him a sidelong glance, then let out a small, plosive chuckle. "Yes, well. When someone who you know has robbed and fucked people up, then shows up at your place in the middle of the night wanting to party, you start to rethink your choice of friends. Doesn't feel so much like *material* then."

The two were driving around in downtown Detroit one night, fairly drunk, hitting some of the dive bars in the Cass Corridor, when Boyle said it. "I know a place not far from here where we could cop some dope. You interested?"

Steven knew what "cop" meant and he could see that Boyle was serious, but what kind of dope did he mean? He was pretty sure he didn't mean weed. Was Boyle testing him in some way? Finally, Steven shook his head, meaning to just say "nah" in an offhanded way, but ended up sounding much too adamant to be cool about it. The whole idea terrified him.

"I prefer to admire hard drugs from afar," he said, a feeble attempt to save face. The writer Robert Stone had said this, but Steven was happy to take credit for it.

Boyle shrugged. "That's cool. Will you take me there?"

Steven had driven that night. For the most part, downtown Detroit was a great place to drink and drive. The police were generally occupied with more important matters than busting drivers who were a tenth of a point over the legal blood-alcohol limit. Unlike the suburbs, where both of them lived, where cops laid in wait down every dark side street poised to pop some incrementally swerving driver, impound their car, and send them off for a night in the slammer and a costly court date. Steven had no desire to spend a night in jail anywhere, especially Detroit. He would be devoured there. Still, Boyle coaxed him into driving to the place, an abandoned-looking apartment building on Cass Avenue, down past Temple, a building with a faded ghost sign painted on one side:

HOTEL ANSONIA
Rooms by Day or Week—Reasonable Rates

When Boyle told him to stop the car, Steven actually sped up. They shot past the building.

"What the fuck are you doing?" said Boyle, his voice rising. "I said *stop*."

"No. I'm not going to take you there," said Steven, shaking his head.

"Why not? I'll just be like two seconds. In and out."

"No. I'm not going to do it. Drive yourself if you want to do this."

Initially, Boyle looked pissed, then his expression changed. It was the first time he had looked at him with what Steven now recognized as respect.

"Fuck it. Let's go get a nightcap at The Comet," said Boyle.

■ ■ ■

Whenever they went out together, it seemed like Boyle was always trying to pull Steven toward some territory he feared to tread. In a way, Steven liked that. They seemed to balance each other out. When he was with Boyle, he always drank more than he usually did or ended up somewhere he normally wouldn't have ventured. An example: a bachelor party at some downtown condo for some guy Steven had never met. (He wasn't really sure Boyle knew him either.) The party featured a "show" of two drugged-up prostitutes engaged in *soixante-neuf*. ("Is that even possible? Or is this some other French number?" said Steven to a shushing Boyle.) Though one might have thought that any red-blooded, long-married, porn-sneaking, middle-aged American man would enjoy this, Steven actually found it sad.

During the few minutes that he stood there watching, trying to find something vaguely arousing about it, some anonymous, aging-frat-boy account executive came up to him and said, "Pretty fucking hot, huh?"

It was all Steven could do to not say: "No. In fact, I can actually feel my penis retracting." Instead, he just nodded numbly and stumbled out to the back porch, away from the cigar smoke and fumes of spilled booze and lady-funk, where he found Boyle crouching over a patio table, snorfling a massive rail of cocaine.

Cut to Boyle weaving his way north on I-75 at four in the morning. (Steven made a mental note that in the future he would always, *always* drive when he went out with Boyle.) Luckily, the downtown drink-and-drive rules had prevailed once again—there were no cops out and they made it home safely. The next morning, Steven's wife, Sherrie, who normally was pretty liberal in matters of his going out, said that he smelled like "death."

Yet, a few days later, when he told the story to someone at work, he was perversely pleased that he had been through it. Here was an interesting anecdote. He thought that maybe he could fit it into a story at some point. It made him feel like he was a different kind of man than he actually was.

While Steven was being pushed into unknown, troubling places, he conversely felt that he was keeping Boyle from heading too far toward the edge. Truth be told, when it came to drugs or drink, the man didn't seem to know when to stop. Steven remembered something that the rock critic (and cough-syrup addict) Lester Bangs (who was definitely in the shrine) had said to a friend once, after the man had stopped drinking for the night: "Why are you stopping? Don't you want to seek oblivion?" Bangs eventually found it (with the help of Romilar and Darvon), and Steven sometimes thought that it could be that way with Boyle, always traveling further south, searching deeper in the shadows.

During that year that he and Boyle hung out too much there were mornings when Boyle actually thanked him for not letting him go too far. The first time

Steven met Boyle's wife, Laine, a willowy but slightly hard-edged blond with a Grosse Pointe bob, she thanked him for being "the sensible one." It made Steven understand the symbiotic relationship between he and Boyle, which made him feel useful yet weak, because it was so obvious that ol' reliable, temperate Steven was the opposite of everyone in the shrine. The most interesting creative people were exactly the ones that were out of control. He tried to remember if William Blake was on the wall, but it all had something to do with that well-traveled road of excess, down which Boyle was currently swerving.

As fascinated as Steven was with Boyle's excess, he couldn't quite bring himself to actively participate in it. There was always something in him, observing him, the voice telling him not to drink so much, not to snort that massive bump of coke, not to hit that blunt soaked in promethazine, and certainly not to do what Boyle had surprised him with one night, during yet another night of drinking, when he told him to pull over to the side of the street.

"Here?"

"Yeah, just for a second."

Steven pulled the car over. Again they were downtown, in the Cass Corridor, near the remains of Detroit's old Chinatown, next to an abandoned red-and-white restaurant tattooed with gang tags. Boyle then pulled out a piece of aluminum foil and a clear tube, deftly folded the foil, shook powder from a clear packet into the fold, held a lighter beneath it, and sucked up the smoke through the tube. The process was complicated, but Boyle completed it as quickly as one would open a candy bar. Steven sat there watching for a stunned moment.

"What the fuck are you doing?" Steven finally said. He looked in the rearview mirror to make sure there were no other cars around.

After Boyle inhaled, he didn't speak. It wasn't until his head rocked back on the headrest and his breath slid through his teeth that he spoke. Even then Steven couldn't understand what was said, a muttered pair of syllables. He was too distracted by the strange smell in the car—burnt and vinegary.

"What did you say?" said Steven. He had never seen Boyle so relaxed.

"*Chui lung.*" He exhaled a long, almost inaudible breath.

"What is that and why are you doing it in my car?"

A sigh. "Umm. You may know it as *chasing the dragon.*"

Steven put the car back in gear. "Fuck *me*. You're smoking heroin? I wish you would have told me that you were going to do that."

Boyle smiled drowsily. "Why? You just would have stopped me."

"Yes, I would have. Asshole."

"You want some?"

Steven thought of the shrine and all of them there looking down at him, watching him. "No. No, thank you."

■ ■ ■

All their heroes were fuck-ups. Was it wrong to admire someone for doing the things that you were curious about but incapable of doing? So much art by junkie geniuses had had a sinister effect on Steven. He had always been fascinated with these artist addicts and their mythic, myriad ways of hurting themselves, but he himself had never had the gumption, the need, the balls, the compulsion, the courage, the stupidity, the madness, the *whatever*, to seek that particular oblivion. Why? Was the need to self-medicate some sign of brilliance? Was it the talent that made the drugs necessary? Or was it the drugs that made tolerable the blistering awareness that birthed the talent? After so long idolizing these people, these artists, these dead legends, these fuck-ups, it only made him think that they were something he would never be. Talented. Driven. Dark. Complicated. Real.

How could not taking drugs make him feel all this? He should have been feeling superior to Boyle, but it was just the opposite. As the weeks went by, he found himself seeking out Boyle less and less, avoiding his cubicle and that stupid shrine on the wall. And just as quickly as the two had become friends, they stopped hanging out together. Soon it was easy because Boyle was showing up to work less and less. Every once in a while, Steven would catch a rumpled glimpse of him in the coffee room. Or they would run into each other in the hallway. Steven would act glad to see him but always had an excuse not to talk for long. Boyle seemed different now, his clothes more truly frayed, his eyes hooded and oily but strangely worldly, as if by slipping deeper into addiction, Boyle had achieved some authenticity that Steven himself would never find.

■ ■ ■

Not long after Boyle's cubicle was mysteriously cleaned out one day, Steven tried to call him on his cell and left a voice-mail message. He wasn't really sure what to say, so he just asked Boyle to give him a call when he had a chance. Steven never heard back. It was a relief, but a few weeks later, he tried again. Then he stopped altogether, wary of what it might now mean to be friends with Boyle. What was he like now? Was he one of those people who would show up at his house in the middle of the night? *You start to rethink your choices.*

Some months later, on a whim, Steven called again and actually got a hold of Boyle. The sound of his voice was a shock, for he had expected either his voice mail or a disconnected line. They shared awkward conversation for a few minutes, and then Boyle surprised Steven by wanting to meet for coffee on Saturday. Steven almost balked, but he was truly curious about Boyle and what had happened to him.

Saturday, Steven waited for close to an hour at Avalon, a coffee shop in the part of the Cass Corridor that was slowly being gentrified. Luckily, he had brought a book, Frederick Exley's *A Fan's Notes.* He'd backed off on the junkies lately since his dealings with Boyle but still loved his dipsos. Just as he was about to leave, Boyle appeared, looking haggard but all right. Boyle bought a cup of coffee. Steven got a refill and they sat out front on a concrete bench. Their view was of a row of old brick homes across the street, most in the process of being renovated, except for the one closest, which was slowly falling apart, its windows busted, chimney crumbling, still a victim to the elements.

"Where you been, man?" said Steven. In direct sunlight, Boyle looked pale yet dewy, as if he had just ran wind sprints.

He shook his head and took a sip of his coffee. "Sorry. I had to catch a ride with someone."

Steven almost asked about his car, but didn't. "So. Haven't seen you in ages."

Boyle pulled out a pack of Newports, shook one out, grabbed it hard between thumb and forefinger, and pressed it into his mouth. He lit the cigarette and inhaled deeply, dragging down the smoke like it was a relief.

"I've been out of circulation," said Boyle. "I was at a place. Briarton."

Steven had never heard of the place, but he nodded anyway.

"Laine got me in there. On her insurance." Another bottomless drag.

Steven squinted at him. "I don't understand. You were sick?"

"Jesus, dude." He sighed. "I guess I have to say it. It's fucking rehab."

"Are you kidding? What happened?"

"Everything happened," said Boyle, shaking his head. "I started to get prescription drugs over the Internet."

"You can do that?"

"Yes. Of course you can," he said, practically rolling his eyes. "It's easy."

Steven was half-shocked and half-amused. This was classic Boyle, yet he wasn't quite sure if he was buying the whole thing. "It is? Like what?"

"Vicodin, Oxycontin, stuff like that."

"Well, isn't that safer than smoking heroin?"

Yet another long, deep inhalation. "Oh, I was doing that too. And crack. Pretty much anything I could get my hands on."

"Oh." This was now sounding a little too real.

"Laine found out. She was not pleased."

"Yeah. Um. I'm not surprised."

"The shit started showing up on the credit statements. She let it slide at first, because she knows I like my drugs, then she saw how bad it was getting."

Steven had no idea that Laine was this tolerant. "What did she do?"

"Said she was going to leave and take everything if I didn't get help."

Obviously, Steven was sorry that Boyle had gone through this, but there was more. Excited, he felt a sudden burst of pride. *I know someone who's been in rehab*. He felt like a more interesting person. "How was it?" he said. "I mean rehab."

Boyle looked bewildered by the question, but also annoyed that Steven would ask it. "Fuck. I don't know. It was rehab. It's not what I would call fun." He pulled back his sleeve with his finger and glanced at his bare wrist. "I can't stay long, man. I got to go to a meeting."

"Meeting?" said Steven. "Did you get a new job?"

He just stared at Steven. "N.A. meeting."

Steven nodded. "Oh. OK. Where is it? I can give you a ride."

"It's just off Selden. Not too far. I can walk."

"You're going to a—what? A Narcotics Anonymous meeting downtown? Aren't there going to be a lot of, like, pretty hard-core people there? Junkies and crackheads?"

Boyle didn't bother to hide his incredulity. "It's a fucking N.A. meeting, Steven. Of course there will be."

"I mean, like, *street* people."

"Yeah, so what?"

Steven was going to say something else, then stopped himself. Then said it anyway. "Well, shit, aren't you going to be the only white person there?"

"I don't know, maybe. Probably. So what?"

"I don't know. It's just . . ."

"Just what?" For the first time, Boyle had some emotion in his voice. Everything else, he had delivered in a dispassionate monotone.

"Nothing." Steven tried to leave it alone, but somehow he couldn't. "I mean, that isn't your world. Who are you trying to be? You're a white guy from the suburbs. You think you're a gangsta or something?"

Boyle looked at him, disbelieving. "No, I don't. It doesn't matter at the meetings. It's just where I feel comfortable, Steven."

Steven crossed his arms. "Really? I have a hard time believing that."

Boyle shook out another Newport and very deliberately inserted it between his lips. "Gosh, I'm so sorry that you don't like it."

"I don't *not like it*. I just don't get it."

"No, you don't. Obviously." Boyle shook his head and looked at his wrist again. "*Fuck*. What time is it?"

Steven looked at his watch. "Almost three."

"I gotta bounce." Then Boyle got up and headed toward Cass. Steven stayed there on the bench. Looking down, he saw that Boyle had barely touched his coffee. He sat for a moment, then pulled up the plastic lid and drank from it.

Why did this all feel so unreal? Why did it feel like Boyle was playing this up for all it was worth? What was he doing going to N.A. meetings in the ghetto? Had he really been in rehab? But then, the guy was smoking heroin in Steven's car, for god's sake. Of course he would become an addict. It just seemed somehow impossible. Yet how could he believe that writers and musicians did such things, but not believe that actual people like Boyle did them too? Why William S. Burroughs or Kurt Cobain, but not Boyle Petersen?

Why did Boyle seem so different? Why was he acting as though he was better than Steven now? Like he was a badass or something? Even though Steven was still the one with a job and a working marriage, and not going to rehab. How could he have that aura of superiority?

Steven did not feel like going home yet. He drove around the corridor, nowhere in particular, sipping coffee, trying to clear his head. He thought about stopping off for a beer, but he wasn't sure what was open this early. He drove far down Cass Avenue, half looking for Boyle, half never wanting to see him again. Meanwhile, the neighborhood was getting worse: more boarded-up buildings, and homeless people loitering in front of empty, weedy fields, straddling both the sidewalk and the street. He drove farther, burst through a flock of low-flying seagulls that circled a littered area, down past Temple, toward the old apartment building where Boyle had first taken him to score drugs. There Steven slowed down, examined the faded sign on the side of the building.

Rooms by Day or Week—Reasonable Rates

Steven pulled over to the side of the street and turned off the engine. Someone appeared in the doorway. After a moment, Steven started the car again and pulled away. He crossed over the freeway, turned left on the service drive, turned again on Woodward Avenue, and headed north, away from the city.

THAT STORY

Jack Driscoll

WHEREVER MY MOM FINDS THESE ARTICLES I HAVEN'T A clue. All I know is that she clips them out and hands them to me to read. "Look, Fritzi, another miracle," she says, the most recent having occurred somewhere outside San Francisco.

For a good laugh I pass them along to Dieter and Brinks while we smoke in my dad's Plymouth Fury, the odometer frozen at 172,605 miles. The car is up on blocks, transmission shot and hubs painted purple. Rear risers but no tires, and snow up to both doors so we have to crawl inside, like it's an igloo or a fort, and always with some half-wrapped notion of someday firing it alive and driving hell-bent away from Bethlehem. Not the one in Pennsylvania, but a town so remote you can't even locate its position on a USGS map.

And therein resides both the irony and the farthest far-flung implausibility that somebody hereabouts discovers a visage of Christ in a lint screen at the local laundromat, and that then, along with our name, we got ourselves a shrine and a destination to boot. "Imagine it," my mom says, but a million pilgrims desperate to put a knee down in this nothing town suddenly adjacent to God and heaven confounds even the dreamer in me. And yet, as misguided as such an influx sounds, it's what she's apparently banking on. Which might explain why she's hand-painting all those baby Jesus Christmas ornaments, preparing to make a fortune off the endless caravans of sinners soon to arrive here in the provinces. But she says, "Nope. Uh-uh." They're nothing more than another scheme designed to fill and quiet time. Besides, she says, each month at the diner she always manages to sell at least a few to the truckers to take home to their wives.

I hate to admit it, but a miracle is precisely what it'll take to hire a lawyer high profile enough to enter an appeal and get my dad's sentence overturned from first-degree manslaughter to self-defense. Guilty or not, my mom maintains, when a married man slurps bar vodka from some strange woman's navel, he's going to pay a heavy price somewhere along the line. I remember how, right after the trial, she sat me down at the kitchen table and held both my hands and said, "Fritzi, listen to me. All premature deaths are wrongful deaths. But some, like this one, they're so senseless it makes them more wrong than the others. It makes them," she said, "eternally unforgivable."

Their divorce, final come May, has for a long while now been inevitable and therefore OK, I guess. Except for Bobby Bigalow, my mom's new boyfriend. Every word that falls from his loud mouth is either a rule or a sermon, and whenever he mentions my dad I can feel him present in my balled-up right fist. I know all too well that a single punch placed perfectly to the temple can kill a man, and so I afford Bobby Bigalow a wide berth. I'm only five foot six, but place a bet that I can't hoist a frozen hay bale over my head and you'll lose. Not that I'm prone to feats of strength or violence, but if he ever touches me or mistreats my mom I swear I'll take that first swing and at least rearrange his dentistry, that sneer of a smile, those tight snake lips. Maybe send him packing with a jaw wired shut and eating through a straw—though of course there's my mom to contend with, and thus the quandary.

Dieter and Brinks and me can't see him, but we know he's standing not ten yards in front of us, eyeballs straining, and so in unison we drag all the harder on our Lucky Strikes, imagining ourselves magnified behind the windshield. Tough guys you come at with a length of pipe and who leave teeth marks in the metal.

A fit father or not, my dad taught me to never take one backward step, no matter what, and for starters there's that tradition to honor and uphold. Besides, I've never been fingerprinted or booked on even a single juvenile misdemeanor charge.

Flat-out lucky is Bobby Bigalow's take, and I'd second that—but never face-to-face the way he'd like. He's the type, you confess anything and he dangles it in front of you like a noose. What he wants is for me to shape up, to shit-ditch what he refers to as my attitude and lack of focus, and commit to a new start before it's too late. Beginning with my friends, "those ones," as he calls them. He means tribal kids. (I'm one-quarter Ottawa on my dad's side, my hair shiny blue black just like his. The resemblance in our facial features, however, is not all that close except in the eyes—"like night minus the moon," as my mom in happier days used to proclaim.) We've grown up together, all three blood brothers, and when Dieter's snowmobile is up and running we like to shoot the glass insulators from the tops of the telephone poles with our pellet rifles. Or ding the silver dining cars mere inches below those lighted windows where couples leaning forward keep toasting their lives, the train whistle within minutes fading into the invisible distance.

Right now, we blow slow-motion smoke rings above the head of the Day-Glo dashboard Saint Christopher, perpetually open-fingered and palms up, who seems to say, OK, fine. But you're fifteen years old, for Chrissake, and so just what, pray tell, is the goddamn battle plan going forward?

It's late February and the ashtray is packed with a fat stack of Trojans, like it's a free, customized in-car dispenser. We've got a bottle of Thunderbird, which Dieter scored on the reservation. Like my dad I've got no alcohol tolerance, so just a few quick hits and I envision a fig bush flowering inside Gloria Masterson's skintight Levi's. She's never afforded me the time of day, but there's a buffalo robe on the backseat just in case, and even the thought of it warming those impossible contours of her body accelerates my heart rate by plenty.

I can see my mom peeking out through the living-room window, her hands cupped to her face like blinders. Everybody staring at everybody else, and no one advancing or uttering a single sound. A virtual standoff. Our prefab is a repo, two bedrooms and the wall so thin between them that some nights I can hear the static of my mom's nylon stockings as she undresses for bed after a double shift at the Honcho out on old Route 668, just north of the four-way stop. Out on the void, as she says, where idling, slat-sided transport trailers shake the entire parking lot like some low-grade version of the San Andreas Fault. I've seen it firsthand, the plates and silverware rattling on the Formica tables and countertops. My mom gets long hours and low pay, but jobs are tough to come by, and because we're barely hanging on she's locked in there against her long-term wishes. She's first on the seniority list, and I can't recollect when she last called in sick. Or when her credit card wasn't maxed to the hilt.

In one of the articles she gave me, a waterspout somewhere in South America spewed up coins of solid silver and gold. Not a thing you'd think to hope or wait around for, but there it is to consider, as opposed to the cash register that she tends day after day, all sticky with pitted nickels and dimes and quarters. Her dream is to someday see the Himalayas, though she's never even one time in her entire life left the state. Mark my words: Bobby Bigalow is not her ticket to anywhere you'd read about in a guidebook or travel brochure.

He's from Texas, an ex-rodeo cowboy out of Amarillo—or so he claims. He's got a slightly stooped back, so I calculate it's possible some pissed-off Brahman bull whiplashed him into early retirement a few lifetimes ago. Dieter's verdict is pisswilly on that, and Brinks agrees: Bobby Bigalow's just a self-glorified blowhard. He's got hair like General George A. Custer, wavy and blond, and I don't blame my mom for wanting company, but when the metal storm door opens and he steps back inside, I say, "Fuck him."

"And the horse he rode in on," Brinks says, though it's a Chevy Silverado he drives, and sometimes he'll rev it up real loud before he leaves, glasspacks growling, always the near side of midnight. Always after a few beers on the couch with my mom, arm around her neck or waist, and as she closes the blinds now I can see the vibrating blue waves cast by our secondhand, widescreen Sony Trinitron.

At least for the time being the arrangement isn't live-in, and so I suppress any impulse to tell my dad about what's transpired on the courtship front. I will, however, as a last resort if at some point I need his counsel. On the final Sunday of every other month is when we talk. 7:00 p.m. sharp. And it's only because he inquires that I betray my mom's whereabouts. Battalion II Bingo, I tell him. Same exact routine replayed in every single solitary conversation. "Yes, she drives herself," I say, but what I withhold is that it's also where Bobby Bigalow calls out the numbers that have sent my mom home a winner these last few times in a row. It's where they met. An omen, she says, that against all odds she and I are fated for a life of lesser burdens.

During those allotted fifteen contact minutes, my dad says her name a lot, "Laila," in ways that turn each next sentence lonelier than the last. He's never denied that trouble feeds the passions of bad men, and on the witness stand he said simply, in his own defense, that he did not, first off, consider himself to be among them, leastwise not by intention. Just some nobody, he said, with a pint in the glove box and a drinker's lack of judgment—and, no, he conceded, he was not ignorant of a record of arrests too long to overlook after a Sunday night bar fight turned deadly.

"Then you're spared now to contemplate a different life going forward," the judge said. "But for the one you've mangled thus far, Mr. Boyd, you've run your quota of last chances. For which I hereby sentence you to eighteen years in a maximum-security prison without the possibility of parole." Bars and razor wire and turrets and armed guards—that's how my dad describes the joint. The big hole, he calls it. He says piss in the chili long enough and right here's where you end up, all dulled out and dead to the entire world.

"Bum rap," Brinks says. "I ask you, where's the justice?" He means that another weekend's shot, and we're out of cigarettes, the smoke so thick inside the car that I crack the window. There's a ladder that leans against the house, and a path I keep shoveled up to the roof peak for when the motor on the rotating TV antenna seizes. Mostly all it takes is half a dozen cupped breaths and a single knuckle rap to get it started again, but I refuse to watch the tube in Bobby Bigalow's presence. Dieter, as if he's reading my mind, says, "Well, you want this waste out of the picture or what?"

The honest answer's as dumb as trying to stare down the sun. The night air is frigid and still, and as my dad sober used to say, a man's mind in winter isn't meant to be enlightened, or sought after, and any attempt then at decision-making only invites grim and sorry thinking. I'm eye level with the snowdrifts that the wind has sculpted, the temperature's double-digit at best, and it's beyond me why I say what I say, but I do, inviting trouble of a magnitude that we don't need and yet sometimes covet. I say, "Yeah, big-time," both hands locked on the Fury's steering wheel, and envision running Bobby Bigalow off the road and deep into the frozen turnip fields stretching away in all directions.

"It'd at least break the boredom," Dieter says. "There's that." He's got a deep voice and braids that sway when he walks, and every single paper he writes for English class is about the vanished nations rising up again. At school we stick close together, and if anyone wisecracks about the amulets he wears, we're a small war party to deal with. The same goes for Bobby Bigalow, who's a grown-up version of that same small-minded, small-town bully. He potshots us and takes cover behind my mom's loneliness, never smiling or offering to drive Brinks and Dieter home so they don't have to snowshoe those five miles each way just to sit in a backyard beater in the bitter cold.

"Why would anyone in his right mind do that?" Bobby Bigalow asked a few weeks back, and in my best attempt at a nasally Texas drawl, I said, "'Cause we ain't got a rowboat. That's why."

"Hah, hah, hah," he said. "Talk that bullshit and you and me, pal, we real plain and simple got us a problem to reconcile."

He leaned so close to me then that I could see the pockmarks on both his cheeks flare crimson. A grown man's glare I'd never seen fastened on a kid before, but I thought, "Hate-stare somebody else, you Lone Star loser." The only scare tactic that had ever worked on me was when my mom threatened to leave. And sometimes she did go off for a day or two, with my dad stammering in her absence, "Honest to God, Fritz. Honest to God," like it was a double vow to fix everything that had, for years, spun further and further out of control. Speeding tickets and DWIs and racking up points enough to have his license revoked ten times over. Resisting arrest, disorderly conduct, urges that over the long haul define, as my mom insists, a weak man's feverish nature.

Brinks says, "The Quonsets. Let's blindfold him and escort him there."

That's where the turnips are temporarily stored after harvest, on dirt floors cut deep like bunkers. No windows, and even in summer it's always cool, the perfect place to build our ritual fires. Shavings and sticks and just enough flame to get our knife tips glowing. Check out our inner arms and you'll witness remnants of an ancient art, the raised scars long and blade-thin and climbing almost up to our elbows.

Bobby Bigalow's got matching spur tattoos on his biceps and a silver belt buckle big as a shield. And those gaudy western shirts with fake pearl cuff and button snaps. He's a sorry-looking stand-in for anyone I might consider habitable company for my mom. She's thirty-eight, strawberry-blond and narrow-hipped, and still pretty enough for men to get the fidgets when she walks by. So, sweet-talking Bobby Bigalow into relocating somewhere else won't be an easy sell. He's already acting like a stay-around, helping himself to beers and snacks from the fridge, and sometimes shuffling the mail as if searching for something that's his.

He complains that if he doesn't time it perfectly he gets caught at the crossing gate, warning lights and bells and those freight cars throwing up sparks, and I'm halfway thinking right there's our optimum ambush spot: on the far side of the rails, so that after the sleepers and the caboose get past, there we'd be, the single high beam of our snowmobile bearing down like a phantom train about to pancake his sorry ass.

Dieter's waiting on parts so he can rebuild the carburetor in auto shop. He figures by midweek. But for right now, before he and Brinks trek home, he mimics the man in Spokane whose reattached left arm at nightfall points involuntarily at the Northern Cross, according to one of my mom's articles. Not that we buy any of it, that's for sure, but it nonetheless provides us some hilarity. Holy Mary, Mother of God, you lose a limb and sew it back on and all you can think to do out there under the heavens each night is reach up and thank your lucky stars?

Brinks says, "Man, if it's me I hit the casino and honk down on the lever of a thousand-dollar slot and watch the place light up like a munitions factory."

Dieter's all over that and I am, too. A little revenge for the years our dads lost to the gambling and the booze, for those declarations to change everything that ever hurt or harmed us if only they could. One summer, our faces streaked with war paint, we sent up smoke signals to the gods on our dads' behalf. If certain girls happened by, we'd turn to them and tom-tom the drums of our flat, naked stomachs, hoping they'd stop and maybe dance for us.

That failed to happen, then or ever, and here we are, me and Dieter and Brinks. When we bother to attend, we each maintain a steady C-minus average in a much-lower-than-average school district so far north that the cloud light hovering some nights turns the landscape a bluish-gray shade either gorgeous or violent, depending on your state of mind. Ours hasn't been that great of late, and to make matters worse my mom appears more and more dazed by bogus notions about Bobby Bigalow.

"He lies," I tell her. "He's a bully and a sneak." But her standard comeback is that he treats her well and that I shouldn't begrudge her another chance with a man.

"Those flank steaks," she said. "He's the one who bought them, not me. Please, don't judge him so harshly, Fritzi, inasmuch as you can't possibly know in advance how a thing might turn out in the end."

I figured she'd interject my dad as a negative example, but she didn't. Which in its own cruel way made him appear even more expendable in our lives going forward. It's as if Bobby Bigalow's got her under some spell. I've seen her turning this way and that in front of the full-length mirror, her hair down, wearing nothing but red lipstick and a slip, and making silent-still music with her hands on her hips.

Dieter says that you can crush dry gumroot and swamp irises into a fine yellowish-blue powder and boil it into a tea that forces the fork-tongued to speak the truth or else their skin pusses up and peels away. But he can't recall the exact mixture or the other herbs, and the tribe's last medicine man died long before we came into this life. And anyhow, if we wait for late spring all might be forsaken.

"We'll figure something," Brinks says as he crawls out the window, and half a dozen snowshoe lengths later he and Dieter are out of sight. They come and go in silence, leaving no tracks or drag marks, because a few weeks back we attached a horsehair tail to the ass end of the snowmobile. The two five-tined pike spears we carry with us are spoils from a raid over on Lake Tonawanda, where we war-whooped and circled the shanties to make certain nobody was inside when we finally kicked open the door. Nobody other than those nude centerfold pinups, of course, tacked to the wall and staring back at us, with their slightly parted lips all glossy and blistered in the blue flames of my dad's brush-chromed Zippo, and Brinks and Dieter's pilfered Bics. And so go ahead and try following them across the stark windswept pastures and fields of white moose and deer and coyote, and just see how long before you're completely turned around out there where the spirit world is everywhere alive.

■ ■ ■

Here's my mom's best one yet: a capstone gets jimmied from a long-abandoned well in the Ozarks and blind lungfish cry out in the voices of angels.

"Poetic," Dieter said.

"Downright inspiring," Brinks chimed in, all crocodile with a case of the weepies. Wet-vac all the way and, right, real funny, but maybe all miracles are a matter of need and deceit—all honest Injun horseshit, as Bobby Bigalow says about Dieter and Brinks, and sometimes about me, though never when my mom's within earshot. I've seen him fingering her Christmas ornaments and eye rolling and shaking his head. I've seen him drink milk straight from the carton and then stare at those missing children in a way that blames everyone but himself, my mom's personal savior. And mine as well, if only I'd offer up some measure of contrition and a commitment to believing in forces other than myself and my two pull-trap friends. Yeah, we've got a few illegal beaver and muskrat sets, but so what? Not that Bobby Bigalow'd know a thing about where they're at. If he did he'd turn us in first thing to Church Stoner, the CO who's been itching to bust us for years, but even he—who's grown up in these parts—can't track us.

But a week or so after that night in the Fury we tracked Bobby Bigalow, and it's possible that he and my mom went dancing like she said this past Friday night, but Dieter hit seventy-five miles per hour on the snowmobile to position us at our outpost on Summit Hill. We could see the lights of town. The crisscrossing of the streets, the dull red pulse of the Grand Union sign, and Bobby Bigalow hooking a right toward that strip of drive-ins and cut-rate, off-season motels. Which merely reinforced that nothing is sacred or safe with him around. I suppose I could have waited up to interrogate my mom, but to what end other than to start my own blood throbbing? And I backed off on the attack front anyway, so as not to arouse or inflame suspicion.

Until this morning when, before boarding the school bus, I said, "It's my house, too," and she did not say back, Of course it is, or it always will be, like I'd anticipated. She said, "Yes, within reason," but anyone reasons this out and they've identified the source of all our impending anguish and grief. She doesn't see it and no doubt won't if I don't intervene on her behalf.

"It's not an open subject, Fritzi, and I'm tired of feeling so disenchanted and god-awful all the time. I've been too long at my wit's end, but I'm dating someone now, and it's not as if they've arrived in twos and threes. Have they? I know how resentful you are, but I don't want us to face off like this all the time. And whatever happens going forward, I want you to promise not to hold it against me."

I remained silent and stone-faced. We both did, and then she said a thing I knew might someday prove to be accurate, though to hear it spoken conjured in me a consideration I hadn't until that moment ever fathomed, and hoped I'd never in a different situation have to again. She said, "If you want to blame someone, blame your father. And if he asks, you tell him the truth. That he, and he alone, is the one who led us to where we find ourselves on this very day. As crazy convoluted as it sounds, he's the one who introduced us to Bobby. Tell him that, Fritzi. And tell him that except for a man being dead, I'm glad in the end that he did."

Dieter met me as I stepped off the bus, and said, "Everything's still a go?" and I said back, "Full bore," and we both nodded. We've stashed two sickles and a roll of electrician's tape in the Fury, and the wolf headdress that he signed out from the tribe for next week's history-class show-and-tell, plus a peace pipe that we've been sucking without success for residual effects.

The forecast is for a blow out of Canada. A foot or more of snow, and you watch—that'll be Bobby Bigalow's ruse to finally spend the night. And I don't mean on the couch, and I don't care to wake to that next morning, and breakfast, and the final rubble of my dad's last possessions boxed and banished to Goodwill without me even getting to go through them.

I ditched early, right after civics class, and by late morning I'd already stopped obsessing about what our civics teacher Mr. DeSclafani called a God-spot, this bay in the brain that functioned to dial back the onset of anger and treachery and revenge. I didn't raise my hand, but if I had I would have mentioned the afghan that Bobby Bigalow unfolds and drapes around my mom's shoulders just to tick me off. And how sometimes he even winks at me from right there behind the couch. In my head I hear my dad's old rant: "Give ground one time to that and you'll be doing it on a daily basis," and so it only makes sense to "bring 'em on, all comers. Every last Fo, Fuck, and Fum."

And tonight as Dieter and Brinks and I see it, we're going to right some wrongs is all. If things foul up maybe we'll move on Dieter's backup plan to screw a spigot into one of those giant wine casks we've seen stacked on the boxcars and drink our way West on the rails to the Columbia River Gorge. Out where his dad lived for a short while after a stint in the service. And where he fished for king salmon that danced on their silver tails in the froth and the sunshine, right there below what he called the great nonstop booming of the falls. Last we heard he was living outside Montreal, and I suppose someday that might be a destination for us, too. I can't legally visit my dad until I turn eighteen, but like Dieter says, at least there's no guesswork concerning his whereabouts.

My mom's scheduled to work a double shift, and she left wearing a polished, silver-veined quartz stone around her neck. I've never seen it before. A gift from Bobby Bigalow no doubt, who just last night complained about the lousy water pressure like somehow he owns that right. The pipes not being buried deep enough under the frost line's the problem, and so we have to let the faucet slow-drip whenever the mercury dips below fifteen degrees. Sometimes I'll place an empty, upside-down ice-cube tray directly under the tap in the kitchen sink just to drive him batshit. I spare him not one reminder that in my eyes he and my mom are maybe hot-wired for the short run but are destined for an abrupt chill down.

He's clueless that Dieter and Brinks tracked him home to some double-wide off Tapico. Off Arrowhead. Off a no-name two-track that backs up to state land where the proposed hydraulic dumpster was supposed to go. All that's there is a giant hole half filled with the dead weight of ruptured appliances and bedsprings and bald tires. TVs with bullet holes through the picture tubes. Plus a few metal shopping carts that we hauled out for the caster wheels we used to build ourselves three suicide skateboards.

We've remapped our attack-and-capture strategy in favor of just happening to be in Bobby Bigalow's neck of the woods later tonight. You know—to search the clearings and snow fields for a high-stepper who might teach us how to make our squaws go dumb between the bedsheets—a phrase he let slip that caused the first time I'd seen my mom flinch in his presence, her mouth muscles going taut. I wanted to say, "There. That's who he is outright. A croaker always running his lily-livered mouth, and why parlay the likes of him into heartbreak? Why him?" But they're a twosome, plain and simple. And, like Brinks says, all love's a fluke either temporary or lifelong, and without incentive Bobby Bigalow ain't about to scare or bugger off anytime in our immediate future.

But as I wait for Dieter and Brinks to pick me up, I'm all Indian, and the sickles are razor sharp and already taped to the insides of my wrists for a better grip. Like curved tomahawks or talons. And the wolf's skull plate a perfect fit, my face smeared with lampblack from the inside glass of the kerosene lantern my dad always used whenever we dipped smelt in Otter Creek.

There's a full moon and the air's frostbite cold, and I remember how my dad said years ago, when I inquired, that he'd proposed to my mom under a meteor shower, the tracer tails so intense they turned the skyways platinum. There's Orion, the hunter. And this is the car in which my parents first dated, first kissed, and only since Bobby Bigalow does my mom, without a second's hesitation or any apparent regret, say straight-faced that it was all a colossal mistake, "a marriage so doomed and misguided." Think on that awhile like I do: I pull up short of calling her a liar, but she's nonetheless knocking a lot of careless and hurtful wrong words about.

That's a fact, and rather than let her pawn her wedding ring, last month I zinged it with my slingshot as far into the constellations as I could. And is that not, when I hear the muted roostertailing of Dieter's snowmobile up a certain draw still half a mile distant, why I roll down the car window and crawl outside without a second thought? Yes, on all fours, dressed in furs and wolf fangs and ready, finally, to move out across the frozen tundra, under the miracle of these winter stars.

■ ■ ■

"No mercy," Brinks says. He's holding a ball-and-claw table leg, and Dieter's brandishing one of the pike spears. There's no barking dog to quiet, but there is a second vehicle in Bobby's driveway. It's definitely not my mom's Cherokee, and it's parked directly in front of the pickup, which appears to be sniffing the Jeep's hind end like it's got in mind to hump it.

We're standing back a short ways from the slider. No blinds and the kitchen lighted up, but nobody's stepped into view yet. I've never seen wallpaper like this before. A jungle-clot of jonquils—all summery and yellow—and flocked here and there amid them are a few oversize roses the dark blood color of mulberries.

"Some weird shit here," Dieter whispers, and it's true that the icicles hanging halfway down in front of the glass distort this woman who appears out of nowhere like a ghost among the vines and tangles. She's stark naked, and she stops at the stove and leans over and turns her head sideways to light a cigarette from one of the front burners. Then she leans against the counter and folds her arms over her breasts like she's shy or cold, or maybe even afraid and cowering.

No one says so, but we despise Bobby Bigalow all the more when he swaggers in zipping up his pants. What I notice most, though, is the ceiling textured and flecked like ours with fake chips of mica. And how this woman is knock-kneed and shivering as the moon disappears and more snow starts to fall. It's the exact same posture I've seen my mom assume too many times—though bundled up of course. I imagine all four gas jets open full, and the oven turned on the way we always have it to survive the night whenever our furnace conks.

"It ain't his place," Brinks says. "He don't live here, Fritz. It's hers, and now how the fuck may I direct your call?"

The only one I'm certain owns a cell phone among us is Bobby Bigalow—some new fancy-ass gadget that takes snapshots and that he keeps holstered on his hip. I've heard it ring, though never have I seen him use or answer it.

What I flash on instead is one of those old-fashioned cameras, a bellows and a black hood and that slow, handheld explosion of gunpowdery light. This would make a one-in-a-million portrait, a classic: three armed and angry young chieftains standing side by side, the single threat of each of us tripled in the camera's eye.

"Let's dial this up or duck out of here," Dieter says, ice forming on the black buzzard and eagle feathers in his hair.

"Your call," Brinks says. "Either way." But when he passes me the wine skein it's my dad I imagine, half-drunk and fury-fisted and cleaving through the snow toward whatever door that Bobby Bigalow is about to exit.

Like father, like son, and it takes only a matter of seconds for me to calculate that weeks or months or years from now I might own up that "Here, overtaken by rage and revenge, is where I pummeled and perhaps maimed or even killed a man." Or, "Here's where I stood with my only two friends on earth one February night. The snow suddenly coming down so hard that a man my mom believed mattered passed unaware within ten feet of us after being with another woman. We could smell her perfume, her nakedness, his beery breath, could hear him hiss between his teeth as we watched him disappear."

Neither is a confession whose details can redeem a thing. But have I mentioned the jukebox at the Honcho? Merle Haggard and Mickey Gilley, and truckers who change dollar bills into quarters, and my mom who's destined to start humming those heart-drain tunes again real soon, one way or another, no matter what goes down here.

When I give the word we sneak away. Dieter starts the snowmobile. "Hang tight," he says, and it's as if nothing can touch us as we tear-ass into all that whiteness, flying blind and the trees coming at us out of nowhere. There's an abandoned cellar hole we somehow avoid, and then we're airborne over the not-so-high rock-face outcropping we've survived at least a hundred times. The snow's coming in waves like wings, and we rise, I swear it. Three lost-cause kids in crazy getups, straddling not the wide seat of a Polaris sled, but rather a bareback horse, its black tail combed shiny by the wind.

That story. The one riddled with God-spots and paybacks and love full-blown for women we might someday make giddy and, despite our best intentions, betray. Thunderbird and muscatel. Dads who've gone missing, and a mom who, against all the evidence, believes in miracles she's determined to pass along to her son.

THE MIGRATION

Matt Bell

AFTER EACH KILLING THE MIGRATION WOULD QUICKEN.

The men killed one and another migrated. The men killed two, and a dozen left. This was the method of the migration, of its start and its continuation and its quickening.

This is what the men who killed believed. This is the belief they killed for, for which they continued to kill.

■ ■ ■

Over some number of nights the men killed a man and then a man and then a man and then two men, then another number of men they did not count. They killed them with ball bats and pipe lengths, with bricks held in leather work gloves, by pushing them over the railings of overpasses. They ran some others down in the streets, dragged their bodies like dolls beneath the carriages of crowded cars, accelerated quickly, braked hard and late.

The men who killed, they did not make anything look like an accident, because they did not want those who would migrate to believe anything was.

The men who killed talked about killing more, killing faster, about buying dynamite, about making firebombs, but mostly they could not afford to kill if they could not use what they already owned, what they found ready inside house and garage and basement: one killing they made with a crowbar, a tool meant to tear drywall and to lever apart two objects, a tool that worked the same upon a person. Like rope, like wire, like a hammer.

Throughout the killings, there were some who used their boots and some others who used their fists, and afterward some of those men scrubbed themselves raw in the long dark of their sleepless hours. Some of these men who could not sleep had their doubts, but they did not give these worries voice nor allow the others to voice theirs, not even after the killing of the woman, after what happened because of her killing.

The men who killed the woman had not meant to kill the child inside her, had not known she was with child. They had not *seen* her, not as they laid their hands upon her, not as they held her down, not as they pinned her legs, not as they wrapped their hands around her face, quieting her mouth with heavy fingers. And not in the first minutes after either, when they stood around in the pooling dark, their eyes aglitter.

This child inside the woman was the size of a fist, and already there were so many fists that what was the presence of one more? Below them the woman became obscured in bruises or the coming of bruises, after the boots were removed, after the bat stopped its swinging against her body. Later there were flowers in the wet street, and the prayer cards around the flowers wetted too, damp from a hose sprayed against the stained sidewalk, those gallons spent to wash away those pints. And after the child was found beneath the layers of its mother's bruises, then some men in uniforms arrived at the many doors of the men who killed to bind them with cuffs and herd them into the locked backs of waiting cars, their heads pushed low to keep them from getting hurt.

They had not meant the second portion of what they did, were even some of them sorrowed, but they were not sorry enough, and for this crime they were locked into a building they could not escape.

■ ■ ■

The men who killed knew they had been locked up because they would not stop the killing, because even if they were freed they would not leave the city.

No, they said. They were not the ones who would migrate. They were the ones who would return, who would stay and kill more, because they wanted the migration to continue, wanted it to quicken and quicken.

Even with the men who killed locked in the building, even then it did quicken, and everywhere it went there were televisions, and everywhere the televisions were there were other men behind their screens, men in suits who said the killers had killed out of some long hate, out of old wrongs come back around and gone bad again.

But that was not what the men who killed said.

The men who killed were sometimes in the television too, and in the television they said they did not want much.

All they wanted, they said, was this where this went, that where that should go.

It is not complicated, they said. Just us and them. Not together but separate.

We are not the same, they said. They said, We do not belong together.

■ ■ ■

Some of the men who killed agreed with those experts on the television, the men in suits and ties who did not believe the migration would ever be finished, because those who would migrate were not all of one mind.

Some were stubborn, the experts said, and would require more killings to be quickened, if they could be quickened at all.

The experts said that before they became those who would migrate, many of those who lived there had been trying to get out but didn't have the money to leave, nor the good credit to borrow the money, and so no matter how many were killed some number would always live there.

In the ways of their finances and also in other ways, the men who killed and those who would migrate were not so different, but this the men did not believe.

Different is all we are, they said, all we will be.

The experts explained that the houses of those who would migrate had long ago been the houses of men like the men who killed. They had been the houses of women and children, of families, a father, a mother, children or else the absence of children, the trying for. The men who killed thought this was the way it had always been, the way they wanted it always to be. But that world seemed no longer to exist, no matter who they killed, no matter how many were made to migrate.

The sorrow this brought the men, it made them sorrier than killing the woman and the child ever had, but this they did not tell to anyone. They did not need to. They had already said it, in every manner but speech.

■ ■ ■

According to one expert, you could tell the kith and kin of the men who killed from those who would migrate by some matters of degree.

They were skinned differently, for one thing, and their skins did not take the same dressings.

Also there were matters of music, another expert said.

The men who killed did not like the music of those others who lived among them, of those who would migrate. They did not like even one single note of that sound, but their daughters did, and so also their sons. The music had grown louder and now if the men who killed heard this music moving down the street they would yell from their porches, their yards, their sidewalks; they would grind their teeth, harden their hands to fists. And when their hands were hard enough the men would use them to kill.

Just a theory, the expert said. Just a story, how we got from there to here.

■ ■ ■

The migration continued even without the men who killed, and without them the world bloomed and then burnished, went orange, and the women of the men did not know what to do. Their houses were hot with what their men had done, with what the women had known or not known, and in the heat they sweated in their kitchens, sweated in their bedrooms, sweated wherever the television held the faces of their men or else those who spoke for them, about them.

It was always their men they thought of, and their anger or disbelief or fear, and the heat already in the air and on the street entered and dwelled within the women until they struggled to work, to care better for their children, to gather peaceably in churches where they might see each other's faces, the facades of those left behind.

The women of the men could not be fired for having a man who killed but they could be made to quit and so some of the women quit, while others stayed and bore it, bore it as they bore the capture of their men, as they bore the sudden embiggening by absence of a family they had to care for all alone. In the bars where some worked a man would buy them a drink and then another drink and then he would say maybe you need help at home and sometimes the women did and sometimes they did not and sometimes they were not sure and so they took the men home anyway to see what use they might be and then afterward they sat in the beds of the men who killed with these new men who had not and together they watched the television say fair trial and impartial jury and change of venue, and in those repetitions the women heard how even after it was over it would never be ended, not the migration and not the heat and not the women of the men who killed getting by less well and less often.

And what could the women say and what could the women do?

In the supermarkets some women worked and some women shopped and it was not the same women at the same time. Some women went to work in the factories where their men had once worked and some where those who migrated once worked, but maybe some of the women got worse jobs than the others, because of the differences in who they were, in who they replaced.

On the evening news an expert said there were differences in their lunch boxes, in the food they chose to bring for lunch. What parts of the cow they ate, how they prepared their potatoes.

Another expert straightened his already-straight tie and said they did not drink the same drinks, and he was right on this as he was on the surface of all things.

Sometimes when the women of the men who killed left work early to pick up their sons and daughters from their schooling, sometimes they saw them playing with the sons and daughters of the killed.

And what this meant to the women.

And how hard it was to watch.

And how hot it made them to tell their sons and daughters no, to tell them never again, to tell them what would your father say. And then it was summer and there was no more school and the differences between burned all the brighter, for being farther apart, for being harder to see.

■ ■ ■

Those who would migrate were women and children, and also men who had lived, who had not been killed. Maybe these men did not want to migrate, but maybe their women did, maybe their children deserved it, and anyway because there was no more work, even less work than when the migration had begun, because the factories and the shops and the supermarkets were migrating too, closing down, locking up. Some of the men did not have the means to take their families away, lacked exactly what the television experts said they lacked, and so the men who would migrate did so without their women and their children, went to other cities to build for less what they had before built for more.

The men who migrated alone lived in smaller apartments than they had when they lived with their women and their children, and it was hotter where they went or it was colder, and some of them were still killed there, even though there was no migration happening yet in their new city.

One expert said, This migration will not be isolated. It will not be insulated. It will spread city to city, until it is finished or until it is stopped.

But another asked, Where will those who migrate go? Who will receive them, house them, take them in?

The men who killed, they also spoke again from within the television, from within the building where they were guarded, and together they said, Someone else, and, No one, and, We do not care as long as they migrate, as long as their migration quickens until it is finished.

Some others had less reason to stay or to return, and so they locked their front doors for the last time. Their migrations were the easiest, because their reasons to remain were the weakest—although they were not nothing—and still there was cost—and those without men or children or women left their houses and their apartments, and then those homes sat empty, their windows black accusations, and then no one would take their place, no one would move into their emptied but still-hot rooms, their fallow chambers of wallpaper coming unglued, come crumbling down.

■ ■ ■

In the courtroom, the men who killed were not allowed to wear their own clothes, and so each man sat dressed in the same colors, shod in similar shoes. They tried to appear changed, different from the days when they slept each in their own houses, beside their women or else alone, but different was not always an improvement—and when the photographs of the woman before and the woman after were shown on the screen only one of the men who killed cried—and then they were each called by name, were one by one sworn in and sworn at, and afterward the men who killed offered their testimony, which was of two parts, always or almost always.

We killed the woman, they said. We had warned her before. She shouldn't have been out so late.

During the day, she could have gone to the store or the laundromat, and we would not have seen her. We would have then been decent men, working men. Not yet the men who killed.

At night, we killed the woman, but it was her fault too, for being where she was not wanted, and if so then also it was her to blame for the death of her child, a bump we could not have known.

They should have left, said the men who killed. They should have migrated. They should have been quicker to do one or the other, they said, and all this was only always the first part.

■ ■ ■

Now the city was emptying, its citizens leaving by the freeways, and in the television the experts said there were no more jobs anywhere, not in the neighborhood or in the city or the county, not even in other states, and those who were migrating would not all find anything better than what they had once had.

One expert said this was the year the factories closed and then reopened, and maybe you got your old job back and maybe you didn't, but if you did it was not the same job anyway, not at least in matters of pay, of benefits.

And then his image was replaced by footage of the trial, of the judge and the men and the women of the jury, and also the men who killed, taking the stand and taking the stand, a progression of men who had killed, of those who were left, who had not been killed themselves by those other killers also imprisoned, the ones they were most afraid of—and again there were problems of rough description, problems of calling this rightly what it was, because so few men were made different enough.

Identifying marks, an expert said. This is how you tell them apart. There are tattoos and scars, each located on a particular part of the body, and each differentiated in purpose by class, by education, by neighborhood and affiliation.

Fear, said another. The tattoos are about fear.

But the men who were killed had tattoos too. Like the men who killed.

Yes, agreed the experts. Yes, and all such men are afraid of each other equally.

■ ■ ■

The migration continued, quickened by the trial, the reminder of the killings enough, and there were reminders everywhere in the neighborhood, even before the television began its broadcasts, its color commentary:

Here was the street where a father was dragged behind a sedan, the same model sedan he had once built in the days of his working, when there were still places in which work was being done.

Here was the alley bar where a brother was struck with a pool cue, a glass mug, a boot, where no one saw anything even with the blood sprayed, stained in dark-brown arcs across the billiard-green felt.

Here was the house where a son was choked with rope, choked out of his house and into the fenced-in square of his yard, where he was lifted into his only tree by the rope slung over the thickest branch. And when that branch broke first, then here was where they lifted him again and again, until a stronger structure was found to hold.

Here was the laundromat where the woman was leaving with her clothes in her basket, with her baby in her belly, a sliver curled beneath, and here was the distance away where we were too, we who must not pretend anymore that we were not there, and here was where we heard the sirens and here was where we were when we knew they wouldn't get there in time, and also where we never called out, never begged anyone to help, to stop what was coming.

Here was where we were, when we did not stop what was happening to these others, who were not us or ours.

Here was where we did not help because we did not want to be made to migrate too, here was where we decided whether or not to join the men who killed, our brothers and uncles and fathers and neighbors, who we had never stood apart from before, who now we would have to pretend we always had.

Here, and here, and also here and here. These were the places where we did or did not act, where we did or did not speak, and all around us remain the consequences of those actions or inactions: the migration, and also its quickening.

And if we cannot reckon with our lack of punishment, deserved for all we did not do? Then to require one who can be blamed until he might stand before us scapegoated, so his shape might be broken and his limbs torn from his unforgiven and sacrificial body, an act best accomplished by deed, or else by law and letters, the judgment of myth.

■ ■ ■

What the men who killed now knew: It was possible to be sure you were right and still to be punished for what you had done wrong. This is what they told themselves, when they were alone in their cells, through the nights stretched so long in the building where they were guarded, where their worst parts twisted in around the remains of the better.

In the courtroom the prosecution said there was danger in the men who killed, and if they would not claim it for themselves then it was the duty of the state to place it upon them. To set them apart and then to punish them for their apartness. There was evidence against them that could only be mitigated by matters of degree, by dividing accusations of who had held the weapon the longest, who made the most blows against the body of the woman, and this was the second part of their defense: not the difference between not guilty and guilty, but between this guilty and that guilty, the determination of which was worse, the killer who did most of the killing or the killer who waited from behind a steering wheel for it to be done, or the one who kept watch, ensuring it would not be interrupted.

One of the men said, I would never kill a woman. I could not look either, or stand too close to listen.

But the migration, he said. And so me, waiting on the sidewalk, watching the street, protecting my friends.

My wife left, he said. She took my children and I don't know where they went.

It wasn't her I was trying to make migrate, he said, and haven't I been punished enough, and this was the man who had cried, and now he cried again, and in his tears he knew it was not enough, that it would never be enough, and he did not know how to stop his begging, his wanting for what mercy he did not deserve or understand.

Another of the men who killed took the stand, and then another and then another, one who placed his hand upon a Bible and then denied placing his same hand upon the bat.

Only her mouth, said the man. I held her head in my lap, held her screaming inside her while the others did what they did, what I will not tell you whether they did or not, or who did what part.

I did not murder the woman, said the man. I only quieted her a while, until she was quiet herself.

Another admitted it was his bat—those were his fingerprints, among and under the fingerprints of the others—but he did not admit to anything else.

This man, he did not admit to swinging the bat over and over, did not admit to the breaking of the ribs and the breaking of the fingers and the breaking of the femur and the hip.

The bruising of the organs, the prosecutor said, and the man said, That wasn't me either.

And the baby, the man said. I had nothing to do with what happened to that baby.

The baby, he said, was someone I didn't even know, and why would I want to hurt what I didn't know?

■ ■ ■

Not all the men who killed had been caught, locked up, brought to trial. Still there was the one who remains.

The one who remains, still he was housed with his woman and his children, still he was employed at his place of work, still he was engaged in the drinking after, in dollar draughts and well whiskies.

The one who remains, he smoked or did not smoke. He marked his woman or did not. He loved his kids, probably, but maybe he did not even have kids—and we have to admit we do not know, we have not thought so far ahead. We argue that it does not matter. Whatever separated him from those around him, even those skinned as he was skinned, clothed as he was clothed, it was perhaps very little. Whatever it was, he could have been anyone. He drove a car or he took the bus or he walked, because his house like all the other houses stood in the shadow of the factory where he worked, the factory he'd told the others might cut his job, might terminate their employment at any time.

The one who remains, he might or might not have played ball, but either way he knew how to swing a bat.

On the television, he watched the prosecutor move his accusations across a chart, explaining the configurations of the men who killed, the proportions of guilt each might hold—but the figures did not add up, skewed inaccurate.

The prosecutor said, Someone is lying about what he did, but perhaps the prosecutor was wrong.

The one who remains, he sucked a splinter from his thumb, then the blood from the splinter's wound, what was left behind. When he removed his mouth, the blood welled, stained the skin around his thumb, darkened it darker.

The one who remains, his skin was the same color as the men who killed, his skin was different than that of those who would migrate, and it was the surface of a man only different by chance, and what differences there were within were believed to be of another category, created by a man's own designs, his own making—or else this was only what we told ourselves, and always the one who remains had been this way, a man who kills, even from the first of all the many times he moved among us.

■ ■ ■

In the television, we saw the men and the women of the jury, bored and restless.

The men and the women of the jury were united in purpose, anything but in mind. And what that meant for arriving at conclusions, consensus. And how there were some who believed in the guilt of the men who killed and some who believed only in the difficulty of their prosecution, in the lack of clear blame—and should the man who held the woman down be sentenced the same as the man who drove the car as the man who swung the bat, if that man was even on trial, a now doubted assertion?

What is proof, the men and the women of the jury asked.

What is enough proof, they asked each other, and their words seemed so familiar, and each man and woman worried at this, feared some assigned and acted-out role, but each day they said nothing to any other, and what good could these thoughts have done if voiced, and so despite their doubts they voted, and then the vote was split and then the men and the women of the jury admitted to the judge they had not yet made a decision and they were sequestered in rooms that did not contain their families when all they wanted was to go home to rooms that did. *Sequester* as a synonym for *imprison*. In the night the men and the women of the jury laid awake and this was the night they decided they would change their vote and then after all those long and stalling deliberations they at last voted as one, and then in the morning the men who killed stood to hear the foreman read the jury's decision, the foreman sweating with heat under his collar, a hotness that did not abate when he finished speaking, when the end of his speech set off what was always coming after.

Now all the men who killed were crying or else stricken silent, temporarily ghost white, and around them the room erupted into hot sound and hot fury, against which the banging of a gavel had no good effect.

■ ■ ■

On the steps of the courthouse, one of the experts faced the camera and said, Now the migration will never end. Now it will quicken and quicken and worsen.

Another said, The savagery of man. The fault of the police. The incompetence of the prosecution.

A third expert looked nervously at the camera, then nervously away. This is the summer of rage, he said. This is the summer of the furies. Now they will take to the streets, righteous and terrible, and who knows where they will stop.

■ ■ ■

The streets already hot when the verdict came down, now getting hotter, burning up with what rolled across their cracked and potholed surfaces: Heat coming out of television sets and radios. Heat coming out of car engines, out of automobiles long ago assembled by the men who had killed, by the same hands with which they had killed. Heat coming out of the doorways of their homes and the doorways of those who remained but not the doorways of those who had already migrated, whose houses sat empty, shut up.

Then the hot heat getting hot in Oakland, hot in Detroit and Flint and Saginaw, hot in Chicago and Mobile and Oxford and Cincinnati.

Then the hot heat getting hotter, hot in St. Louis and Bismarck and Lincoln, hot in Albuquerque, hot in Pittsburgh and Bethlehem and Baltimore.

Then the hot heat hottest in the neighborhood where the men who killed once lived, where their women and children lived still, where those who would migrate remained in great numbers, despite the danger and the anger, caught in the constraints of finance and gravity. And how hot they were now, at the end of the summer, at the end of the trial, at the ends of this city, at the terminus of one city the city might have been, and then the heat, the heat, the heat, consuming and containing and contained as it came up off the concrete and down out of the sky until it filled the space in between, and anyone caught on the street near burst with it, their skinned bones wet with sweat begging to get out, and when the houses were too hot to hold the men and the women and the children then each house was opened by the doors, and each spilled its inhabitants out onto the street, where they became a crowd—and then the crowd filled the streets—and then the crowd in the streets began to move.

■ ■ ■

The crowd in the streets moved not as one body but as many bodies moving together, and while some were angry at the sky others were angry at the ground. Some were angry at store windows and shattered them with bricks and stones and pipes and boards, some were angry at the objects inside the stores and so they smashed them too, or else carried some objects off into the streets, where they were also smashed or secreted away. Some were angry at automobiles, and so together they worked to overturn one and then another and another, and to set them ablaze, and some of the vehicles they burned were ones they had built themselves in the last days of their working, and in the flames of brake pads and air bags and child-safe seat belts there was burning some part of themselves.

Some were angry at their god, but whether they prayed or cursed there was no one to hear but themselves, all others made blunted, mad, and mute, smote dumb by watching.

Some were angry at those who most resembled the men who killed, and they dragged them from the cabs of their trucks or from behind the counters of their shops. And so again the killed and the killers became confused, and in their confusion they died or were made dead, and the city burned, and the men who killed were still not released, because it was not safe for them on the streets, and each man cried out in his solitude, for what was happening was stronger than he had ever imagined the migration would be, and he knew he had done his part to make it so.

■ ■ ■

The men in uniform were armed with weapons that did not kill but would injure, carried grenades that did not burn but would choke. They did not want to fire these weapons, or at least they did not all want to fire all of them, but then the crowd in the streets arrived, at first standing a distance from these men, a divide too small. On the other side a uniformed man with a bullhorn and a helmet told the crowd to go home, saying, No one needs to get hurt, but he said it with such a quaver no one had to believe him, not if they didn't want to, and there were those who did not, who would never again believe anything any man in uniform had to say. And so instead they threw their voices and they threw their rocks and they threw their bricks and when the men in uniform began to fire their weapons into the crowd then most of the crowd ran, but some few rushed the wall of uniforms and shields, falling beneath boots and batons wielded by men who were not supposed to kill unless they had to, unless they were threatened, but who nonetheless sometimes struck with the same force as the men who killed, broke bones in those who should have migrated, the same bones others had broken before.

■ ■ ■

And what now, asked some expert, sweating before the camera. And what next? What would there be? What could there ever be again?

■ ■ ■

The one who remains stepped out of a bar or a house or an automobile, smoking or not smoking. He knew where his woman and his kids were or he did not. He wore a shirt with his name on it but still we do not know his name, or else we will not speak it—or else it was an invention, and also it was invented that he had tattoos and scars, but not such that identified him for what he was, for who he is.

His hands were big, but perhaps his body was not. Again there was a baseball bat in his hands, probably, and steel sewn into the toes of his shoes, more than likely, and always there had been migration in his heart and always he had worked to quicken it, this separation of men from men, first alone and then with others.

The one who remains did not have his bags packed. The one who remains did not plan on running away. The one who remains did not know if he would be arrested, if his blows upon the woman and the baby would ever be properly counted and accounted for, translated into punishment, imprisonment.

The one who remains, he *remained*. He did not run, he did not move, he did not migrate.

The one who remains, this was his house.

This was his street.

This was his neighborhood, this was his store and his bar and his laundromat.

This was his factory, where he had spent all the working days of this life, where by some hard grace he worked still.

This was his city, and he would not leave it to those he wished would leave, nor would he forsake it to their music and their foods and the dressings of their different skins.

This was his city, as long as he remained, as long as he remained and they were made to migrate, quicker and quicker, and now he walked out among the others, a new bat hanging loose and easy from his hands, and at first he was not visible although he should have been, because everything he was made of cried out from the etchings of the lines of his face, from within the black parts of his eyes, and around him and ahead of him the crowd in the streets surged against a wall of shields, those men in uniform, and there was gas and rubber bullets and beanbags fired into and through the air, and everywhere the one who remains strode there was crying and running, and also fire, flames lit amid broken skins and broken glass.

The city burned, and the one who remains did not smile at the sight. His face was a slab of slate, his eyes a killer's eyes, black and blank. His movements were those of a ghost, and he thought of himself in this way, not flesh but this other thing, ghosted. The one who remains, this was his city, and yet he stayed invisible to it until he acted, until he swung the bat, until he connected its heft with the head of one of those he wished would migrate, and then there was blood on the wood, and there were splinters, and the action vibrated through his arms and into his shoulders, a feeling so quickly expanding it nearly split him, and perhaps it would have done so, had he not made of himself an empty room, had he not earlier pried loose so many other holdings, the ones that might have made him different than he was.

■ ■ ■

In the television there was video from the sky, video from the streets, and on the streets as in the television a man in uniform brought his baton across a teenage face and the crowd in the streets circled a car on fire, surrounded the shirtless man atop it, glory gory triumphant, and all around there was paint sprayed on the bricks and blood sprayed on the paint and there were killers in the crowd and also mothers and fathers and sons and daughters, revolted and revolutionary, and those who would migrate were the crowd in the streets but they were not all the crowd, and all there combined into one creed, and this creed contained among its verses the absence of love and god and the possible death of every man and woman and child and the destruction of the city, and the heat was still so hot the air shimmered and sung, and the men in uniform gassed the crowd in the streets and the crowd in the streets charged through the gas, and the houses burned and the fuel stations were firebombed and the fire trucks were not numbered enough and the men in uniform were not enough either and the crowd in the streets contracted and hardened, until it was all right to steal and it was all right to hurt and it was all right to sink to your knees with your hands in the air and your face streaming down your shirt and it was permitted to hold a trampled child and to comfort even what was not yours and it was permitted to rend your clothes when the gas streaked your eyes and you did not know which way to run; and it was permitted to run, so the crowd in the streets ran, so the men in uniform ran after, uncareful, each man maybe losing his head beneath his helmet so that he fired behind the backs of those who were running through the lists of smoke, who were falling to the concrete, bodies breaking upon the hard miles of the city even as the day dwindled toward the dark, and beneath the last rose of the dusk the one who remains continued on, further against the sundered city.

■ ■ ■

The one who remains, he swung his bat against some new skull and sternum, against some other femur and fibula, and all bones gave way beneath his blows, and those cracks were the loudest yet, and at last some others heard, at last some of us still scrapping turned to stop him instead, to stand opposed to what he was—and this is the story we tell ourselves about ourselves, a testimony sworn to, retold as often as we need it to be so, whenever we regret what else we remember we were: Down the street came a crowd made of one purpose, armed with bricks and stones and loud voices and bodies all around, and when the one who remains did not heed their call to stop they filled the air with more shouting, new throwings. When they reached his shaded shape they saw all he had caused, and in their anger they knocked him to the ground and they lifted him from off the paved earth and they pried at the bat fisted within his hands, and the furious crowd tried to identify his face but he was no one anyone would recognize because while his face was still whole he looked like everyone else, and because while there was difference in his heart it was not always visible on his skin, which did not color with blood the way others did, and he thought as he was struck how of all the made beasts only humans blushed, flushed with shame or excitement or fear, but even caught his face did not bloom, would not no matter how he might rage, and as the crowd in the streets and all around him became a single rushing awful mass, the one who remains declined again to flee, but turned into them instead, grinning a joyless smile, and as they beat him he gave up his fingers to be broken from off the bat and he gave up his teeth to be booted from his head and he gave up his cheeks to be dashed against the sidewalk and he gave up everything without giving up, and when they at last made him cry out the crowd in the street saw what they had become, and the one who remains saw too and was gladdened, even as his body came unsocketed by their hands, and by his long command he knew some in that crowd would yet die before the end of the day and some of them believed they would live forever or close enough, and those that lived would be the ones who remembered, and as the crowd in the streets left what was left, as they ran away from what animals they had made of him and of themselves, then they knew that at the end of those hot days there would be no answers and no punishment either, no reckoning except what remained of the migration, paused but not stopped, except the crowd in the streets cooled, removed from each other, made again those who migrate, made again the women and the children of the men who killed—and before the one who remains could die some men in uniform came down the streets in their helmets, locked side by side behind their shields to empty the crowd of its last resistance, and the flying rubber and stinging gas forced the people in the streets back home, back into their houses, each a powerless space where no lights burned, where no one waited for their return, where for some the word *home* would never apply again, and outside the city smoldered, and everywhere there was less than before, and it was not just people who could be made to migrate but all good things, and the sun and the stars and the moon were absent from the sky for a span, hidden by a foul tower of smoke—but then for some time the sun returned—and by its pink light other men found the one who remains, what of him there was, but they too did not know his name, nor how to recognize what was left, and some say that because they did not name him right then he never ended either, and some say he went ever on, anonymous, and the men in uniform lifted him onto a stretcher, lifted him broken into an ambulance, lifted him into surgery and repair and rest, and later he would leave the hospital unseen, wholer and still wrongly unaccused, and later the men who killed were for a time made free men, and all the city's citizens were unsatisfied anew, despite what they too had done, and at the release of the men who killed a new expert spoke, said the migration was not finished, that forever it would quicken and quicken. The migration did not require men to continue to kill but only to not stop killing, and walking among us there were some who never would, and at the last they might be all that there was, men who killed turning in upon each other until perhaps there would be only one, and all around that one some city like this city, ruined and burnt and spent, broken off its bones, heaving haggard its best breaths, and those gathered did not want it to be this way, wanted to cry out some rebuttal, but if there was another story to tell then it was lost to us that day, made wrong-shaped by our guilty intentions, and so still even our best-meant speech is often defeated, too soon turned again to wailing and to whimpers.

DEATH OF A MARRIAGE COUNSELOR

Eileen Pollack

LORETTA PULLS INTO THE LOT. JENNA CLIMBS OUT OF HER car and turns to thank her for giving her a lift. She is startled when Loretta gets out with her.

"I still can't believe you're seeing a marriage counselor who has his office in a railway station," Loretta says.

"It used to be a railway station," Jenna says.

"Are those or are those not railroad tracks? Are those or are those not hoboes?" Loretta points to two women with faces as weathered as reused lunch bags; they are walking on either side of the tracks, snatching up bottles and cans and chucking them into the black plastic trash bags they drag behind them. "Where did you find this guy, handing out coupons on Main Street?"

The rents down here are cheap, Jenna says. Her therapist can charge his clients whatever they can afford. Besides, she is not about to make an appointment with one of the fancy analysts who have offices in the tower above the fancy clothing store on Main Street. They make her sick, stacked like a bunch of Yertle the Turtles in some Dr. Seussian-Freussian pond.

"At least the turtles have their doctorates in psychology!" Loretta says. "What is this guy, an MSW? He's a social worker, am I right?"

Jenna isn't sure Dr. Neal even has an MSW. She only calls him "doctor" because otherwise her husband would refuse to see him. "I don't need someone with a psychiatry degree from Harvard to figure out what's wrong with my marriage. If I want to see Navajo rugs and Southwest pottery, I'll tell my troubles to Martha Stewart."

"That's exactly whom you should be telling your troubles to! Five minutes with Saint Martha and you would stop complaining about having a fantastically smart, hardworking husband whose only fault is that he spends too much time in the lab."

This is what Jenna has to put up with—everyone assumes that because her husband works in a lab, he must be curing cancer. What Stu does is study an infinitesimally tiny speck of DNA that codes for some protein that codes for some tiny part of the mammalian rodent eye. Apparently, there is a strain of dwarf mutant mouse, and most of these tiny mice are born with normal eyes, but every so often one comes into the world with no eyes at all, and Jenna's husband is trying to figure out why. He raises mutant eyeless mice. They cower in their cages, and Jenna's husband reaches in, he lifts them like a god, he yanks their tails and snaps their spines and guillotines off their heads and studies their DNA. That's why her husband can't pick up his two adorable children from day care. Or eat dinner with them. Or read *Horton Hatches the Egg* for the millionth time.

"You married a man who has a PhD in biology," Loretta says. "What did you expect, he was going to become a shoe salesman?"

"What about my degree?" Jenna asks, barely restraining herself from adding: I graduated from the Yale School of Drama. One of my plays was put on at the Rep. If we had stayed on the East Coast, I would have a decent career by now. "I'm a playwright," she says, "and I work for *Car and Driver*."

"Playwright," Loretta sneers, "playwright" being a word that no one—not even a playwright—seems able to say without a sneer. (You're wright! Jenna wants to apologize. I only play at wrighting!) "It's not as if you're not getting to write your plays isn't important," Loretta says, which leaves Jenna trying to untangle the triple negative. "But compared to curing cancer—"

"Cancer!" Jenna says. "If my husband were curing cancer . . . If I thought for a minute he could help our therapist."

"What's wrong with your therapist?" Loretta asks, and Jenna answers, even though she knows her friend will give her a hard time, because how can you not tell your best friend that your marriage counselor is dying of lung cancer?

"Oh my God," Loretta says. "Does he smoke?"

"No! Why do people ask that? He runs marathons. There's a photo of him climbing straight up a fucking cliff with his son."

"That is so sad," Loretta says. "I don't know what my Vera and Edna and Tolly would do if Barry or I . . . Ugh, I can't even bring myself to imagine it."

Actually, Jenna had been hoping Loretta would be able to imagine it. By bringing up her therapist's son, she hoped she might kindle some sympathy for the man. She is about to say this, but the two women collecting trash have worked their way to the section of track where Jenna and Loretta stand. The women give off the autumnal scent of smoke, moldering leaves, and stale beer, although it's possible the smell of beer is coming from the cans. The taller of the two hands Jenna a card that says, "I am a deaf mute," then motions back along the track, smiling and opening her eyes wide to invite Jenna's approval.

"Why yes," Jenna says, "it does look much better. Thanks for collecting all that trash." The woman smiles and nods, then motions toward Loretta, then toward the section of the track that lies before them. "I'm sorry," Jenna says. "I would love to help, but we don't have the time."

The shorter of the two, whose hair reminds Jenna of a hank of cheap gray yarn, croaks and says, "Oh, no, dear. She means we're going to Chicago. She's never been there before. We're planning a night on the town. You're welcome to come along. But I doubt either of you would make it very far." She points down. "Not in those shoes." The taller woman pats Jenna on her face, then signals excitedly down the track, at which she and her companion continue dragging their bags, stooping to pick up litter.

Loretta seems oblivious to this interaction. "You're going to stop seeing him, aren't you? Please tell me you are going to stop seeing this man."

"Stop?" Jenna says. "How can we stop?"

"It isn't depressing enough you come down here to Hobo Town once a week to talk about your dying marriage, you need to be treated by a dying man?"

Jenna hates to admit it, but she has come to dread these appointments. Every time she and Stu see their therapist, he's lost another fifteen pounds. His color has gotten worse. His cough . . . God, that cough. "But there's something else," she tells Loretta. "It's hard to explain, but the fact that he's dying . . . No matter what Dr. Neal asks us to do, Stu and I promise that we'll do it."

"Great," Loretta says. "That's just great. Don't you realize your therapist dying is perverting the entire process? Let me call Barry's cousin—he'll refer you to someone good."

Jenna doesn't bother to explain that she doesn't want to be referred to "someone good." Whenever she needs a doctor, a car mechanic, a plumber, she looks for someone who has spent his or her life struggling to keep up with the other doctors, car mechanics, or plumbers, believing that a lack of natural aptitude forces whoever it is to develop an entirely different set of skills. Patience, say. Stick-to-itiveness. An ear for the malfunctioning valve or blocked pipe. "Look," Jenna says, "if I thought Stu was finding a cure for cancer . . . But my husband couldn't cure a mouse of lumbago."

"He's working on a cure for blindness."

"In mice," Jenna says. She starts to chant the nursery rhyme, but Loretta cuts her off.

"I'm not saying you'll never get your chance. When the twins are in school and Stu has won his Nobel Prize, you can sit around in your bathrobe writing plays."

"Stu lives off grants," Jenna says. "The money could dry up any time. I can go days without seeing him. This is a man who says he'll be home for dinner at six and doesn't show up until seven—the next night."

"At least you know where he is."

"You sound like my father. 'He doesn't run around. He doesn't beat you up.' And Stu's mother! She said it's bad enough I complain about taking care of my own children, how can piddling around with my plays compare to anything her son might accomplish in his lab."

"Piddling? She used that word? Piddling?"

"The same word she used when we potty trained the twins. 'Irma? Max? Don't you want to go piddle in the potty for Grandma Glen?'"

"Oh, sweetie, I am sorry. I want you to stay with Stu. But not because your therapist is dying." She gets back in her Volvo. "I do like your plays. It's just, if you left Stu, would you get to see him more often? Would you trust him to take care of the twins? You made your bed, sweetie, and I am afraid you are going to have to keep lying in it. With your nerdy but might I add utterly adorable husband."

It occurs to Jenna that she never asks her friend's advice because she doesn't want to hear it. Loretta's mother named her after the movie star

Loretta Young, who, in the fifties, hosted a television show in which she waltzed out in front of the camera in a fabulously stylish gown, introduced that week's episode, then waltzed back at the end to offer the moral of the story, embellished with a quote from Shakespeare. Jenna's friend does the same thing—the waltzing in, the moralizing—and people take it from her because, as Loretta's mother hoped, she grew up to be both beautiful and stylish. Or tall and blond and well-off, which are much the same thing. But Jenna finds herself chafing at the morals Loretta offers. She would rather die than end one of her plays with a moral. All you really need is a memorable parting line: "I have always depended on the kindness of strangers." Or "Attention must be paid!"

By now, Loretta has driven off—if she was going to offer another moral, Jenna didn't hear it. The wind picks up, sucking leaves in its wake like an invisible train, and Jenna thinks the real trouble with her therapist having his office down here is that she can't stop seeing the tracks as the backdrop for a play. All those miles of steel rails, stretching to infinity, threatening to come together but leading parallel lives forever. A stagehand blowing a harmonica. Whoo-whoo, whoo-whoo. The train that carried Jimmy Rogers home.

Disgusted with this descent into melodrama, she forces herself to go inside and take a seat on one of the benches. Jesus, couldn't Dr. Neal have put in a few chairs? You can still see the space above the door where the schedules must have hung. You can almost see the bald guy in the visor selling tickets. To pass the time until her husband shows up—late, Jenna hopes—she rehearses that week's complaints. But then, because Loretta is right and she shouldn't be looking for reasons to leave her marriage, she forces herself to tabulate the reasons she should stay. For instance: the biology class Stu insisted she sign up for in college, the way it opened her eyes to all those worlds within worlds, entire cities of Whos living on specks of Whovilles, carrying out their intricate little industries of nitrogen fixation and photosynthesis. Also: the many weekends Stu took the train up to New Haven to accompany her to all those masterfully staged productions by all those masterful old masters—Beckett, Brecht, Chekhov, and Chayefsky—whose names Stu said reminded him of the wheezes and hacks on a ward for consumptives; the way he leaned forward in his seat, eyes wide, as if he, too, were glimpsing worlds he hadn't known existed; the way, during the final act of one of her own plays, Stu wiped away his tears before rising from his seat and clapping, which, Jenna is moved to recall, inspired at least a few other audience members to do the same.

Unfortunately, this leads to the grim truth that Stu can no longer stay awake even on the rare occasion they hire a sitter and go out to see a movie. And these aren't snoozy French existentialist dramas she's talking about—these are blockbusters in which the White House and Statue of Liberty get blown to smithereens. A few weeks ago, Stu walked the twins across the street to the neighbors' Halloween extravaganza. By seven, when Jenna turned out the lights and headed over to join him, he was stretched out in the middle of the Sampsons' hardwood floor while a frenzied herd of seven-year-olds raced around and stepped over him and the children's parents eyed Jenna as if to say, Is Stu all right? Shouldn't you do something?, until Jenna wanted to scream: What should I do? Drape a sheet over him and say he decided to come as a corpse?

Something flashes by and Jenna looks up to see a man on a bike—it's like the scene in *The Wizard of Oz*, except that, instead of a witch, the rider has the shape of someone Jenna could love. When he comes in, they exchange a hug made awkward by the helmet he is carrying and the backpack on his back. Then again, it is no more awkward than the hugs she has seen soldiers exchange with their wives, and hasn't Jenna always been moved by such reunions? What if she were the wife of a marine who had just spent a year in Iraq? Would she complain about her husband's absence then?

"Jenna," Stu says. "I'm sorry, I should have called."

"It's fine," she says. "You're only a little late."

"It took me hours to get hold of someone at the consulate who could extend Daniella's visa. She's the best technician I've ever had. If Daniella gets sent back to Haiti—"

"I like Daniella," Jenna says. "I would hate to see her get sent back." The relief that crosses Stu's face makes Jenna feel even worse than the cringe that came before. "But maybe you could have called the consulate earlier in the day?" Stu cringes again, and Jenna says, "No, I know, you had no idea how long it would take."

"Right!" Stu says. "With places like that, bureaucracies . . ." He glances at the clock. "When I didn't see the car, I thought you'd given up and left."

"The muffler?" she says. "The transmission?"

"Oh," he says, "right. But then, how did you get here?"

"Loretta?" she says.

"Oh, right. Loretta. That was nice of her. How's Barry?"

Barry? Why is Stu asking about Barry? Stu thinks Barry is pretentious, and Barry can't stand the way Stu can't or won't make small talk, not even about sports, but if someone mentions anything to do with science, you can't shut the guy up. As for Jenna, she would rather share a house with a man who keeps his thoughts to himself than a know-it-all who can go on for an hour about the relative merits of the two wheels of French cheese he brought for that night's dinner. "Barry is Barry," she tells her husband.

Stu motions to Dr. Neal's office. "He hasn't been out?"

Until now, Jenna hasn't acknowledged how worried she is. But seeing that Stu is worried, she realizes how worried she has been all along. "Do you think we ought to do something? I'd hate to be standing out here while he's in there . . ." She can't bring herself to say, Lying dead on the floor. "Stu," she says, "do you think you could tell him we want to see someone else?"

Stu plucks the bicycle clip from his leg. "I guess. He did tell us at that first appointment—"

It hadn't been at their first appointment. Back then, she and Stu had just assumed their therapist had the flu. It wasn't until their fourth visit that Dr. Neal told them he had been diagnosed with a recurrence of his cancer. He gave them the option of switching to a colleague. But what were they supposed to do, take him up on his offer? "Yeah," Jenna says, "but he also told us he intended to beat the odds."

"The odds," Stu says. "As if anyone with this particular form of cancer—"

"That doesn't matter," Jenna says irritably. "If someone tells you he intends to beat the odds, you can't very well come back with: Well, we don't think you're going to win this particular bet. He said it himself—there's nothing he would rather do with however much time he has left."

"And the income," Stu says. "If all his clients stopped seeing him, how would he support his family?"

"Well," Jenna says, "his wife could support them."

"Right," Stu says. "Except their son is, what, sixteen? Seventeen? They'll need to pay tuition."

"I'm sure Dr. Neal has life insurance."

"Life insurance," Stu repeats, and Jenna guesses that once again he has forgotten to sign them up for a policy. She is about to tell him that if he doesn't sign them up for life insurance she will kill him, but she wouldn't write such an obvious line for one of her characters, so why write it for herself? Besides, their therapist has just poked his head into the room.

"Sorry, guys. I dozed off. It's this last round of chemo. I'm fine in the morning, but by this late in the afternoon . . . You two are my last session. Just give me a minute. I'll duck in back and make some coffee."

"Sure!" Jenna says.

"Sure!" Stu echoes. "Take your time!"

But when they hear his cough echo from the back room, Jenna covers her ears and says: "I can't stand it! I can't stand listening to that cough! Not while we sit there and complain about such trivial shit."

Stu nods. "If nothing else, you want to make the poor man happy."

"Right!" Jenna says. "You don't want him to go out thinking he failed."

"But that's crazy," Stu says. "It's not as if we're throwing him a good-bye party and we're thinking of what gift to get him."

Jenna stops, struck that sometimes her husband does come up with perfectly good lines of his own. "You're right. He told us himself—a marriage counselor's goal isn't necessarily to ensure that a couple stays together. He said a victory might consist of an amicable separation. A husband and wife caring for their children like two responsible adults."

"Yeah, but you know what?" Stu says. "That's the same kind of goody-goody lie parents tell their kids so the kids don't care who wins the T-ball tournament."

"When was the last time you went to a T-ball tournament?"

"You only notice the times I don't show up."

"Fine. You went to a T-ball tournament. The point is, Dr. Neal said our staying together isn't necessarily the outcome he has in mind."

"But how could he want a couple like us not to stay together? And Jenna, it's not as if I want us to split up. You have to know, I would do anything to keep us together."

"Anything except—"

"I told you, I can't give that up."

"Taking off a few hours a week isn't giving up a career!"

"Yes! That's exactly what it is. Do you think it's just me? Do you think I'm the only one there on Saturday nights? Do you think I can just kick back and tell my experiments I'm taking the afternoon off?"

"Jenna? Stu?" Dr. Neal appears at the door, his head so white and vulnerable it might have been sculpted from papier-mâché. Inside, he lowers himself into his chair and tries to find a comfortable position. To avoid watching, Jenna looks around the room, wishing Loretta hadn't made that remark about Martha Stewart, because now all she can see is the hideous plaid sofa on which Stu has taken a seat, or the rubber tree by the window—so neglected Jenna needs to stifle the urge to trace "dust me" on the leaves—or the bookcase with the veneer coming off, the titles indicating that their therapist hasn't read anything more current in his field than *Sybil, I Never Promised You a Rose Garden*, and *I'm OK, You're OK.*

"Stu?" Dr. Neal says. "Why don't you go first."

Stu picks up a geodesic puzzle—other weeks, he has chosen the Rubik's Cube, or the plastic square with tiles you shift to form a picture. "Uh, sure. This week went better than I expected. I finally figured out what was wrong with that gel. The enzyme was bad. Daniella was worried about getting her visa renewed, and she forgot to make a fresh batch. Once we got that straightened out, I mailed off my paper to *Cell.* But that made me fall behind on the grant I was telling you about." He shrugs. "If I stay up most of tomorrow night, I can get it done."

"Stu? When I ask how your week went, it's okay to talk a little about what's going on in your lab, but mostly we're here to discuss your marriage."

"Right," Stu says. "Sorry." He sits there working at the wire puzzle, as if, should the pieces line up, all their problems will be solved. "You know, it's not as if I'm the one who has any problems with it."

"I understand that," Dr. Neal says. "As long as Jenna is happy, you're happy."

"Exactly! But she never is happy! And I don't know what I can do to make her happy. So I just go around feeling bad all the time. And I don't even know why I feel bad."

"So you stay in the lab. And Jenna here feels more and more . . . Jenna, how does it make you feel when Stu doesn't come home?"

How does it make her feel? It makes her feel like a fucking shrew. She has said all of this so many times she can't bear saying it again. Instead, she tells Dr. Neal about the last time Stu forgot to pick up Irma and Max from day care. "I rush in, they're sitting there, trying not to cry while some poor woman who earns minimum wage stands looking at her watch. And you know what they say? Don't be mad at Dad. My life has been reduced to a title by Dr. Seuss. There's *One Fish, Two Fish*. There's *Hop on Pop*. And now there's *Don't Be Mad at Dad*."

"Are you mad?"

"Of course I'm mad! I feel mad, and sad, and very, very bad. I feel mad and sad and bad all the fucking time."

"Does she think I wouldn't rather be at home playing with my kids?" Stu says. "How could she not know how much I love the kids? If one of them got sick, or if Jenna came down with, you know, a debilitating disease, I would give it all up. But if Jenna really loved me—"

"I wouldn't ask? If I did ask, you wouldn't do it!"

"She keeps cutting me off," Stu says sullenly. "Just because I'm not as—"

"God," Jenna says. "A person could grow old and die waiting for you to finish a sentence."

"Jenna? You promised you wouldn't—"

But Dr. Neal can't finish his own sentence. He coughs and coughs, until Jenna blurts out, "Sorry! I do cut him off. Go ahead, Stu. I won't—"

"No, no," Stu says. "It must be frustrating to sit there and listen to me try—"

Their therapist struggles to his feet and goes out for what Jenna assumes to be a glass of water. To pass the time, she gets up and studies the photos above his chair. "Did you ever want to do anything this dangerous?" she asks Stu.

"They're wearing ropes. It's not as if—"

"I'll bet Dr. Neal doesn't really like to climb. He only climbs because his son . . . You know—if you can't beat 'em, catch 'em before they fall off the cliff?"

Stu gestures that Dr. Neal is coming back, and Jenna hurries to her chair. "Your son," she says. "He's what, seventeen?"

"Michael will be nineteen come August."

"Does he still . . . ?" She points to the photo.

"Climb? Oh, yes. He's very good at it. He's taking the year off to work for one of those Outward Bound type tours. My wife arranges them for her clients."

"He's out West? Doesn't he want to be with you when—" Horrified, she catches herself.

"A young man needs to live his own life. Your children may seem very vulnerable to you now. But when the time comes, when they're as old as Michael—"

"I guess," Jenna says. "It's just hard to imagine them so old. Although, if we hadn't . . ." She looks at her husband. "We never told you this, but when Stu and I were younger—"

"Jenna, don't." Stu sets the puzzle on the table. "I knew you would find a way to work this in. No way we were going to see a marriage counselor and this wasn't going to come up. Honestly, I don't see the relevance. Why can't you just—"

"Forget it? You want me to forgive you everything. You want me to take care of the kids. You want me to be patient, patient, patient. You want me to wait to write my plays until the kids are all grown up and leave for college. It's just a hobby, right? That's what everyone thinks. When Stu and I were engaged, his mother threw a lunch in my honor, and one of her sorority sisters took me aside and said it was a good thing that I had a hobby because being a doctor's wife could get lonely and wasn't it nice that I had something to keep me occupied. As for her, she painted rocks. Not that there's anything wrong with painting rocks! My own mother suggested I combine my talent as a playwright with my experience as a mother and write plays for schoolchildren."

Dr. Neal holds out one absurdly thin arm. "And what's wrong with—"

"About a squirrel! There was this squirrel she'd seen hanging around the bird feeder. And it didn't have a tail. My mother suggested I write a children's play, in verse, about a squirrel who lost his tail."

"You say that with such scorn."

Oh no, Jenna thinks. Not you, too. Aloud, she says, "Do you see anyone asking David Mamet to write a play called *The Squirrel Who Lost His Tail*?"

"Of course not. But if drama for adults has value, then why not drama for children? Dr. Seuss has had more of an impact on our culture—"

Again, he is cut off by his cough. When he has finished hacking, Jenna says, "I get what you're saying. Dr. Seuss has probably had more of an influence on more generations—"

"Jenna, you do not need to placate me. I'm not saying you ought to write plays for children. I'm making the case that Stu isn't the only person in this room who doesn't value what you do."

"Oh, you are both so full of crap," Jenna says. "If Dr. Seuss thought it was such an honor to write doggerel for children, then why did he cook up that pseudonym? Why the fake medical degree?"

"Touché," Dr. Neal says, laughing.

But Jenna takes no delight in winning. Dr. Neal just likes to prove he isn't taking Stu's side because they're both men.

"Stu, don't you think Jenna has the right to be angry if you don't pick up your children?"

"No!" Stu says. "I mean, if I were doing it on purpose. If I were doing it to be lazy. If I were doing it because I'm sexist."

Jenna is about to say, Of course you're sexist, but she sees their therapist shift in his chair. Stu must notice, too, because he says, "She has the right to get angry. I just wish she wouldn't exercise that right."

"No, I get it," Jenna says. "I should be more understanding. Because you don't mean to forget."

"Right!" Stu says. "You have the reason to be angry. But if you would choose not to be angry . . . All day, I'm running, running, there's one emergency over here, and another one over there. Then I come home, and it's like living in a wind tunnel. The wind is howling around my ears, and I don't have the slightest room to . . . I can't so much as . . . breathe."

Dr. Neal nods. "You feel as if you're a rock getting buffeted by the wind. And Jenna, you feel like the angry wind that's always howling around that rock." He motions toward Jenna. "The wind feels frustrated." Then he motions toward Stu. "And the rock feels buffeted by the wind. But Stu, I have to say, the rock gets the better deal. The rock never needs to change. And don't you think it might get frustrating for the wind to be living with a rock? Trying to make the rock listen? Trying to make it budge?"

Jenna wants to hug the man. At that moment, she loves Dr. Neal far more than she loves her husband.

"Of course," their therapist says, "the wind might be better off if it realized how futile it is to keep howling at a rock. The wind might realize some other approach is called for. Because Stu isn't going to change, Jenna. Most people don't. You knew when you married Stu that he was going to spend most of his time in the lab."

When he says this, Jenna can't help but see Loretta nodding with satisfaction. In fact, she sees Loretta walk right through the wall of the train depot and stand where she would be standing if this were the play Jenna wishes she had time to write.

> LORETTA: I don't mean to rub it in. But, sweetie, how much writing are you going to get done if you leave Stu?
>
> JENNA (grumpily): I don't see why it's always the woman who gives in. (To Stu.) You think you're such a feminist. But you know what you want? A selfless little wifey like Loretta.
>
> LORETTA: Wifey? I made *Law Review*! I got hired by the most prestigious litigation firm in the Midwest!
>
> JENNA: Yes, and you quit the minute Vera was born. I know, you hated the hours. The partners were assholes. But to give it up? Admit it, it was just easier to stay home and let Barry pay your way.
>
> LORETTA: That is so not true! Just because you have no compunctions about leaving your children with strangers. The women who work at places like that, what do they care whether my little girl takes her insulin? Is it so wrong that I prefer spending time with my kids to defending the phone company from a lawsuit by the cable company?
>
> JENNA: If you love your kids so much, why aren't you home with them now? If you're such a concerned mother, why don't you take your morals and your advice and waltz the fuck out of my therapy session right now, okay? (Loretta makes a face, but Jenna gestures toward the wings and Loretta exits.)

"You should have married someone like Loretta," Jenna tells Stu. "Someone who wasn't so fixed on her own career."

"But the thing I loved about you was that you had something you felt passionately about!"

"So I wouldn't bother you in the lab?"

"If the positions were reversed—"

"But they so rarely are. All these years, and no one has gotten around to reversing the positions."

"I don't think Jenna questions that you're passionate about your work, Stu. What she wants to know is that you're equally passionate about her."

"I would give up everything, if I had to. I just—"

"You trust me not to ask. Which means you aren't really prepared to give it up!"

"I would," Stu says. "It's like when God said to Moses—"

"Abraham," Jenna says. And when Dr. Neal raises his eyebrows, or the space above his eyes where his eyebrows would be if he hadn't lost them to chemo, she explains that it was Abraham, not Moses, God asked to sacrifice his son.

"Whatever!" Stu says. "God wanted to test how much Abraham loved Him. But Abraham had to know that any god he loved wouldn't put him to such an impossible test."

"That's bullshit," Jenna says. "It's easy to say you would make a sacrifice if you know you'll never be called on to do it. You would never give up your lab. And I would never ask you to give up your lab. But you expect me to sacrifice what I love every single day." She turns to their therapist. "Do you know what he asked me to do? We're not talking about Abraham maybe being asked to sacrifice Isaac."

"Here we go," Stu says. "She always tries to blame me for—"

"Whom else should I blame?"

"I'm a little out of the loop here," Dr. Neal says.

"We would have had another child," Jenna explains. "A grown-up child. He would have been twelve by now. Or she would have been twelve. We were married, Stu. It wasn't as if you got some idiot teenager pregnant."

"Stop it," Stu mutters. "Did I take you there by force? Did I hold you down? I shouldn't have asked. But you didn't want that baby any more than I did."

"Jenna? Any comment on what Stu just said? That you wanted the abortion?"

"I didn't want it. No woman wants an abortion."

"Poor word choice. You didn't want it. But you were as reluctant as Stu to have a child."

Jenna feels the room vibrate, but she can't tell if this is because a train is coming, or because her heart is hammering in her chest. If only she could have afforded to take time off from the botany magazine where she had been working. If only she could have counted on Stu to help. If only the managing director at the Rep hadn't hinted that if she finished and revised her second play, he would make sure that Al Pacino and Edie Falco saw the script. How could she have squandered that opportunity? But how could she have admitted that she wanted to abort a pregnancy so she could finish a play?

Then again, what if she had aborted a pregnancy to complete *MacBeth*? Or *The Cherry Orchard*? Or *Death of a Salesman*? "All I know," she says, crying, "is that whenever I look at Irma and Max, I wish that we had had that child."

"Honey," Stu says. "I didn't mean to accuse you. I can't believe I took you to that place, then brought you home and put you to bed and went back to the lab. You were so white. You were obviously in pain. But I felt so guilty. So helpless. I didn't know what to say."

"So you left Jenna and went back to the lab?"

"What was he going to do for me?" Jenna says. "I told him he might as well go in and save his damn gels."

"But you didn't mean it," Stu says. "Even I knew that. Bad enough I went back to the lab. But then, going off to Paris."

Jenna looks out at the graffiti-splattered shed across the tracks. "Why shouldn't you have gone? I didn't want to see you anyway."

"A genetics conference," Stu explains. "I was supposed to present my first big paper, and I couldn't make myself give it up. But when I got there, all I could think was . . . I skipped the poster session. I was sitting on this bench, and all these beautifully dressed French children . . . I called and tried to tell Jenna what I was feeling. I tried to tell you, Jenna."

"It was the middle of the night," Jenna says. "He woke me up, and I didn't understand what he was talking about. Something about the Tuileries, a little girl in a frilly dress. What did you think, Stu? I was going to go back to the clinic and tell them, Oops, my husband made a mistake? Some things can't be undone, Stu. You can't just whip up another batch of enzyme and run the experiment a second time and get the results you want."

Stu starts to say something, but the therapist cuts him off. "Undone?" he says. "You want to know what can't be undone? What I've got, okay? That's what can't be undone. The two of you could just get up and go home to those two beautiful children—You could— You could—" Dr. Neal writhes in his chair. He doesn't cough. He doesn't seem to be able to cough. He doesn't seem to be able to breathe.

"Oh my God!" Jenna yells. "Stu! Do something!"

Her husband springs awkwardly from the sofa and eases their therapist to the floor. "Call 9-1-1!" he says. But Jenna is still trying to understand what is happening. She has this odd impulse to walk over and nudge their therapist with her foot. It's like one of those nature shows where elephants gather around a prostrate member of their herd and murmur uneasily, prodding it, caressing it with their trunks. What does an elephant know about death? What does Jenna know? She has never seen a dying man. How can this wonderfully engineered if wildly improbable conglomeration of chemicals, cells, and enzymes simply stop working? Shouldn't she be able to prevent this from happening, the way she once saw Max about to roll off the changing table—until then, neither of the twins had been able to roll—and she screamed and lunged forward and caught him, not at the level of the changing table, but an inch above the floor?

"Jenna!" Stu yells, and she pulls out her phone and dials.

"Hello?" she shouts. Someone on the other end says something, and Jenna stammers what she believes to be a coherent message about their therapist collapsing in his office in the old railway depot at the corner of Novi and Third. "He has lung cancer," she tells the dispatcher. "My husband is giving him CPR."

Except that Stu isn't doing anything of the sort. He is kneeling beside their therapist as if he, too, has never seen a dying man. Dr. Neal's fine white hair floats from his scalp like waves of heat, or spirit, or soul. His glasses are askew, and with the lack of eyebrows, it's as if his eyes have been erased. When Stu unbuttons the top buttons of their therapist's light-blue cotton shirt, Jenna flinches. The skin on Dr. Neal's chest is the same blue as his shirt; the ribs poke through, and every time he gasps, the muscles twitch in a way Jenna can't bear. Do something! she thinks. Why can't her husband do something?

And that's when it hits her. If you're lying on the floor, struggling to breathe, or if someone you love is lying on the floor, struggling to breathe, you would much prefer that the world be filled with doctors and medical researchers, even researchers who spend their time curing blindness in mice, than a bunch of fucking useless playwrights.

An ambulance sounds from what Jenna can't help but think of as offstage right, and she revises her opinion. If you're lying on the floor, trying to breathe, you don't want a playwright or a scientist. What you want is an EMT.

Dr. Neal is no longer moving. Stu puts his ear to the man's chest. "No," he whispers. "No."

Jenna wonders if their therapist is dead, but suddenly, in a movement that nearly shocks her off her feet, Dr. Neal throws open his arms and rasps, "Michael! I have you!" And Jenna thinks: Yes. That's exactly what it's like to be a parent. Even when you are dying, all you can think about is your son falling off a cliff, and you not being there to save him.

A pair of EMTs blunder in. The men huddle with Stu, then apply an oxygen mask to the therapist's face. Maneuvering the gurney to the door, they knock the coffee table and send the puzzles on its surface flying. Jenna runs after the men, then watches as the EMTs slide Dr. Neal into the ambulance. She feels such an overpowering tenderness for the man that she confuses him with her husband. The tall, dark-haired stranger standing beside her is just some passerby who doesn't know any more about first aid than she does. Why is he still here? What does he want? Why doesn't Jenna have a car so she can follow the ambulance to the hospital and sit beside her beloved, cancer-ridden husband, hold his hand, make sure that he doesn't die?

"Now you see why it's safer for me to be working on mice," Stu says glumly.

Jenna stares at him as if she is seeing him through the wrong end of a telescope. From such a distance, he seems infinitely pitiable. She wants to reach out and take him in her arms, if only her arms would reach that far. More than that, she wants to start loving him again. Shouldn't she be able to do that? To start loving him again? The nauseating truth is that one day Stu will die, as Jenna herself will die, as one day—she can barely force herself to think it—Irma and Max will die. What do any of their piddling—yes, piddling—grievances matter? Why shouldn't she and Stu simply love each other—and love their children—while all of them are still alive?

But that doesn't sound right. Just because you and your spouse are going to die, your differences shouldn't matter? That would mean that anyone who had ever married anyone else should stay married to that person, regardless of what either party did.

"You don't think he did it on purpose," Stu says. "To keep us together?"

Jenna shrugs. "If you're right, that was quite a performance." Again she feels the urge to put her arms around him. Or maybe what she wants is for him to put his arms around her. But that would be cheating, wouldn't it? To ask her husband for comfort after all the terrible things she said?

Instead, she goes back inside to retrieve her purse. Stu trails after her. He picks up his helmet and then his backpack. But neither of them seems able to move. They stand there, stricken by their therapist's empty chair, until it seems to Jenna that someone is reaching inside her chest and squeezing grief from her heart, pumping it like an accordion, and the wailing from her heart is filling her chest, filling the room, until yes, the train is coming, and then the train is there, the train is passing a few feet from the building, not the Amtrak from Detroit, but a freight train waddling to Chicago with its load of who knows what. Looking out at the rusty cars, Jenna experiences that unsettling sensation where the train seems to be standing still and the room is what's moving. Years ago, Stu used this phenomenon to illustrate the theory of relativity. If he were on one train and Jenna were on another, and they each looked out their window . . . But Jenna had lost the point of the illustration because all she could think was that if Stu were on one train and she were on the other, she would jump off her train and onto his.

She looks out again and is startled to see the faces of cows peering between the slats. Do the cows know what awaits them in Chicago? Do they think they are headed there for a night on the town?

"Jenna," Stu says. "I would trade everything I know to be able to describe what it feels like to have a man dying in your arms and not be able to save him. Or the twins . . . I can't even describe what I feel about the twins. I need you, Jenna. I need you to—"

"Finish your sentences?"

"No," Stu says. "I can finish my own sentences. What I need for you to do is . . . Look, there's no excuse for me forgetting to pick up the kids. But if you'll cut me some slack. If you'll try to be more forgiving. If you'll try to see things more from my—"

"Perspective?"

Stu nods, and Jenna thinks that if this really were a play, she would be tempted to have the Stu character ask whether they couldn't stay together, if not for his sake, then for—

JENNA: The twins?

STU (nodding): Right. The twins. But not just the twins. You know. For— (He motions to the empty chair.)

JENNA: You mean for Dr. Neal?

And the Stu character would say: Right! For Dr. Neal! But the truth is, she can't bring herself to write such soppy claptrap, any more than she can go through any of this again—listening to their therapist cough, wondering if he is going to keel over and die right here in the office. If he isn't already dead.

The last few cars of the freight train rumble by, and the silence is jarring. There's so little time for anything, Jenna thinks. To write a play. To cure the blindness of a single mouse. To figure out what's out there, beyond the bars of the freight train that's taking us to Chicago. But where does that leave any of us, she wants to know. Was she supposed to go through life without children just because society hasn't yet evolved to the point where a woman can raise some kids and still have time to write a few plays? What if she hadn't married Stu? What if she had stayed single? What if she were the one lying there on the floor, gasping for breath? Who would call the ambulance? Who would administer CPR? Who would be the one to write the perfect parting line for her?

CRETIA'S GAL

Bill Harris

1.

Saturday, April 1, 1854. Caledonia Plantation, Mardalwil County, Alabama.

It was cloudy that morning. It would be raining by that afternoon.

At the top of the hill inside Highland House in the drape-shrouded parlor Sophy's boy baby, Cretia's Gal's charge, crawled in random patterns through the thick legs of the pianoforte.

Cretia's Gal, twelve, active, intelligent, lady's maid, accustomed to cleaning, waiting on table, sewing, sat straight-backed at M's Esme's shiny instrument. Her eyes closed, her dark fingers, choreographed by the echoing in her head, rollicked in the air above the keys in an exact replica of the capering patterns played last night by the French man.

Untutored, she did not know the melodies' names, their origins, nor their forms. Being under strict and direct orders from M's she had never touched the piano keys, other than with a feather duster.

Sophy's boy baby, the inattentive audience for her pretend concert, cooed, and crawled in random patterns through the piano's legs.

2.

M's Esme, bemoaning boy Jube's stupidity, reprimanded his response to every order as they pruned and patted in the formal garden. She was unable to see for the life of her why she put up with the oddling little nigger. Whistling as if gabbing to himself; dumb as a fish; couldn't speak a word—never had as far as she knew. What she should do is send him straight to the fields, see if McCready could teach him a thing or two.

Maybe his muteness was why she put up with him. Meant he couldn't complain or lie like the rest of them.

Her constant wiping of her brow with her kerchief and the sleeve of her tunic had knocked her bonnet slightly askew. It tittered on her head like the cornfield scarecrows. The sight was enough to make Jube want to laugh.

She did not listen, boy Jube thought. She did not listen to nothing, to no-body. Not even to her uncle Goodsire half the time, not to the Candytufts, who wanted to be in the sun, or the Bleeding Hearts, who did not, or the Foxglove, who wanted moist soil, or the Fragrant Solomon's Seal, who could stand dryness.

She had listened last night though. To that French man's drumming piano playing, pounding like the thunder of heavenly horse hoofs galloping out of the body of the pianoforte. His music stampeded out of the parlor and off in all directions: down the entrance lane, and off through the gardens and fields and orchards and forests and low quarters and swamp of the Caledonia's three thousand or so acres. She heard and listened to that pianoforte being played last night, all right, and instead of cooling with the mirk of night he could see it had simmered and rerisen in her, renewed with the graying dawn. She was still angry from it, snapping like a bulldog on a short chain.

Jube sat on his haunches. He patted dirt around the seedlings.

Earlier, as every morning, he was back from his ramblings, as they called them, and finished with hauling the cookhouse fireplace ashes and replacing the firewood, in time to see Cretia's Gal as she came down the stairs to empty M's Esme's chamber pot.

She had signaled to him that there might be trouble from the mistress because of last night.

3.

The nerve of him, Esme thought, dark-eyed man that he was, bringing that–that savagery (she refused to call it music) into the parlor, extolling. It condoned the vile and the ugly instead of evoking tears and flutters of the heart. That was what music should be. Instead, what had come out of the pianoforte pounded, thrust, heaved, and throbbed like something back of the barn in the middle of the night. Vile. It was an insult to music, an offense to civilization, contemptible to a White person's home. The parlor must be aired of it, the same as if a skunk had spewed its spray from corner to corner.

Uncle had no business bringing that dark-haired, dark-eyed man with the foreign name and fancy ways into the house in the first place. Bringing him from off, like so many of the other items or gifts Uncle brought on his return from his travels away from Caledonia. They were never quite the right size, style, or shade, but all the same he brought them, proud as a cat depositing a fetched dead rat.

4.

Unmindful of the quiet in the house, or the muffled reprimands of M's Esme toward Jube in the near distance, and without Cretia's Gal realizing it, her hands, weighted by the echoing music in her head, lowered themselves and made contact with the keys that she was forbidden to touch other than to gently run a feather duster across them once a day.

Her fingers ceased their air dance and were still for a moment, as still as the house, and then, to her surprise, her fingers began to move to touch the forbidden black-and-white keys, moving in the exact patterns that Monsieur Gottschalk's had moved last evening as she played exactly what he had played.

5.

Esme felt a raindrop on the back of her hand. She had to will herself not to lick it off. Instead, she snapped at boy Jube, contradicting her last order.

He silently did as he was told. Till, for an instant in the graying morning, he sensed all sound cease—the cheeping, peeping conversations of birds; the impatient worry of the sodden wind whispering to the young leaves about the rain to come and the resultant rustle as it brushed past, and the scurry and hunkering down in the undergrowth; the moist plop of the scattered *smirr*; the wanting fragmented lilt of distant field-hand shouts; the sounds of work from the house; the lo and bark and whinny—ceased, and Jube raised himself from his hands and knees to a squat. He tensed like a hound at the anticipated hunter's shot, and then–sound again: the rhythmic pounding burst from the parlor through the window and doors.

Music.

At the first notes Esme looked up and around, her nose angled like a hound's at the smell of prey.

She might have pretended not to listen to the piano playing last night, Jube thought, but she heard it this morning, without pretense.

Esme thinks it must be a conspiracy of some sort. Cretia in on it. Snuck *Monsieur* Gottschalk back and inside to provoke her. After he and Uncle had arisen before sunrise to start off on horseback for the distant train and finally to New Orleans. This, yet another attack on her patience by her body slave, this time direct rather than the usual nerve-racking, slow-grinding, day-by-day insolence.

Esme spat a single word as she took off running, rushing, a raised storm toward the house as if lightening had struck the tail of her dress, and she rushed straight through the bluest anemones and the Indian pinks, toward the parlor where the piano was.

The word was, —Him!

6.

Cretia's Gal, still only hearing the echoing sounds in her head, was the only one in earshot of the piano not to realize it was she who was actually playing it. Playing for the first time in her life.

Polishing the pianoforte was her favorite household chore. Smoothing the oiled cloth back and forth about the dark wood: The part with its gold-scrawled letters spelling Boardman & Gray, which her mama Cretia had taught her to read. The top that lifted to show the wires and little cotton-covered heads of the hammers inside, the curved sides, the heavy carved legs, until it reflected her own darkness back at her. But never touching the ivory-and-ebony keys except to feather dust them with maternally possessive strokes. Warned about it by her mother. Threatened about it by M's Esme. To never fool with the piano keys. Never. Playing now, note for note, the music the French man had played the night before. With the same enthusiasm and volume. The same pounding, rhythmic drive.

M's Esme, her bonnet clutched in her fist, her forehead wet from rain and sweat, entered looking about, stern and confused by what she saw and did not see. Jube was on the porch, at the open window, looking in at Cretia's Gal.

—Where is—? *Who?*

Cretia's Gal stood, wide-eyed as if shaken suddenly from a sound sleep. She stood looking at her hands trembling in spite of her tightly intertwined fingers.

There was a moment of almost hesitant embarrassment, as if each of them had caught the other engaged in a shameful activity, but neither of them, for the moment, knew what it was or what they should do.

—Where is he? M's Esme demanded, unsure this time. She looked at Cretia's Gal.

Sophy's baby cooed, and crawling on his hands and one knee moved toward the woman, then stopped and plopped on his behind and sat looking from one of them to the other, as he began sucking his right index and middle fingers.

—Who was playing that piano? Esme asked.

Sophy's baby made a gurgling sound as he pulled his fingers from his mouth and pointed them toward Cretia's Gal as if he were answering the woman's question.

—You, she said to Cretia's Gal, whether or not she was convinced on the strength of the baby's identification. —Did you play that piano?

The girl stood, looking down at her hands.

—Answer me.

The girl looked up at her mistress.

—Do not stand there looking at me. Did you play that piano?

The girl didn't move.

—I want to hear you play something.

Still did not move.

—Do what I told you.

Cretia's Gal was confused, not sure that she had played, and if she had that she could do it again, and if she did, what she could or should play, nor what would happen then.

Sophy's baby rolled back to his hands and knees and scooted back under the piano as Cretia's Gal did as she was told and sat at the instrument. She closed her eyes and began playing not what the French man had played, but the tune that the woman staring at her from the doorway had been practicing for the last few days.

—No, M's Esme said, almost calm, as if Cretia's Gal had misunderstood her request. —Not that. The other. Play like him again.

Cretia's Gal did.

Cretia, who had not been there, was now, in the parlor doorway.

—*Who taught you that? Who? Her?*

—No-body, ma'am, Cretia's Gal said, her voice steady.

—No-body . . . ? To Cretia: —Was it you?

—Did a'body teach you? Cretia asked her child, reassurance in her voice.

—You do not answer me by asking her a question, M's Esme snapped at Cretia.

—If you'll let me I'll find out, Cretia said.

—I'll find out, M's Esme said. —From her. Or I will send her to the fields. Now who taught you, and when?

—No-body, ma'am.

—Then how did you learn it?

—I do not know, ma'am.

—Are you a mockingbird?

—No, ma'am.

—Then a'body taught you, and I will find out, whoever it was, on Caledonia or not. They made a terrible mistake. That mistake will be paid for. Do you all hear me?

—Get me Mister McCready. McCready, she said to Jube. —Get Mister McCready!

Jube looked to Cretia. Cretia nodded slowly, indicating for Jube to go, but to take his time.

—A'body take her, M's Esme said, indicating Cretia's Gal, —and get her out of my sight, and keep her somewhere till McCready gets here.

Jube ran out into the rain.

M's Esme moved to the piano and grabbed the child awkwardly by the wrists. Cretia's Gal did not actively struggle nor did she passively resist. Her body, for the instant immobilized by fear, confusion, and dawning astonishment, was simply dark flesh, blood and bones, an object with weight and form occupying space.

In M's Esme's attempt to pull the child away from the instrument, the force of the girl's nonresistant but noncompliant mass caused M's Esme to stumble a step forward and hit her hip against the squat black instrument, and in a lurching half roll, attempting to regain her balance and avoid stepping on Sophy's baby crawling from beneath the piano, she caught her foot on one of its bulbous legs, and with a grunt, pitched headfirst, like a feed sack shouldered from a wagon bed, her left hand, nearest the piano, grasping at but hitting and dislodging the slanting vertical rod bracing open the angled piano top, opened last evening by *Monsieur* Gottschalk, striking it with the full weight of her forward fall and thus with sufficient force to dislodge it, causing the blunt force of the shined solid-mahogany top to slam down with a gunshot-like report, as she, to break her awkward fall across the baby, jammed her wrist against the floor.

The wire strings in the instrument's shuddered innards raised a whining quiver, like the after-shiver of an ax stroke in the trunk of an oak tree. It droned in an eerie harmony to M's Esme's cat-like howl.

Cretia knelt beside her, gripping her uninjured forearm.

. . . and Esme looked into the great twin pits and was consumed and sank deeper than the lowest hell into their burning blackness and the sorrows closed upon her, she was naked and empty, and in her distress she heard them say, there will be slaughter and overthrow, and all that is solid will perish, and the foundations will be compressed into dust.

M's Esme swooned, her face as white as late May cotton.

In a few minutes M's Esme regained consciousness to the sight of Cretia's Gal staring at her. Her eyes. —*Malocchio,* she almost screamed. She covered her eyes with her uninjured right hand and screamed, —Face her to the wall. Turn her away from me. Face her to the wall. Convinced of what she had suspected all along—the girl had *Malocchio*. The evil eye.

Cretia's Gal's just-displayed sorcery of perfectly played passages from Monsieur Gottschalk proved that she was somehow connected with evil. It was the only explanation of the piano playing. M's said she did not want to set her eyes on Cretia's Gal again until she had been punished. Hoping that being whipped would drive the evil out of her. The gal had never, as far as she could remember, had a beating. That was what had let the dark spirit get in her. That and her sullen mammy, of course.

7.

The word went down: Bring them up. Bring them all up to Highland House after supper.

Just for the beating of a child?

Must be more to it to be called out in the rain.

When there was bailing out and patching up to be done.

Some: Let's just get it o'er with. So we can come back and get on with our doings.

Some: Just a child. E'en if Cretia's Gal.

Some: She needed to be taught a lesson. Same as ev'rybody.

They went, motley, sodden. Grudging.

The paths muddy, the grass slick.

Trudged up from the bottom in twos and threes and random clots and clusters, nigh, they hoped, the chafing end of a galling day.

8.

Esme wore the sling Cretia had fashioned from a piece of an old petticoat. The swelling was gone and there was no pain even when she flexed her wrist, but she had retied the sling as a reminder to herself and to them.

A lighted lantern on the table behind her, she sat in her second-story window seat and looked down on them as they slowly assembled in the yard.

Their coming together looked to be as resented and labored as her journey to understanding the thing that had until the last few hours preoccupied her life.

9.

—She's mine, Cretia repeated.

—We'll know whose she is when I write my name on her back, McCready said. Then to Asch and Caesar standing on either side of the girl's mother: —Now get Cretia out of my sight, and lock her down. Or I swear I will beat the skin off all of you, first to last!

—Do not let him, Cretia said, a statement to anyone.

Nowhere nigh a proper plea, M's Esme thought. Ought to make her stay and watch. But something warned her not to.

—Whup me! Cretia ordered. —Not her. Me! As she was hauled away by the two mechanics.

—Hold some light here, McCready said. —I want to see what I'm whupping. Don't want to waste my time whupping air.

A couple with lanterns moved closer, the rings of illumination bobbing like fishing lures on a black river.

Cretia howling like Bryce's dogs, Jube, half-bare, thought, and we standing here. No better than bales of wet cotton.

Cretia's Gal sank to her knees and Moon and Odum laid her facedown on the ground.

Seeing Cretia's Gal whipped, hearing Cretia's screams, Jube was, for the first time, and only for an instant, glad he had no parents to witness their child being beat.

During, Cretia's Gal remembered once, after a scolding by M's Esme, when Jube, whistling to himself, had seen her crying and had shown her what at first she thought was how to listen to plants grow–lying flat against the earth, each of them with an ear to the ground, until she had shook her head and admitted no, she couldn't hear a thing, and he'd laughed and shook his head.

No. That was not it.

—What then?

He had pointed at her then and wiped his fingers under his eyes and shook his head to show no tears. She had realized that because of his diversion she not only was no longer crying, but that she had forgotten all about her hurt.

She had smiled at him.

He had nodded and put his hand to her lips to stop her from speaking, and at that instant M's Esme had shouted for her lazy bones, and she had turned and run for the house, but when she looked back before entering he was gone. Disappeared. As he could do. Leaving not e'en a silence where he had stood.

The drizzle wetting her lash wounds, Cretia's Gal laid, her face in the mud.

She listened for the sound of grass growing.

But e'en after the whip had ceased its snap and slash and Cretia had stopped screaming and had gone to McCready's cabin and returned to Highland House, they still heard her in their sleep, in the bottom, in the grieve's house, and in the main house too. Screaming.

—*She's mine*!

10.

Cretia was weary. Slave weary. Too tired to spit or swat a wasp.

She had done what she could. Tonight, and the thirteen years that had come before, when each of those days and nights her primary purpose and thought was to get Cretia's Gal away to possible freedom. She did not e'en consider her good fortune in having had her child for that long to teach and give hope to. Many mothers did not have half that. Many had nothing.

But was it enough? Had there been time enough? Nagged like sore joints or dreams of flying. Was there an *-enough-*?

She remembered her own mother.

Saint Thomas Caribbean woman, carried into southern slavery.

Cretia born in slavery, but bred on her mother's stories of revolt in the Caribbean and of freedom in the north, stories passed on to Cretia's Gal in fact, parables, and sewing riddles as they had been passed on from Cretia's mother to her.

Would the child call on the lessons? Could she use them? Would they serve her? Be her guardians?

Once Cretia's Gal was gone, Cretia would never know. Had known that from the beginning.

Would never again see her. Or hear word of or from.

Who would she be? Where?

She would never know.

Never.

Never.

That was the way of it. To be sold away was, for those left behind, a beginning that had no end.

Cretia was weary tired.

All she wanted now was quiet, and the strength to wait and to gather her strength, for when McCready came back without her child she would kill, she would be strong enough for that by then.

11.

Jube watched Cretia. He did not know what she would do. He did not know what he could do.

He remembered the sound only a few hours ago of the liquid being squeezed in the gourd and her word in the black of the cabin as she soothed the girl. —Remember, was the only word she said, and something had passed between them, mother to daughter, something that he had not been able to see.

In the moments before their final separation they, with McCready and Jube in half shadow watching them in the lantern light of the servant's cabin, mother and daughter had moved without looking at each other. It was as if they had long ago rehearsed the moment of their parting, and ev'rything necessary had been settled between them.

As McCready led Cretia's Gal out, to take her to his cabin and then away, Jube was gone.

It was raining again.

12.

Jube was crouched, hunched on his haunches at the edge of the cornfield. With his naked arms wrapped around his naked knees he watched Cretia's Gal in the illumination from the faint lantern light from McCready's cabin. He marveled at how erect she sat on the surrey seat, waiting as McCready loaded his second satchel into the surrey.

Jube had been planning, as soon as he had time, to make up a secret language just he and Cretia's Gal could understand. It was to have been a language without words. Thought talk. So they could speak anytime, whether they were together or not. She in the house, him in the garden, she on her pallet, he on his.

He closed his eyes and imagined it was in the morning, after the *pour*. He and Cretia's Gal would be in the stable, watching a mama cat deliver a litter of six, as they had done one time, and in their secret, no-word language he would say to her, —What can go round the house and look in ev'ry window, but do not make no tracks?

She would smile at him, and without shaking her head would say she did not know.

—Guess, he would encourage her.

She would think some more, and still smiling would say-think she couldn't guess. —What?

Then she'd hear him think-say: —The sun.

Cretia's Gal would turn her head slightly, but still looking at him, and still smiling, admiration shining in her eyes.

—Ask another one.

Then he'd say-think: —All right, what goes all around the house and do not make but *one* track?

They'd go through it all again, Cretia's Gal looking at him and smiling in wonderment.

Finally he'd tell her: —A wheelbarrow.

She'd wonder how he knew so much . . .?

Jube opened his eyes as he heard McCready close the door to his cabin. The lantern was out. It was dark.

McCready's hound yipped once as its master hiked the surrey horse.

Man and girl rode off in the rain.

Cretia's Gal was gone.

Mud-covered and naked, a beating in his chest like Ashe's hammer on the anvil, Jube blinked in the downpour, and licked the tears and raindrops from his lips.

13.

A candle in the center of the dirt floor.

Cretia and Jube sitting cross-legged, side by side.

—We've had it hard, she said, —from a baby up.

She told him a tale he did not understand, that her mother had told her about a rat in a barrel of uske. A cat helped it out and the rat ran away through a borehole; and she went on, telling him about her mother's life in freedom in Saint Thomas, and about her own life. She went on and on in the flickering light but all he could think of was moving through the dark after Cretia's Gal and being with her and dreaming about freedom they would run away to one day, e'en if they had to move through the darkness with her clinging to him, feeling freedom just thinking about it. Cretia saying she understood, she understood how he felt, could feel how he hurt because she had hurt, just like him. Telling him to let it go. Let the past be the past. Let it fall away like petals from a stem, let it go, or it would forever hold him down, telling him to be proud of the way he had learned to walk the dark. Be proud of the way he could help flowers grow. She was rubbing his hand and she was crying and he was crying, and they were crying together and he was breathing, breathing as if it were his first breath, as if he'd been slapped, had the breath slapped in him, and she was rubbing his hand, and he was breathing, and his face was wet but he was not crying anymore, and his head hung down, almost to his lap, and he was breathing, just breathing, not crying, not hurting, his eyes closed, sleepy, and she was rubbing his hand, and he was as tired as he had ever been. She put something in his hand, smooth, round, and cold, and he clenched it in his fist. A bead.

Was that what she had given Cretia's Gal? He wondered as he slumped sideways and laid his head in Cretia's lap . . .

14.

Cretia did not sleep.

Cretia looked up, as if she had been called. Not snappish like from M's Esme, but soft, like a butterfly, or a whiff in the air. She eased Jube onto the floor and moved to and opened the door. Listening. Alert. Trying to still her mind and concentrate amongst all the confusion of the past day. She closed her eyes against the night darkness and inhaled deeply, holding it as she felt her blood in her veins. She exhaled, thinking of rippling water. Lifting her face, eyes still closed, thinking of her mother, thinking of star glint. Motionless for a moment. Listening. For something beneath the night stillness, something softer than the silent pulse of growing, and sleeping for renewal . . .

She opened her eyes.

She nodded.

Yes, she thought.

She breathed easier.

But she did not sleep . . .

. . . Jube slept.

Dreamed honeysuckles. Growing out of his chest, and dogwoods sprouting from his mouth, red, orange, yellow, purple and pink, and roots growing from his hair, his fingers and toes, and running away, faster than Bryce's dogs, to connect with roots growing from Cretia's Gal, and he thinks her name, and for a flash Cretia's Gal is there: a butterfly glimpse as she, darting from one room to another, smiles like the North Star. It is like the sugary dance of candy on his tongue, and he thinks her name, and she hears him in camellias and evergreens.

But when he awoke he lay with his head in Cretia's lap, the bead in his fist, and Cretia's Gal was there, but Cretia's Gal was gone.

THE TATTOO

Bonnie Jo Campbell

AT THE COUNTY FAIR, MACGREGOR BOUGHT A LONG STRIP of tickets from a man with one arm, and he and Silvie Ross climbed aboard the Tilt-A-Whirl and then the Zipper, the Starship 2000 and then the double Ferris wheel. They swooped, circled, and spun so wildly that they all but set themselves free from gravity. As they perched momentarily at the top of the Ferris wheel, MacGregor kissed both of Silvie's flushed cheeks and then her lips. Beyond her pretty bare shoulder he saw the whole world stretching out, full of possibility. Then the huge contraption heaved them toward the earth, and MacGregor, caught up in the excitement of falling, shouted, "Marry me!" He didn't even consider that they'd only been dating a few months or that he had no ring to offer her. Apparently Silvie didn't think of these things either, because at the bottom, she said yes. The embrace that ensued on the way back up nearly knocked off MacGregor's glasses.

As they reached the top again, MacGregor glimpsed his home to the east, a quarter mile from the fairgrounds, the house he'd just inherited from his parents, may they rest in peace. He held Silvie close and pointed out the visible bit of gray-green roof not shaded by the big sycamore tree; they couldn't see the white clapboards or the dark-green trim, but recognizing that familiar place just now, just after the woman he loved had agreed to be his wife, brought tears to his eyes. His parents had lived in that house until seven months ago when they were killed in a car crash in Nevada, their first vacation since visiting the Wisconsin Dells on their honeymoon. MacGregor had never meant to be president of MacGregor Ball Bearing Inc., where he had worked every position from delivery boy to engineer, but he knew that fifty-three employees, including Silvie, the head of accounting, were depending on him to keep the company going.

MacGregor and Silvie returned to the ground and took their time moving along the midway, seeing each other in a new way as they strolled through the balmy evening, holding hands so as not to lose one another in the throng of teenagers and families. They stopped at the shooting gallery, and MacGregor went first. He picked up the BB gun and aimed. The tin bird cutouts seemed to slip around even while he had them in his sights. Then it was Silvie's turn. When she aimed, MacGregor marveled at her solid stance, her heavy mane of nearly black hair, and her slim figure that felt strong and sweet in his arms. Her first, second, and third shots hit home, and she chose a polka-dot snake and wrapped it around her neck.

"I'll put this behind the door to stop drafts in winter," she said.

She was the practical one between the two of them. People said MacGregor was a daydreamer, not suited to run a company, but with Silvie at his side, he thought he just might be able to do it.

At the coin toss, it cost MacGregor four dollars to win a shell-shaped ashtray.

"I can help you quit smoking, you know," Silvie said, dropping the ashtray into her purse. "And if you do, it'll take down the company's insurance rates." She had wanted him to quit smoking since he'd met her, but it meant something different to him now that they were going to be married. For the first time, he felt as though he could really kick the habit.

They entered a tent with a sign advertising a "World of Natural Wonders" in which they saw a tiny pony, too small to be ridden even by a child. A young carnival worker came in while they stood there and put a striped kitten on the pony's rump, and the kitten lay down and curled up sweetly there. There was a goat with five legs, a calf with two heads, a pig so fat it couldn't stand, but MacGregor felt uneasy looking at the animals' deformities and their drooping eyes. Just past the mirror maze, they found another tent with a sign whose peeling paint read, "The Illuminated Woman."

"I'm not sure," MacGregor said when Silvie pulled him into the line. He felt shy at the notion of ogling a tattooed lady in front of his bride-to-be.

"Oh, don't be a prude," Silvie said. Silvie, his future wife! Her face was incandescent in the fading light. He wrapped his arms around her and lifted her off the ground. He'd long known her mind to be sharp as an ax—though she was only thirty, just three years older than him, his father had made her head of the accounting department—but until they'd started dating, he hadn't known how kind she was, and how much fun. His mother used to accuse him of living with his head in the clouds, but this was the closest he'd ever come to feeling that buoyant.

He doled out a few more tickets, and they entered the twelve-by-twenty-foot tent. MacGregor expected to see a big woman posing in a bathing suit, her skin covered entirely with tattoos, but the woman in profile seemed of average height and size, and she wore glasses. She seemed young, or certainly no older than MacGregor. She was paying no attention to the half dozen carnival patrons in the tent, who were mumbling and pointing at her, but was instead engaged in writing in her notebook. Her hair was pulled into a sensible bun, and she wore a backless black evening gown that revealed the brilliant colors stretching from her tailbone up to her hairline. MacGregor noticed that the images on her skin appeared to be moving.

"They must be playing a film on her back!" Silvie said, moving closer to the burgundy velvet rope, of the type found at old-fashioned movie houses. It was the most elegant piece of equipment at the fair, MacGregor thought, but it kept him eight feet away when he wanted to move in and get a closer look. The sign dangling by a gold chain warned that patrons stepping over or under the rope would be *violated.* He stood behind the woman and waved his hand around, trying to locate the beam of light from the projector he thought must be directed at her.

Playing across the young woman's back was a scene of a man and a boy paddling a canoe on a pristine river. Aspens quaked in a light breeze, and weeping willow tendrils dragged in the water. MacGregor leaned over the rope and saw fish moving beneath the surface, dozens of speckled trout and whiskered catfish. It'd been years since he'd been fishing or canoeing, though he and his father had gone most weekends in the summer when he was a boy. His father had loved being outdoors, and it pained him whenever they found trash caught in a snag or saw the remnants of a dirty campsite on a sandbar. Now, in the scene on the young woman's back, a blue-eyed, dark-haired boy in the front seat turned, and MacGregor started at the sight of the familiar face. Could it be him? Could that man in the back of the canoe with the round face and salt-and-pepper hair be his father? Oh, how he missed his father! Was that his mother, waving from the riverbank? Was there some alternate universe in which his parents were still alive to advise him?

Silvie elbowed him and pointed out a pair of mallards landing on the river, and MacGregor shook away the crazy idea that his own life would intersect with a carnival illusion. In a matter of months, the momentum of his decisions would carry him down a road he'd never anticipated traveling. He was the president of his father's company! About to marry a bright, beautiful, accomplished woman! When he was the age of that boy in the canoe, he'd dreamt of being an astronaut, of exploring other planets and maybe even alternate universes. But it had been a foolish desire, considering how poor his vision was and had been since third grade; astronauts, like all pilots, needed excellent eyesight.

"This is just marvelous!" Silvie said, her face aglow.

MacGregor loved seeing Silvie enthralled, and so he often feared he was boring her with his melancholy talk about his parents and his musing about the properties of ball bearings. Just today as they'd driven to the fair, he'd been explaining to Silvie how radically they could reduce friction and extend equipment life through the use of enhanced surface finishes and special coatings.

"Look, it's changing," Silvie said. The young woman's back seemed to waver, and then they could make out an old-fashioned steam train coming around a curve. It passed through a stand of woods, beyond which a herd of deer was grazing on the side of a hill.

As the train chugged over a river, MacGregor pointed to the tattooed woman's shoulder blade, upon which a couple was eating drumsticks and potato salad.

"Maybe that's you and me," MacGregor said.

"We look very happy and handsome," Silvie said, jokingly.

MacGregor could tell from the way that she put her hand on his arm and sighed that she was ready to leave the tent. But he wanted to stay in order to understand how the pictures were forming and reforming. To him it didn't seem like a movie. For starters, the movement was slow, and the scenes were perfect in every detail, and when the scene had changed, it hadn't done so abruptly. For a moment it had seemed each cell on the surface of the woman's skin contained both the previous image of the river and the new image of the train, before becoming fully the train and its landscape. MacGregor couldn't help thinking the scene was moving by some power of the young woman's body. As he watched, the man and woman on the picnic blanket moved away from one another. Their faces had gone serious. The man's eyebrows were drawn down, and the woman seemed to be saying something angrily. What might they be arguing about? He took Silvie's hand and pulled it to his heart. What could they possibly argue about in such a beautifully illustrated world?

As MacGregor and Silvie watched the scenes move across her back, the tattooed woman remained engaged by whatever she was writing. MacGregor tried repeatedly to get a glimpse of her notebook, but each time he adjusted his position to see over her shoulder or past her arm, she would shift slightly (deliberately?) and block his view. He was moving along the velvet rope, his eyes on her curved profile, when, without warning, tears began streaming down her cheek. The hand holding the pen continued to move across the paper as she quietly cried.

MacGregor stepped back a few feet from the rope.

"Poor girl," he said to Silvie. "It must be exhausting to be in a sideshow."

"Well, at least she's got a job," Silvie said. "I worked with girls like this in Scouts."

"Girls like what?"

"Girls without a solid upbringing," Silvie whispered. "A job helps them make sense of their lives, helps ground them."

MacGregor nodded. After being a Girl Scout for years, Silvie had volunteered as a troop leader, and she now sat on the local board of directors. She was a woman who cared about the people around her as much as she cared about the figures in the red-and-black columns at MacGregor Ball Bearing Inc.

"Let's go look in the 4-H animal barns," Silvie said and moved toward the exit. "I love seeing which chickens and rabbits won the blue ribbons."

MacGregor looked over his shoulder at the Illuminated Woman one last time and saw the father and son in the canoe again, except that now the canoe was plunging over a waterfall, and the fiberglass canoe was crashing onto the rocks. Half of the canoe bobbed in the frothy water where the limp bodies of the father and son floated. MacGregor didn't turn away until Silvie took his hand and led him out of the tent.

That night, MacGregor lay alone in his bed, unable to sleep after the excitement of the day. He had tried to persuade Silvie to stay with him, but she'd wanted to go home and call her mother to tell her the good news. When MacGregor closed his eyes, he saw a brief image of Silvie's face, but then that image wavered and he saw again the colorful visions on the Illuminated Woman's back, the water flowing more dramatically, more realistically than real water had ever flowed. The sun shone on the river to make it sparkle, to reveal the gleaming fish below, and the man and boy in the canoe sparkled too as they paddled. He saw once again their broken bodies at the bottom of the falls and felt again the sorrow he had experienced that afternoon, but he had never been afraid of sadness in a story. The last image, the ruined canoe bobbing alongside those bodies, made him think and worry and reflect. He didn't know why the story of the canoe trip had been interrupted by the story of the train, unless someone from the train was going to see the tragic scene and make a wise observation.

He wondered what stories would play across his body if he had such a tattoo. Maybe the images would play out the history of ball bearings, culminating in his future successful development of new hybrid ceramic ball bearings that operated so smoothly they would last a thousand years without lubrication or replacement. Maybe an image would appear of his crowning achievement: a machine the size of a three-story building that purified polluted air using almost no energy—he and his father had invented the bubbling, humming antipollution machine during one of their jaunts on the river. He imagined cars that flew along the ground and then rose up into the sky effortlessly. He imagined a rocket ship taking off, its destination another galaxy. Then he saw Silvie shimmering in her wedding dress. He saw his mother's wedding ring gleaming on her finger. He hoped he and Silvie would be as happy as his parents had been, growing closer and more affectionate over the years. He wanted Silvie to gaze upon him with pure delight, as his mother had gazed upon his father, as his father had gazed upon his mother in return.

The following afternoon, Silvie was tied up with an audit and had to stay late at work. MacGregor kissed her good-bye and started to go home but then decided to return to the fair. He walked along the midway with his hands in his pockets. He bought a short string of tickets and handed them over at the entrance to the tent of the Illuminated Woman. There was no one else inside. He approached her with his eyes focused on the grass so as not to get distracted.

"How are you doing that?" he asked from behind the velvet rope, but got no response. "Psst. Hey, miss? Please. Is there anything you can tell me?"

"Why are you interrupting me?" the young woman said, and her simple clear voice charmed MacGregor. She spoke with an unfamiliar accent, and he wondered where she was from. This afternoon she was reading a big book called *Greek Mythology*.

"How are you making your tattoo move?" he asked. "What's the trick?"

"Can't you see I'm working?" She barely glanced at him before shaking her head and going back to her reading. MacGregor saw that there was a light shining on the pages of the book. He realized that the light was coming from a tiny bulb she wore on her necklace. He admired it because he liked to read in bed, and something like that would come in handy. Silvie read too, but only for fifteen minutes each night, which was exactly how long it took her to read a chapter of one of her romance novels.

"Do you spend all day in this tent?"

"My aunt and I trade off. Not that it's any of your business."

"Don't you get bored?"

"How could I be bored?" She nodded toward a stack of books and a smaller stack of spiral notebooks on the table next to her. MacGregor kept looking at her, and she finally put down her book, turned to him, and pushed her glasses up along the bridge of her nose. "What do you want?"

"A tattoo like yours. Just a small one." He saw that her glasses were as thick as his own. His mother had told him he'd ruined his vision by reading in the dark.

"Do you want to be in a sideshow?" she asked, narrowing her eyes.

"Heck, no. I'm a company president."

"You're too young to be any kind of president." She glanced over at the entrance, as if to assure herself nobody else was looking in.

He blushed. "I know. My father died, and I inherited the company. I shouldn't admit it, but it doesn't really play to my strengths." It felt strange to say it out loud. "But I'm trying, because I know he'd want me to."

"What about what you want?" she asked. "What would you be doing, you know, if you could do anything you wanted?"

"I'd be in space. On my way to Mars."

"You'd better write to your senator, then. The human space program is in the toilet." She softened her words with a smile, and he saw she had a blemish, maybe a pimple, on her chin. She unpinned her hair, which was almost as dark as Silvie's but uneven, with stringy bangs. She combed her fingers through it, pulled it up again, and repinned it with her barrette. After all that, it looked the same as before.

"I have written my senator," he said. "And my congressperson. And the president."

She continued to smile at him. "Your shirt is buttoned up wrong," she said.

"Oh." He unbuttoned and rebuttoned.

"Usually when men undress in my tent, I call security."

"Oh." MacGregor realized he should have turned away from her.

"So you think you want a tattoo like mine," the young woman said. "Well, you'll have to talk to Madame Needles in the fortune-telling tent. She's my mom. Tell her you're a company president. But don't let her see your socks, because they don't match."

"Oh. OK."

"But don't say I didn't warn you. Madame Needles takes things very seriously. She won't even pay me unless I take all my vitamins every day. She's obsessed with vitamins, which means I get to burp up fish oil for the first two hours of every shift."

MacGregor thanked her, and the young woman went back to reading, and finally MacGregor let himself look at her tattoo. Today she was wearing a purple evening gown, and on her skin there appeared a woman with snakes for hair, and MacGregor watched, mesmerized, as they twisted out from her scalp. One of the snakes lunged out suddenly and snapped at him, and he jumped back with a yelp.

A big man came into the tent and told MacGregor his time was up.

"We don't allow screamers in here," the big man said.

When MacGregor didn't move away from the velvet rope quickly enough, the man grabbed him by the arm and pulled him out of the tent. As the man dragged him along, MacGregor saw that he had a tattoo on his biceps and that the tattoo was an image of the man himself. In the image, the man was flexing his biceps. MacGregor was pretty sure those tiny biceps also featured an even tinier image of the man, and so on.

"Did Madame Needles give that you that tattoo?" MacGregor asked.

"Get lost."

MacGregor found the tent with the sign "Madame Needles: Tarot, Fortunes, and Body Art," and when he stepped inside, he found a small plump woman whose skin shone with a strange golden hue. Her hair too, which at first had seemed gray, was gold. Or maybe it was the angle of the sun as it pitched toward the horizon.

He introduced himself and said that the Illuminated Woman had sent him.

"And what can I do for you?" Madame Needles asked, a bright curiosity in her eyes. MacGregor didn't believe in future-telling, but he felt a bit disappointed that she didn't already know. He explained that he wanted a tattoo.

"I'm looking for a husband for my daughter, Mr. MacGregor," she said. She grinned and her teeth were pure, shining gold. "And for that reason I'll give you a beautiful tattoo. You are the first man she's ever sent to me."

"Well, I, ah, I want the tattoo. Very much," MacGregor said. "But I'm already engaged to be married."

"I don't see a ring." She sounded like her daughter, but it wasn't a strange accent; it was more that both women made each sentence seem like the line of a song they happened to be singing.

"But men don't usually wear engagement rings," he said. Or did Madame Needles somehow know that he hadn't bought Silvie a ring yet? "And it's true. We'll be married next May. She's a wonderful woman, my fiancée."

"You seem very single to me, Mr. MacGregor, and May is nine months away."

"Your daughter seems nice. I'm sure she could date if she wanted to."

"Nice? Ha!" The woman stood and shook her head. "She's an impossible child! She's twenty-five and she just reads and writes all day." Madame Needles's scowl marred her exotic demeanor.

"She's mesmerizing," MacGregor said. He hadn't found anything pitiable about her. "Girls don't have to get married these days if they don't want to."

"If you have ideas about despoiling my daughter out of wedlock, forget it."

"Oh, no, nothing like that," he said. "It's just that she seems content as she is, with her reading and writing." The Illuminated Woman had seemed content, although MacGregor did wonder what she'd been crying about the previous day. Had she known how the story was going to end, that the father and son would go over the falls and drown? Did she make the story end that way?

"Soon she'll be an old maid," Madame Needles said, "and I'll never have any grandchildren. I'll die miserable and alone in the poorhouse while she's writing her magnum opus. Better if she were like her aunt. I tattooed my sister, and those tattoos sit still and behave. None of her colors creep around and excite the marks—I mean, customers."

"I want a tattoo that moves."

"You want. You want. Everybody wants." She gave him a sidelong glance. "But how badly do you want it?"

"I want it very much." He said. "Please. Can you really do it?"

She shrugged her golden shoulders. "I'll do what I do, but there's no telling how it'll turn out. The rest is up to you." She opened the drawer in her desk and took out several sheets of paper. "First, I'll need you to sign some forms."

There was a liability release in case he got blood poisoning from the needles and a nondisclosure form, saying he would not to give away Madame Needles's tattooing techniques, and it contained a noncompete clause forbidding him from joining a sideshow. He read through the forms and reached for the pen in his pocket, but Madame stopped him with a hand on his wrist. She lifted his hand and pricked his finger with a needle and then smeared his blood across each of the signature lines in turn.

She named the fee, and MacGregor fought to keep from gasping. It was ten times the outrageous amount he'd anticipated, but he paid it. He described the tattoo he wanted, the size of a playing card, of a red bird perched on a branch above a blue stream, against the golden sun. It was an image he'd seen in dreams.

She pulled a wooden bowl off the table and shoved it into his hands. "This is going to hurt," she said. "You can bite down on the edge of the bowl." She slipped a black satin sleep mask over his eyes and had him lie back in the chair. When the first needle penetrated the center of his chest, he howled. It sank deeper, seemed to enter his heart.

He felt Madame Needles pull back and heard the rustle of the tent flap.

"Does the screamer need an escort off the premises?"

MacGregor recognized the voice. It was the man with the tattoo on his biceps.

"I'll let you know," Madame Needles said. She leaned in close to MacGregor's ear. "Do you want this badly enough?"

MacGregor took a breath. He recalled watching the girl's tattoo, feeling it move his senses, his thoughts, and his emotions. He remembered how it had thrilled Silvie. But it was more than that. He didn't just want the tattoo; he needed it. There was something primal bubbling inside him that needed a way out, and he was sure this was the way, through his skin. He bit down again on the edge of the bowl, nodded for Madame to continue. As she drove the needles in again and again, the pain became surreal, moving beyond any pain he'd ever known. He squeezed his eyes shut, but his tears seeped out anyway and soaked the mask over his eyes. His teeth cut into the rim of the wooden bowl. He did not open his eyes until she was finished. He thought that about a half hour had passed, but when he walked shakily to the door of the tent to look out, the sky was dark, and even the midway lights and music were off for the night. The rattle of cicadas was almost deafening.

MacGregor kept the tattoo a secret until the following weekend, when he and Silvie took a three-day vacation to Sanibel Island in Florida. Their suite overlooked the Gulf of Mexico, and on their first day there they saw pileated woodpeckers, roseate spoonbills, and alligators from their balcony. When Silvie picked up her novel that night in bed, MacGregor took off his shirt, pulled the gauze from the tattoo, and sat before her.

"You got a tattoo!" she said, her expression one of mild alarm. She reached up and touched it. MacGregor had avoided looking at the tattoo himself, even when he cleaned it and applied new bandages. He had wanted to share the experience of first seeing it with Silvie. As he had hoped, it began to move under her fingers, at first slowly: the wind rustled the bird's feathers, the wings opened and closed. They watched as the bird on his breastbone lifted and flew through air. It soared above a boat, which sailed from a port into a blue-green ocean. Waves gently slapped the sides of the boat. MacGregor saw upside down what Silvie saw and marveled at how the tattoo swelled and changed to show every detail.

"It's real," she said. Her smile showed pure delight. "It's marvelous!"

He nodded, but Silvie was less happy a while later when a storm blew in, and the boat capsized, and all the tiny people were pitched into the merciless, shark-filled sea.

"Sorry," MacGregor said, and Silvie opened her book and read a chapter.

The following night, MacGregor posed in front of the mirror, and together they watched a silver airplane take off and soar out of the atmosphere. It made its way around the moon. MacGregor allowed himself to feel a little proud. Madame Needles had seemed unsure whether the tattoo would move the way he wanted it to, but it was working. The ship soared with the sun glinting off its wings until it exploded without warning. A dozen bodies were strewn across space.

"I don't like this story," Silvie said and turned away.

MacGregor did not want to stop watching. He wanted to see how the story really ended, what might give meaning to the tragic demise of the astronauts who had died during their mission. The tattoo seemed to have doubled in area since the story began, and MacGregor wondered if the Illuminated Woman had started out with a small tattoo as well. While Silvie got ready for bed, MacGregor watched the last remaining astronaut plunge toward Earth. When he hit the atmosphere, he became a bright stream of light, a falling star.

Across his skin, MacGregor felt the movement of the explosion and of the man's falling, but that wasn't the extent of it. The pictures showing on his chest were like mushrooms growing atop soil, connected by tendrils to the greater body under the surface. If this were a projection of images, they came from inside, not out.

"I know you wonder why I read romance novels," Silvie said, turning to him later in bed. "You think they're written for foolish girls."

"No," he said, though he did wonder. He had tried to read one of her novels, but he'd fallen asleep in the middle of the first chapter.

"It's because all day long I have to make critical decisions. There's money, livelihoods, resources at stake. I act with confidence, but I can only hope my decisions are the right ones. When I come home, I don't want to worry. I want to know that everything will turn out well and that everyone will be happy and that justice will be served."

"Thank you, Silvie," MacGregor said. "Now I do understand."

She needed life to be worry-free outside of work, and he would make it that way for her as best he could. She already did so much for him. When he was at a business meeting or a cocktail party and veered off onto the wrong track, Silvie would guide him back. He wanted to do the same for her.

■ ■ ■

One Saturday morning in March, MacGregor woke breathless from a dream of flight, still feeling the joyful energy of soaring above his house, moving faster than the cars below him over the street below. He listened to the purr of Silvie's snoring. He smelled her perfume from the day before and slowly turned his head on the pillow to gaze at her smooth face in the gray predawn light. She stayed over every Friday night, and in two months she would be there beside him every night, forever. Beyond her, on the nightstand, lay her current novel, silhouetted against the window. The pages were fluffed out prettily, suggesting her book was part of her decorating scheme that included the handsome off-white window dressings, the ribbed bedspread, and the new, slightly luminescent paint on the walls. She said remodeling made the room belong to them. This had been his parents' bedroom, and MacGregor didn't care what it looked like. He had grown up an only child, and the most important thing to him was having another soul lying beside him, sharing his life. He would go along with any remodeling Silvie wanted to do.

MacGregor's chest prickled. Silvie had recently suggested he keep the tattoo covered all the time. She had walked in on him watching a story at work more than once, and she was concerned about the hold the tattoo had on him, how it was distracting him from more important things. He couldn't argue with the truth of the matter, that the work of being president was tiresome to him, so much so that he had taken to hiding out in his bathroom to revive himself. He had managed to resist looking in the mirror for more than a week now, until this morning, when a vision of flying without aid of any machine had invaded his dreams. If he hadn't felt the urgent prickling, he would have remained in bed, absorbing the pleasures of lying with Silvie, would have wrapped an arm around her and pulled her close. Instead, he slipped out of bed, tiptoed to the bathroom, closed the door, and turned on the light. Silvie had helped him quit smoking, but giving up cigarettes had been easy compared to resisting his compulsion to look at the tattoo. He turned the lock on the door and stuffed a bit of tissue into the oversize keyhole. His heart was pounding as he looked around the small tiled room, at the modest claw-foot tub, at the old-fashioned light fixture covered with a frosted-glass seashell shade. The old bathroom mirror had a fun-house quality; he and Silvie had once stood beside one another and laughed at their distorted reflections.

MacGregor pressed his ear against the painted wood of the door. Silvie's snore was one of his favorite household sounds, along with the toaster popping up and the dryer spinning. In the world outside, he loved the sounds of jets and rockets taking off, though he'd only heard the latter on television. MacGregor unbuttoned his pajama shirt. He slid his arms from the sleeves, and when he looked in the mirror, the color in the playing-card-size tattoo dazzled him. He took a deep breath and let the tattoo expand and rush to fill the smooth skin of his chest. The first mysterious effect of the tattooing process had been that he had lost the modest amount of hair he'd had there, and it had never grown back. He took a deep breath and inhaled the colors, which smelled of air so rich and oxygenated that it filled not only his lungs but his whole being. When he exhaled, all the stress of the week fell away at once, and the picture of the bird and the branch and the stream and the sun began to change.

A rocket sat upon a launchpad surrounded by complicated machines operated by white-coated scientists whose faces glowed with intelligence and focus. MacGregor took another deep breath, and the men and women began to move, to tap their fingers on their whisper-thin handheld computers, to point out and discuss objects of interest around them, to compare calculations. As MacGregor's focus returned to the rocket ship, it increased in proportion to the scene, and the scientists disappeared from view. Somehow, as MacGregor's heart pumped blood out through his arteries and back in through his veins, the point of view moved so he could see inside the capsule atop the boosters, where two women and three men in silver suits were making final preparations and buckling themselves into their seats. To MacGregor they seemed perfect human specimens, strong-bodied and healthy, and their eyes showed a love of adventure. Or was there a shadow of something sinister crossing one man's face? Did the fifth astronaut have an ungenerous spirit, a tendency toward cruelty or sullenness? Was his desire for space less pure than the others'? MacGregor's concern faded as he felt the collective excitement of the other astronauts. He also felt their fear and sadness and understood that they were leaving behind their loved ones in order to journey into the unknown.

One of the men in the capsule resembled MacGregor, with blue eyes and thick eyebrows and dark, unruly hair. So much so that MacGregor was almost sure it was him. Neither of the women resembled Silvie, however. He knew Silvie wouldn't venture into space, not even with him at her side, reassuring her. She didn't like not knowing what was coming next. She was most content when she was following her routine of work and relaxation, having coffee on the patio in the morning or taking a brisk walk in the early evening. She was continually opening windows to let in breezes and wouldn't like the cramped quarters of the space capsule, in which everything was designed for efficiency and maximum function.

MacGregor, too, would miss many things about Earth, especially the familiar objects from his house and his desk at work, the way his tools felt in his hands, but he knew that for him the memories of the objects could suffice in their absence. MacGregor would miss Silvie most of all, but he could take comfort in the memories of Silvie that he would carry into space. Behind and beyond the rocket, there stretched the vision of MacGregor's own planet's beauty: a glittering silver desert and purple mountains. Beyond that, somehow, defying the laws of perspective, he could see the vast and shining ocean. From a high cliff, a giant bird launched itself, flew across the water on golden wings, and on the bird's back was a young woman. Her arms were wrapped around the creature's neck. Her hair whipped around in the wind, and she was laughing. At first he thought it was Silvie, hoped it was Silvie, but when she shook her head to get her hair out of her eyes, he saw that she was wearing glasses and that they were held fast to her head with an elastic strap, like the one he'd worn as a kid. MacGregor laughed with delight, realizing as he did so that he hadn't felt delighted in quite a while. He fell backward against the door, and it rattled.

"Gerald?" Silvie called from the bedroom, and MacGregor's heart seized.

"I'll be right out," he said just loudly enough to be heard, trying not to interrupt the flow of the story. The golden bird vanished behind a hill.

"I'm worried about you, Gerald. Please come out and talk to me," Silvie said. She jiggled the doorknob, and the tissue fell out of the keyhole and onto the floor.

"Just a minute," he whispered. When he was experiencing a story in this way, he knew how life could be extraordinary, how the simple four-chambered human heart and the primitive human brain could begin to understand the universe. And he thought that if Silvie would watch the story unfold with him—if she could shake her fears about how it might end—she would feel inspired as well. The rocket blasted off with a flame more brilliant than a lightning strike. MacGregor gripped the sink as the rocket tore free of the earth with a violence that seemed more than the rocket or the planet, or he himself, could endure—his heart felt nearly wrenched from his chest at the force, and he was out of breath by the time the rocket was airborne. As he watched in the mirror, he could see the magnificent Earth from space, its blue oceans and green lands still beautiful despite the pollution and all the other human folly that threatened to destroy it. As the planet became small as a marble, as it shrank to a pale-blue dot, the scene darkened, and then the rocket was swimming far from home, through the sea of stars. MacGregor kept hold of the sink to steady himself against the joyful energy of barreling through space.

"Are you looking at that tattoo?" Silvie asked. He could tell from her voice that her face was pressed up against the other side of the door.

Silvie had done so much for him. She had carried him through the grief of losing his parents. She had supported him as president of MacGregor Ball Bearing Inc., though she was better suited to run the company than he was. It was her ability to manage money, employees, and schedules that had allowed him to be anything more than an engineer.

"We need to get you some help, Gerald," Silvie said thoughtfully.

MacGregor tore his eyes away from the mirror. He looked down at the tiny hexagonal tiles that made up the old floor, the same cool tile his bare feet had known as a kid. There was a slight rise near the radiator, where the floor had buckled, reminding him of a shoulder blade. As he studied the tiles, he began to see a vision move across the floor. The picture was not as vivid or colorful as his tattoo, but it played out in shadows that brought him feelings from a long time ago. Some boys filled a bottle with dry ice, shook it up, and shot a cork across a pond. They sent a model rocket two hundred feet in the air in the field behind his house. MacGregor both saw and felt himself riding his bike along the sidewalk and then gathering speed on the downslope, and though the adult MacGregor knew the poor boy was headed for a crash, he grinned at the wind in his face. MacGregor still felt like that same kid, twenty-one years later. He heard Silvie move away from the door.

"I saw a giant bird flying over the ocean, Silvie," MacGregor said as he stepped into the bedroom. "Big enough that a girl was riding on its back."

"Oh, Gerald," Silvie said tiredly, "we both know what's going to happen." She was sitting on the bed with her back to him, and the bed was already made up. She wore the pearl-colored bathrobe she kept at his house.

"What do you mean?" he asked.

"The rocket always crashes. The volcano always explodes and kills the villagers. I don't want to see a girl plunge into the icy depths."

"This is a new story. Things might be different."

"Gerald, we've been through this. The lions in the veld tear apart the sweet little gazelle. Cold empty space swallows the astronauts. Somebody is going to shoot that big bird out of the air. I've lived with your stories for more than six months, and my hope has run out."

"The rocket doesn't always crash," MacGregor insisted. "And the gazelle is the lions' natural prey—that can't be helped."

"If the rocket doesn't crash, if the astronauts land safely, then in the next story they go on to kill the peaceful inhabitants of the new planet with their human stupidity."

"Oh, honey," MacGregor said. "So what if some of the stories don't exactly end happily? I just wish we could watch together, to experience the adventures together, the good and the bad."

The sun was rising outside their window, and Silvie's shiny bathrobe exploded with color. Shapes began to form across her shoulders, and MacGregor began to see a vision of himself and Silvie in the future. Her hair was white, and his was gray, and they were holding hands in the garden in spring. He didn't understand how this was happening, how the stories were stretching beyond his own body, appearing all around him. In the vision, MacGregor clung with his free hand to a walker. White-haired Silvie lifted both hands to her head, groaned, and then collapsed to the flagstone path to lie among the tulips and daffodils.

Silvie gave no indication that she was seeing the images on her robe.

"I need my stories to be happily ever after," she said. She picked up the novel from her nightstand and held it in MacGregor's direction until her bookmark fell out. He saw on the cover a muscular shirtless man with long hair and a woman with soulful eyes and even longer hair. "Why can't you create a happily ever after for me?" she asked, tears glistening in her eyes.

"But the stories exist on their own, Silvie. They come to me just as they are." He felt as though he were mainly a conduit for the stories, but maybe he was, somehow, creating them. Maybe his very nature was creating them. And maybe there would be a way to control them by force of will, but that wasn't what he wanted.

"Gerald, I don't think I can live with you this way."

"What can I do, Silvie?"

"I've been thinking about it," she said and stared out the window. "And I don't think I can marry you unless you have the tattoo removed."

MacGregor's heart thudded and slowed. He stumbled into the bathroom and looked in the mirror, and there he saw the color drained from his skin, saw the brilliant visions replaced by a web of scar tissue, the explosion of life replaced by an expanse of angry flesh that pinched and stretched like the residue of a life-threatening burn. He felt physically ill. He bent at the waist, crossed his arms over his chest. He knew what Silvie didn't know, that the tattoo was more than ink on skin. The tattoo could not be removed without gouging out his heart.

He hadn't realized he was holding his breath, but when he breathed again, the sick feeling went away. His skin tingled as the spaceship hurtled through space, and he uncrossed his arms and saw the stars again. Inside the capsule, the five astronauts floated weightlessly and joked with one another. One woman was eating dried cherries, and she tossed one toward the open mouth of one of the men, but the cherry moved in slow motion, and they both laughed and discussed their pea-plant experiment until the fruit finally reached the man, and he bit it out of the air. As a child, MacGregor had tried to eat like an astronaut—powdered drinks and vacuum-sealed protein bars. Now he tasted the sweet sourness of that dried cherry!

When MacGregor returned to the bedroom, he found Silvie dressed and packing her overnight bag with the few things she kept at his house.

"No, Silvie. I love you. You're the most important person in my life."

"I love you, too, Gerald. It's your choice." She finally looked at him.

"See, Silvie, the rocket landed safely on a new planet," he said and pointed to his chest. "It's Mars. Look, four of the astronauts are getting out. Everything's going to be OK this time."

"They all have guns," Silvie said anxiously.

"For protection, or in case of wild animals. Silvie, look at the planet. The sky is red! Can you smell it? The dust smells of flowers and vanilla. Everyone is safe." To his joy, he found he really could smell the dust. He felt the hot breeze on his skin. "Can't you smell the vanilla?"

"They're not safe, Gerald. They're probably bringing germs that will infect everyone on the new planet. Or else they'll try to take away the Martian riches, and a war will break out. I've seen these stories too many times. I can't take any more."

"But look. The astronauts have met a Martian family, a couple and two children. They're all conversing. Everything is friendly. You can tell by their hand gestures." MacGregor noted the hands of the Martians, their fingers long and elegant compared to the stubby mitts of the Earthlings. The sky behind them glowed the rich orange-red of campfire coals. MacGregor imagined the Martians and Earthlings sitting around a fire, and soon enough they were indeed sitting around a fire, conversing telepathically, cooking Martian fish and giant mushrooms they grew in their basements.

"What about that fifth astronaut lurking in the background?" Silvie said.

"He stayed at the rocket."

"He's right there now, drinking whiskey from a bottle. I can even hear him cursing. I don't want to hear it."

"No," MacGregor said, but he knew she was right. The man seemed unlike the others. He was suspicious and angry. And now he was drunk and armed.

"Somebody's going to die," Silvie said. She looked away from him and stuffed her slippers and bathrobe into her bag. "Eventually somebody's going to die. Don't deny it."

"Eventually we all die, honey."

"Well, I can't face it."

"Just look at the light reflecting off the Martian canals as evening falls. It reminds me of your eyes, Silvie." He closed his eyes to imagine the story more vividly, and he heard the door shut. He wanted to run after her, but he needed to see the story through. As Silvie said, most of the stories ended with trouble, just as marriages ended in death or divorce. He thought he might work at keeping a story alive longer, putting off disaster, just as he might convince Silvie to give him one more chance. It occurred to him that he should run after her and beg for another chance. And yet, readers and watchers and listeners needed a story to end sometime.

■ ■ ■

MacGregor and Silvie's separation was as amicable as MacGregor could have hoped. He arranged an emergency meeting of the board of directors, and they agreed with him that Silvie should become acting president, while MacGregor would retain his majority stake in the company but return to being an engineer. He felt relieved to move his things from his father's office back to his old desk in the fabrication shop. At the beginning of August, Silvie drove to his house in a new electric car she'd bought, in order to pick up some winter clothes she'd stored in his attic. She stepped out into the gravel driveway, wearing a trim-fitting pants suit in charcoal gray. She wore high-heeled shoes that barely covered her pretty toes. Her heels sank through the gravel and into the earth.

"I'm sorry things didn't work out for us," Silvie said. "I guess we're another one of your tragic stories."

MacGregor put the last box of clothes into the trunk of her car and invited her to stay and have some coffee. When she declined, he took off his glasses and cleaned them on his shirt. When he put them back on, Silvie was shaking her head at him and smiling as she might at a child. When she backed into the street, MacGregor walked out to the end of his driveway to watch the silver electric car, as sleek as a rocket ship, head down the road, and that's when he saw the billboard for the county fair, August 4–9. He was surprised to realize that the fair was opening that day. His skin began to tingle, and his heart began to flutter crazily. Was it possible that the Illuminated Woman would be there? He'd seen her in his stories and dreams, but he hadn't considered seeking her out. He could hope that Madame Needles had failed in the last year to find her daughter a husband. Of course she had failed, for the girl knew her own mind! MacGregor wanted to see her, to lose himself in her brilliant visions, to listen to her voice sing, to look into the eyes behind her dark-rimmed glasses. He had been ashamed to think of her this way when he had been engaged to Silvie, but now there was nothing to keep him from visiting her and trying to know her better. And maybe now that he had his own stories, she might want to see him, too.

CONTRIBUTORS

ELLEN AIRGOOD grew up on a farm in Michigan's thumb, near a house she believed to be Bob Seger's, based solely on local legend, a long driveway, and a fancy gate. (It wasn't.) She almost left the University of Michigan after her first year to go back home but stayed when her parents offered to cosign the loan for the new fencing she'd need to raise beef cattle on their eighty acres, the only crop they considered feasible. (She was a vegetarian at the time.) She graduated with a bachelor of science from the School of Natural Resources and Environment and now lives on the shore of Lake Superior in the Upper Peninsula, where she writes and owns a diner with her husband. She is the author of three novels published by Penguin Books, including Michigan Notable Book and Midwest Bestseller *South of Superior* (also featured on National Public Radio's Radio Reader) and the award-winning *Prairie Evers,* a Bank Street Best Book for middle-grade readers.

NATALIE BAKOPOULOS published her first novel, *The Green Shore,* in 2012 (Simon & Schuster), and her fiction and essays have appeared in *Tin House, Salon,* the *New York Times, Michigan Quarterly Review, Granta, Glimmer Train, The Millions, O. Henry Prize Stories,* and other publications. She has received fellowships from the Camargo and MacDowell foundations and was a 2014-15 Fulbright Fellow in Athens, Greece. She received her MFA from the University of Michigan and is currently a visiting assistant professor at Wayne State University.

MATT BELL is the author most recently of the novel *Scrapper,* published by Soho Press in 2015. His previous novel, *In the House upon the Dirt between the Lake and the Woods,* was a finalist for the Young Lions Fiction Award, a Michigan Notable Book, and an Indies Choice Adult Debut Book of the Year Honor recipient, as well as the winner of the Paula Anderson Book Award. He is also the author of two previous books of fiction, *How They Were Found* and *Cataclysm Baby,* and a nonfiction book, *Baldur's Gate II,* about the classic video game, published in 2015 by Boss Fight Books. His writing has appeared in *Best American Mystery Stories, Tin House,* the *New York Times, Conjunctions, Gulf Coast,* the *American Reader,* and many other publications. A native of Michigan, he now teaches creative writing at Arizona State University.

MICHAEL BYERS is the author of two novels, *Percival's Planet* and *Long for This World,* as well as the story collection *The Coast of Good Intentions.* He has been a finalist for the PEN/Hemingway Award and has won the Sue Kaufman Prize from the American Academy of Arts and Letters. A native of Seattle, he teaches at the University of Michigan.

BONNIE JO CAMPBELL is the author of *Mothers, Tell Your Daughters* (W. W. Norton, 2015) and the bestselling novel *Once Upon a River.* She was a National Book Award finalist and National Book Critics Circle Award finalist for her collection of stories *American Salvage* (Wayne State University Press, 2009), as well as a Guggenheim Fellow. She lives in Kalamazoo, Michigan, with her husband and two donkeys. You can check on her progress at www.bonniejocampbell.com.

A 2015 Kresge Artist Fellow, DESIREE COOPER is a former attorney, Pulitzer Prize–nominated journalist, and Detroit community activist whose fiction dives unflinchingly into the intersection of racism and sexism. Using the compressed medium of flash fiction, she explores intimate spaces to reveal what it means to be human. Her fiction and poetry have appeared in *Callaloo, Detroit Noir, Best African American Fiction 2010,* and *Tidal Basin Review,* among other online and print publications. Her first collection of flash fiction, *Know the Mother,* was published by Wayne State University Press in 2016. Cooper was a founding board member of Cave Canem, a national residency for emerging black poets. She is currently a Kimbilio fellow, a national residency for African American fiction writers.

PETER HO DAVIES is the author of the novel *The Welsh Girl* and the story collections *The Ugliest House in the World* and *Equal Love.* His work has appeared in *Harper's,* the *Atlantic,* and the *Paris Review* and has been selected for *Prize Stories: The O. Henry Award* and *Best American Short Stories.* One of *Granta* magazine's "Best of Young British Novelists," he is also a recipient of the Pen/Malamud Prize for excellence in the short story. Davies serves on the faculty of the Helen Zell MFA Program at the University of Michigan.

MICHAEL DELP recently retired from the Interlochen Arts Academy, where he was the director of creative writing for many years. He is the author of numerous collections of prose and poetry, with his most recent collection of short stories being *As If We Were Prey* (Wayne State University Press, 2010). He is also the mentor and advisor to the Front Street Writers Program in Traverse City, which operates under the auspices of the National Writers Series, and the co-editor of the award-winning Made in Michigan Writers series from Wayne State University Press. He lives in Interlochen with his wife, Claudia, and splits his time between there and Reeling Waters, his cabin on the Boardman River.

JACK DRISCOLL is the author of ten books. His most recent, *The World of a Few Minutes Ago,* was named best short story collection of 2013 by *ForeWord,* and winner of both the Society of Midland Writers Award and the Michigan Library Award. He teaches on the fiction faculty of Pacific University's low-residency MFA program, and is the recipient of a 2016 National Endowment for the Arts Creative Writing Fellowship.

Since the appearance of his first novel in 1976, LOREN D. ESTLEMAN has written nearly seventy books and hundreds of short stories and articles. Among those books: *Writing the Popular Novel, Burning Midnight, The Confessions of Al Capone, The Branch and the Scaffold.* He recently finished writing the twenty-third installment in the Amos Walker P.I. series, and is currently working on another standalone novel. He has received twenty national writing awards: the Owen Wister Award for lifetime achievement from Western Writers of America, the Barry Award from *Deadly Pleasures Mystery Magazine,* four Shamuses from the Private Eye Writers of America, five Spurs from the Western Writers of America, two American Mystery Awards from *Mystery Scene Magazine,* Outstanding Western Writer, 1985, from *Popular Fiction*

Monthly, two Stirrup Awards for outstanding articles in the Western Writers of America magazine, the *Roundup*, and three Western Heritage Awards from the National Cowboy Hall of Fame. He lives in Michigan.

BILL HARRIS is a Wayne State University Emeritus Professor of English. He received the Kresge Foundation Eminent Artist award for 2011. He is a playwright, poet, and arts critic. He formerly served as artistic coordinator for JazzMobile and the New Federal Theatre in New York and was chief curator at the Charles H. Wright Museum of African American History in Detroit. His plays have been produced nationwide, and he has published books of plays, poetry, and reappraisals of American history. *Booker T. & Them: A Blues* is his latest publication.

An enrolled member of the White Earth Chippewa Tribe, GORDON HENRY has been a faculty member at MSU since 1994. For the past eight years he has served as senior editor of the American Indian Studies series (and the series sub-imprint Mukwa Enewed) at Michigan State University Press. Under his editorship the AISS has published research and creative work by an array of scholars working in a variety of disciplines related to the larger field of American Indian Studies. Henry received an American Book Award for his novel *The Light People*. His poetry, fiction, and essays have been published extensively, in the United States and Europe. He is also a ceremonial helper who has learned and been given permission to do such cultural work by Francis Cree and Louis Cree from Turtle Mountain, North Dakota. He has participated and helped with various ceremonial practices for the past twenty-nine years. Henry has recently released a CD in collaboration with jazz musicians Mike Johnston and Mike Gilmore, aka the Northwoods Improvisors.

LAURA KASISCHKE has published seven novels, a novella, a collection of short stories, and eight books of poetry. She has been the recipient of the National Book Critics Circle Award, a Guggenheim Fellowship, and other honors. She teaches in the Residential College and the MFA Program at the University of Michigan, and lives in Chelsea, Michigan.

JANET KAUFFMAN lives in Hudson, Michigan, and works for sustainable agriculture with Environmentally Concerned Citizens of South Central

Michigan. She taught at Eastern Michigan University for many years and has published nine books of fiction, poetry, and nonfiction, including *Trespassing: Dirt Stories & Field Notes* (Wayne State University Press, 2008) on the factory farm crisis in southern Michigan watersheds.

M. L. LIEBLER is an award-winning poet, literary arts activist, and professor. He is the author of several books of poetry, including *Wide Awake in Someone Else's Dream* (Wayne State University Press, 2008), and an editor of the groundbreaking anthology *Working Words: Punching the Clock and Kicking Out the Jams* (Coffee House Press, 2010). He is also author of *I Want to Be Once* (Wayne State University Press, 2016). He has taught at Wayne State University since 1980.

MARDI JO LINK is the author of three true crime books and two memoirs. She lives in Traverse City.

THOMAS LYNCH is the author of five collections of poems and three collections of essays, including *The Undertaking*, which won the American Book Award, the Heartland Prize, and was a finalist for the National Book Award. *Apparition and Late Fictions—A Novella and Stories*, was published in 2010. The PBS film of "The Undertaking," based on his work and broadcast nationwide in 2007, won the 2008 Emmy Award for Arts & Culture Documentary. He keeps homes in Michigan and in Moveen, Co. Clare, Ireland. (His story in this anthology is part of a longer fiction he may never finish.)

ANDER MONSON is the author of six books of fiction, nonfiction, and poetry. He edits the magazine *DIAGRAM*, the New Michigan Press, and the website *Essay Daily*. Originally from Houghton, Michigan, he now lives in Tucson, Arizona.

THISBE NISSEN is the author of two novels, *The Good People of New York* and *Osprey Island*, and a story collection, *Out of the Girls' Room and into the Night*. She is also the co-author (with Erin Ergenbright) of *The Ex-Boyfriend Cookbook*, a collection of stories, recipes, and art collages. Thisbe's stories have been published most recently in *NANO Fiction*, the *Iowa Review*, and the *American Scholar*. She has taught fiction writing at the New School, Pacific

University, Brandeis, Columbia, the Iowa Writers' Workshop, and Western Michigan University, where she is now an associate professor of creative writing. Thisbe earned a BA in English and Creative Writing from Oberlin College in 1994 and an MFA from the Iowa Writers' Workshop in 1997. Often embroiled in a number of projects at the same time, Thisbe is working on a novel, a few novellas, some short stories and short-short stories, collaged picture books for kids, and a patchwork quilt or two or seven. She and her husband, poet and writer Jay Baron Nicorvo, are parents to one old cat, a dozen sprightly chickens, and one intriguing human child. They dream, one day, of raising goats on their farm outside Battle Creek, Michigan.

EILEEN POLLACK's most recent novel, *Breaking and Entering*, was awarded the Grub Street National Book Prize and chosen as a *New York Times* Editor's Choice selection. Her fiction has appeared in publications such as *Ploughshares*, *Prairie Schooner*, and the *Harvard Review*, as well as *The Best American Short Stories* and *The Pushcart Prize Anthology*. She is a professor in the Helen Zell MFA Program in Creative Writing at the University of Michigan.

JOHN SMOLENS has published ten works of fiction, most recently *Wolf's Mouth*. His stories, essays, and reviews have appeared in publications such as the *Massachusetts Review*, *The Virginia Quarterly Review*, *Columbia Journal of Literature and Art*, the *North American Review*, the *Southern Review*, and the *Washington Post*. In 2010 he was the recipient of the Michigan Author of the Year Award from the Michigan Library Association.

GLORIA WHELAN's short stories have appeared in a number of literary quarterlies as well as in anthologies, including The O'Henry Awards. Her young adult novel, *Homeless Bird*, was a National Book Award winner. The story collection, *Living Together*, published by Wayne State University Press, received the Silver Medal in the Short Story Fiction category for the 2014 IPPY Award.

MICHAEL ZADOORIAN is the author of two novels, *The Leisure Seeker* (William Morrow) and *Second Hand* (W. W. Norton), and a story collection, *The Lost Tiki Palaces of Detroit* (Wayne State University Press, 2009). He is a recipient of a Kresge Artist Fellowship in the Literary Arts, Columbia

University's Anahid Literary Award, the Michigan Notable Book award, and the Great Lakes Colleges Association New Writers Award and was long-listed for the International IMPAC Dublin Literary Award. His work has been published in the *Literary Review, Beloit Fiction Journal, American Short Fiction, Great Lakes Review, North American Review,* and *Detroit Noir*. Born and raised in Detroit, he lives in Ferndale, Michigan.